Changing Appeara

UNDERSTANDING DRESS IN CONTEMPORAR

Changing Appearances

UNDERSTANDING DRESS IN CONTEMPORARY SOCIETY

George B. Sproles
GES Associates
Tucson, Arizona

Leslie Davis Burns
Oregon State University
Corvallis, Oregon

FAIRCHILD PUBLICATIONS
New York

Text Design: Circa 86, Inc.
Cover Design: David Jaenisch

Library of Congress Catalog Card Number: 93:73072

ISBN: 1-56367-014-3

GST R 133004424

Printed in the United States of America

BRIEF CONTENTS

6. SOCIAL PROCESS OF FASHION DIFFUSION   **137**

7. THE MASS DIFFUSION AND TERMINATION OF FASHION TRENDS   **161**

*C*hanging Appearances: Understanding Dress in Contemporary Society is about how and why consumers choose changing appearances—new fashions. Fashion-oriented consumer behavior results from a multitude of behavioral processes and is among the most complex acts of consumer behavior. In this book we have developed a comprehensive multidisciplinary analysis of the psychological, social and economic forces influencing consumers to acquire and use new styles of appearance.

We begin in Chapter 1 with a conceptual look at the nature of fashion processes. In the acceptance and diffusion of new appearances, two processes are paramount. First is the broad process by which a new fashion is born, accepted by certain leading consumers, spread to wider audiences of consumers through processes of diffusion, and eventually terminated. This is frequently termed *the fashion process*. Second is the individual's process of accepting a new fashion, which is frequently termed *the adoption process*. Each individual makes choices, sometimes based partly on his or her individual psychology and often influenced by many external forces, to adopt changing appearances. Those fundamental principles are introduced in this chapter, and are expanded on in later chapters.

Chapter 2 introduces the birth and evolution of changing fashions. There are many major approaches to the study of fashion evolution, and these are properly the subject of lengthy history books and historical accounts. Our purpose in this chapter is to introduce the principal concepts that are fundamental to understanding the birth of new fashions: the concept of historical continuity in fashion, the role of culture and society as shapers of fashion, and the special role of influential individuals including fashion designers and consumers as creators of new appearances.

In Chapter 3 we begin a five-chapter sequence on the diffusion of fashions. This sequence of chapters derives from classical fashion theories and a general theory on the adoption and diffusion of innovations. Chapter 3 summarizes the general theory on adoption and diffusion of innovations, as applied to the specific case of fashion innovations. Chapter 4 expands on the process of diffusion by looking at the concept of fashion life cycles. Chapters 5 through 7 then become key chapters focusing respectively on how consumers lead in the acceptance and diffusion of changing appearances, and the social processes by which this diffusion takes place both in small groups and as a mass collective process in society-at-large. Finally, we also examine how fashion trends end, which is largely through a social process of termination.

Our attention turns to fashion adoption as an individual-centered phenomenon in Chapters 8 through 11. It is clear that fashion is very much a socially influenced phenomenon, yet we must also look at fashion as the result of many individuals making personal (though socially-influenced) decisions to accept or reject a change in their appearances. Chapter 8 examines these psychological dimensions of fashion, and we can see that there are important psychological and social psychological principles explaining the acceptance of change. In Chapter 9 we focus on the symbolic dimension of fashion, the meaning of fashion attributed by its wearers and by people who observe its wearers. We also note the basic fashion concept that the symbolic meaning of fashions is continually changing: old fashions lose their symbolic meanings as new fashions evolve conveying new meanings. Chapter 10 turns to the subject of fashion communications, examining the roles of impersonal communications such as mass media and personal communications such as friends in spreading information about fashions. Chapter 11 looks at the overt decision-making processes that consumers go through in accepting or rejecting specific styles. Consumers receive information and influences from many sources—the mass media, friends, and the marketing system to name key ones—and these integrate to influence the consumer's knowledge and choices.

The most difficult challenge in understanding changing appearances is to forecast what will come next. Chapter 12 closes the book with perspectives on this subject, including general and fashion-specific principles which can be applied to predicting trends. A perspective on the future of fashion is proposed as well.

This book has evolved from the previous works on fashion theory of the first author, principally *Fashion: Consumer Behavior Toward Dress* (Burgess Publishing Co., 1979). Those experienced with that work will find familiar subjects here, substantially expanded in important behavioral science perspectives. We have written this book because we believe that changing appearances *and* the underlying *fashion process* are the most important subjects for understanding dress in contemporary society. It is a modern fact of life that change is inevitable; indeed it sweeps cities, countries and continents in this marketing and communications-oriented world. Today there is extraordinary diversity and individualism in styles of appearances, yet there are themes and similarities in appearances that become very apparent among groups, subcultures, and particular life-styles pursued by people. Fashion has become powerful, perhaps the most powerful force shaping our appearances today. It is important for people to think of appearance in terms of its dynamic and changing nature, and we hope we have achieved the goal of making those dynamic and complex processes shaping change more understandable.

We expect this book will be of interest to academic faculty, undergraduate students, graduate students, and professionals in the fashion business. All have an important need to understand the processes of consumer behavior in changing appearances. Students will find this a particularly useful book for courses in such subjects as "Fashion Theory," "Dress and Human Behavior," or other courses where apparel is a central subject. Career-oriented students in the fashion industry and in retail merchandising need to understand the processes by which fashions are born, spread, and ultimately die, for the very success and failure of their professions depend on this phenomenon.

Many people have assisted in this work and we gratefully acknowledge their support. George Sproles' colleagues at Purdue stimulated his thinking on the subject of fashion early in his career, in particular Charles W. King and Margaret M. Conte. Other colleagues, including Mary Ellen Roach Higgins, Loren Geistfield, Shirley Ezell, Brenda Brandt, Soyeon Shim, Naomi Reich, and Ellen Goldsberry have influenced his thinking as well. George Sproles especially appreciates his coauthor, Leslie Davis Burns, who has brought fresh perspectives and broad knowledge of the behavioral sciences to this new work. Leslie Burns would like to express her appreciation to her colleagues at Oregon State University who have assisted in this work and to her husband, Chris, for his support throughout the project. Special thanks go to Sharron Lennon, Susan Kaiser, and Mary Lynn Damhorst, who have greatly influenced her thoughts on the social psychology of appearance. Her deepest appreciation goes to George Sproles for the opportunity to work on this project and his guidance through its development.

We wish to thank the readers selected by the publisher: Dawna Baugh and Charlene Lind at Brigham Young University; Usha Chowdhary at University of Missouri-Columbia; Mary Lynn Damhorst at Iowa State University; Kim Johnson at University of Minnesota-St. Paul; Sharron

Lennon at Ohio State University; Suzanne Loker at University of Vermont; Kimberly Miller at University of Kentucky; Frances Penalis at Syracuse University; Mary Ellen Roach-Higgins; Margaret Rucker at University of California-Davis; Phyllis Touchie-Specht at Mt. San Antonio College.

Finally, appreciation is extended to Earleen McGrew, our word processing expert who drafted the vast majority of this manuscript to its final form; and to anonymous reviewers who have commented on this text and shaped our thinking for the better. To all who helped we say thanks.

1994

George B. Sproles
Tucson, Arizona

Leslie Davis Burns
Corvallis, Oregon

Changing Appearances

UNDERSTANDING DRESS IN CONTEMPORARY SOCIETY

1

Perspectives on the Nature of Fashion

OBJECTIVES

- To introduce the subject of this book—the processes of consumer behavior in the acceptance of changing fashions.
- To examine the meaning of *fashion*, the many differing ways the term fashion is used.
- To introduce the concept of the *fashion process*, how new fashions are born and spread into popular acceptance among consumers.
- To propose fundamental principals that shape consumers' acceptance of changing fashions.
- To suggest why fashion adoption is an important phenomenon of consumer behavior, and its powerful role in our society, economy, and life-styles.

There is nothing so certain as change. It inexorably enters or invades our daily lives through our professions, possessions, friendships, life-styles, values, attitudes—the totality of personal and social experiences. Perhaps the most visible of changes are the daily, weekly, and yearly revisions of our appearances, the ways we see ourselves visually and the ways we present ourselves visually to others.

This we know as **fashion,** a term related to a variety of consumer products and services; a term conveying many nuances of meaning but primarily centering on the idea and ideal of our continually changing appearances. To the casual social critic or moralist, fashion conjures up images of personal vanity, conspicuous consumption, waste, excess and frivolity.

Superficially such perspectives have appeal, yet the more persuasive case will be made for the importance of changing appearances and fashions. Whatever our perspective may be—that of a scholar, entrepreneur or simply a participant in daily life—we all have a need to understand this human phenomenon of fashionable changes in appearances. These changes represent many things fundamental to our society and lives: Changing appearances set the stage on which daily life takes place, they represent the continuing change of social and cultural ideals, they determine our social relations and friendships, and they are used by individuals to enhance their self images and manage impressions on others. Given a phenomenon of such reach, we need to know the processes of **consumer behavior** that lead to these changes in appearances.

FASHION—WHAT IS IT?

To start, it is valuable to explore the many meanings attached to the term **fashion.** This term can be used to refer to the style of a consumer product or component of the product, the symbolic meaning attached to the product, or the process by which the product is adopted by individuals and social groups. What follows are excerpts from classic definitions of fashion that have been proposed by various authorities. Each of these brief quotations points out the different and often subtle meanings that are attached to fashion (emphasis added):[1]

Fashion is:
- the mode of dress, etiquette, furniture . . . adopted in society *for the time being*. (*Oxford English Dictionary* 1901)
- a series of *recurring changes in the choices of a group of people,* which though they may be accompanied by utility, are not determined by it. (Ross, quoted in Hurlock 1929, 4)
- a concept of what is *currently appropriate*. (Daniels 1951, 51)
- the styles . . . that are *socially prescribed and socially accepted* as appropriate for certain social roles. (Barber and Lobel 1952, 126)
- the *pursuit of novelty* for its own sake. (Robinson 1958, 127)
- an elementary form of *collective behavior*. (Lang and Lang 1961, 323)
- *a process of social contagion* by which a new style or product is adopted by the consumer after commercial introduction. (King 1964, 324)
- *a way of dressing, behaving* . . . that is considered especially *up-to-date* or noticeably following the *contemporary trend*. (*Webster's Unabridged Dictionary* 1966)

 want to fit in.

Fashion represents continuing change in social ideals and individual self-images.
(Elliott Erwitt / MAGNUM PHOTOS, Inc.)

(handwritten annotations: "ould be", "oir", "fro erus", "can be anything")

Summarizing the main points in these definitions, fashion first involves an **object.** This can be a style of jacket, a style of furniture, or an item of novelty. Thus fashion-oriented consumer behavior touches many different consumer products, not just apparel. But changing styles of apparel are most commonly associated with the fashion phenomenon, and apparel is the product most frequently thought of in relation to the term fashion. Thus although we focus on fashions in personal appearances (i.e., clothing, accessories, hairstyles, etc.), it is appropriate to view fashion processes as more general phenomena of human behavior.[2]

(handwritten annotation: "hAs to be appropriate for the era. Temopary")

Second, a fashion is a **temporarily adopted** object. A certain "mode," "contemporary trend," or "prevailing style" will be adopted for some period of time, but ultimately it will be replaced. *Every* fashion eventually comes to its end.

Third, the acceptance of a fashion is based on consumers' perceptions of its **social appropriateness.** Some fashions may gain popularity because they are prescribed as the most acceptable objects for use in certain social situations or roles. Others might be accepted as appropriate through social conformity, "social contagion," or "collective behavior" among many

Fashion touches all aspects of changing appearances.

(WWD, Fairchild Publications)

people who influence one another. Whatever the case, it is clear that a particular fashion is chosen because it represents what many people collectively perceive to be socially desirable behavior.

Finally, fashions are adopted by a particular **social group** or groups, or by some discernible (noticeable) proportion of the group's members. That social group might be all the members of a society, the members of a specific subcultural group, the members of an organized group (e.g., a club, sorority, fraternity), or an informal group of friends. Thus the term social group can include a range of small to large groups, and formally and informally constituted groups. It is not unusual to find that different social groups adopt different fashions. In modern society, however, it is also common for many different social groups to adopt the same basic fashion.

By synthesizing these main points, we offer this general definition of fashion:

(quiz) general def.

A fashion is a style of consumer product or way of behaving that is temporarily adopted by a discernible proportion of members of a social group because that chosen style or behavior is perceived to be socially appropriate for the time and situation.

This definition reflects the fact that fashion is a general phenomenon that can occur in many differing classes of objects (e.g., consumer products, forms of human behavior). This definition can be applied to a variety of fashion-oriented consumer products. Because clothing fashion is the central focus of this book, we will state this definition in the specific context of clothing.

A clothing fashion is a style of dress that is temporarily adopted by a discernible proportion of members of a social group because that chosen style is perceived to be socially appropriate for the time and situation.

(handwritten note: (quiz) general def. difference is the word - clothing.)

One special point of clarification on the meaning of fashion is especially crucial. For any specific fashion, there can be a variety of different designs or interpretations, each somewhat different from the other. Thus the content of fashion may include component parts of the consumer product. For example, the fashion of men's double-breasted jackets may be seen in differing suits, blazers, side-vent styling, no-vent styling, brass buttons, bone buttons, etc. Similarly the fashion of women's short skirts may be interpreted in several specific lengths (mini, micro), colors, fabrics, etc. In each case, we have a *single fashion*, albeit one with many individualistic and seemingly different expressions. Thus, a fashion expresses something similar and in common among its wearers, yet expresses a uniqueness and difference in each as well.

And finally, fashions are present in all dimensions of external appearance. Naturally we think of apparel, but what about hairstyles, makeup, personal grooming, posture, gestures, expressions, body shapes, body forms, body textures, body colors, masculinity, femininity? The total appearance is changed by fashions, though certain parts may command the center of fashionable attention at any given moment of time. At center stage dress is ever-present, and this should not be surprising since it is typically the largest single component in our perceptions of others. But how often do we observe the fashionable and popular acceptance of hairstyles, makeup and other accessories to our changing appearance.

THE SPECIAL LANGUAGE OF FASHION

Fashion has a language all its own, so rich and varied that complete dictionaries (Picken 1973; Calasibetta 1988), encyclopedias (Houck 1982) and directories (McDowell 1985; Stegemeyer 1988)) have been prepared. For our purposes, it is necessary to explicate certain fundamental terms and concepts related to fashion. Particularly significant in the language of fashion is the relationship among the terms design, style, and fashion. Although these terms are sometimes used synonymously, each has a unique meaning.

Components of fashion include silhouette, design details, and material (top left).
(Bob Adelman / MAGNUM PHOTOS, Inc.)

Styles often take on names such as "punk" in the early 1980s, depicting origins of the look (right).
(*WWD*, Fairchild Publications)

A **design** is a unique combination of silhouette, construction, fabric, and details that distinguishes a single fashion object from all other objects of the same category or class (e.g., pants, shoes, earrings). An infinite number of designs can be created. Apparel fashions can differ in silhouette, construction, material, pattern, color, and ornamental details. Each separate design exists as a highly individualistic creation. A fashion design is frequently created by a fashion designer or artist. The designer's goal is to create an overall form that is visually pleasing, socially acceptable, or that represents a cultural ideal of physical attractiveness (Roach and Eicher 1973). The creation of a fashion design may be considered a form of art. When this overall form also aesthetically expresses a cultural ideal of physical attractiveness or a norm of socially appropriate behavior, that design is very likely to become fashionable.

A **style** is a characteristic mode of presentation that typifies several similar objects of the same category or class. Broadly speaking, within a category, a style may include many designs with common features. Items of clothing with the same basic silhouette and construction constitute a single style. Sometimes these styles are given names depicting the social origins of the "look," or the time period when they originated. The words "punk," "preppie," "fifties look," or "Victorian" bring to mind specific styles distinguished from one another by common features unique to each. Finally, the term style is often used more narrowly as well, to describe distinct characteristics of a particular category. For example, there are several styles of pants, including bell-bottoms, capri, hip huggers, palazzo, pedal pushers, and clam diggers.

Of the basic styles that might be identified, only a small number of these will be accepted by a discernible number of people at any time. These limited numbers of styles are **fashions.** Thus we might identify styles such as five-pocket jeans and double-breasted jackets as fashion at a specific time. During the same time, however, other basic styles such as knickers or bustle skirts might not be accepted as current fashions.

Clothing, Apparel, and Dress

Clothing, apparel, and dress are often thought of as synonymous. However, each contains subtle differences in meaning. **Clothing** is frequently used as a generic term for any covering for the human body. **Apparel** is also defined as a body covering, but with the added connotation of a decorative covering. In general, the term apparel is used in the industry to refer to actual constructed garments.

The term **dress** is the most inclusive of the three (Roach and Eicher 1973). Dress includes the total presentation of all coverings and ornamentations worn on the human body. Dressing the body may include the use of apparel, accessories, hairstyling, cosmetics, facial hair, and tattoos.

Component Parts of a Fashion Object

A clothing fashion is composed of three major components: silhouette, design details, and material. **Silhouette** is the physical shape or lines of the style. Though the number of possible shapes can be limitless, examples of basic identifiable silhouettes include tubular, triangular, circular, bell shape, inverted triangle, back-fullness, and hourglass.

Design details are specific elements of construction which make up the fashion object. Details include collars, sleeve treatments, pockets, pleats,

Basic silhouettes dominate fashions in different time periods. The popularity of the four main silhouettes: hourglass, back-fullness, tubular, and inverted triangle can be seen in these illustrations of men's and women's fashions of the past century. (Illustrations by Robin Read.)

HOURGLASS SILHOUETTE

men, 1820s

women, 1820s

women, 1950s

women, 1960s

BACK-FULLNESS SILHOUETTE

women, 1890s

women, 1950s

TUBULAR SILHOUETTE

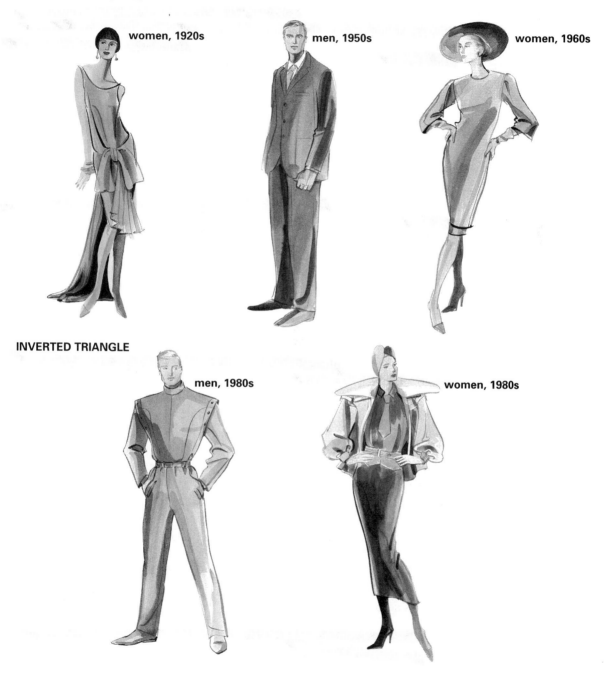

women, 1920s

men, 1950s

women, 1960s

INVERTED TRIANGLE

men, 1980s

women, 1980s

belts, buttons, lapels, and necklines. Price differentiation of similarly styled fashions is often based upon the intricacy of the design details along with the fabric quality.

The final component is **material.** Materials used in clothing and accessories include fabrics, leather, fur, plastics, metals, and gemstones, just to name a few. Aesthetically, the material is a combination of pattern, color, and texture. These aesthetic elements combine to determine the appearance, fitting characteristics, and tactile qualities of the material. In fabric these can be achieved by the design in which fibers or yarns are interlaced (woven, knitted, laced, or nonwoven/felted), and by aesthetic finishes applied through dyeing, printing, napping, or glazing.

Each of the major components (silhouette, design details, and material) may be independently subjected to fashion change. Particularly, silhouettes are subject to the most fundamental and long-lasting of fashion trends. It appears that today new silhouettes seem to evolve every ten to fifteen years. By comparison, design details and fabrics tend to undergo more frequent design changes, often changing every year or two. Therefore, these elements of styling usually have shorter lives as objects of fashion. However, one cannot overemphasize the fact that silhouette, construction, details, and material interact in defining a fashion object. All of these features are crucial in the consumer's decision to accept or reject a fashion.

Fads, Trends, and Other Jargon

Because the term **fad** is frequently used to describe extremely brief popularity of a specific style, it is important to understand the difference between a fad and a fashion. Several analysts have offered perspectives on this difference. Nystrom (1928, 5) suggests a fad is "merely a miniature fashion in some unimportant matter or detail." Meyersohm and Katz (1957, 598) make no distinction between fad and fashion, applying both terms to "transitory phenomena that involve a large number of people or a large proportion of members of a subculture." In contrast, Sapir (1931, 139) states that a fad "differs from a true fashion in having something unexpected, irresponsible, or bizarre about it. Any fashion which sins against one's sense of style and one's feelings for the historical continuity of style is likely to be dismissed as a fad."

Today the usage of fad and fashion differ in ways worth mentioning, and several principles may be employed to help distinguish between fads and fashions:

1. Fads are often revolutionary or extreme in design when compared to the currently existing fashions.

Michael Jackson's sequined glove exemplified the term "fad," 1984 (above).
(UPI / BETTMANN NEWSPHOTOS)

Fads are often popularized by movies. Remember *Flashdance* sweatshirts (1983)? (right) (The KOBAL Collection)

2. Fads are "born overnight" and grow very rapidly in popularity.
3. Fads receive limited rather than massive adoption, and they are accepted only in some special social or subcultural groups.
4. Fads decline rapidly in popularity (perhaps existing only a few weeks or months) and their demise is usually permanent.

Fads often come about from movies (remember torn Flashdance sweatshirts), rock stars (e.g., Michael Jackson's single, sequined glove), and fast growing status symbols (e.g., Vuarnet sunglasses). All of these appear to meet the principles identifying temporary fads from more enduring fashions. However, it also should be recognized that some styles might initially be perceived as faddish, and yet later become widely accepted fashions. For example, in the mid-1960s miniskirts appeared to be a passing fad, but turned into a major fashion trend of the late 1960s and again from the late

Couture fashion is depicted here by Gianfranco Ferré for Christian Dior, 1993.
(*WWD*, Fairchild Publications)

1980s to the early 1990s. The fads of jeans, long hair, and love beads worn by the "hip" or "hippie" youth of the 1960s progressed into mainstream fashions. In the 1980s and early 1990s styles worn by Madonna started out as fads but evolved into larger fashion influences.

It is also necessary to understand the concept of a **fashion trend.** A fashion trend is the direction a new fashion is taking. The trend may be toward a particular new silhouette, material (including pattern, color, and texture), or design detail. A trend can affect a variety of fashion items. For example, we may see a trend toward a tubular silhouette reflected in narrow trousers in both men's and women's wear. Or a trend might be toward a family of colors, as when pastels gain popularity in many different items of clothing. Trends also spread across product categories, for example, when wider lapels become the fashion in men's dress suits and sports jackets as well.

There is much specialized jargon in the field of fashion, and some of this has come into general use. **Couture fashion,** in the true sense of the word, involves the one-of-a-kind, made-to-order collections of famous designers such as Chanel, Dior, Yves Saint Laurent, and Givenchy. Couture caters to only a few hundred extremely wealthy customers worldwide, and though it has become a money-losing venture, it sets the stage for the broader arena of high fashion and mass fashion that is mass-produced. **High fashions** are high-priced, exclusive, "designer-branded" styles. They are often *avant garde* and innovative in their styling; the implication is that these fashions are adopted only by people of high social status and wealth. High fashion includes the collections of famed designers offered through exclusive boutiques; some "high fashion" is now mass-produced as ready-to-wear. **Mass fashions,** on the other hand, are fashions that have achieved considerable popularity. They are mass-produced and sold in large volume in all price ranges through department, specialty, discount, and off-price stores. Styling of mass fashions is usually more basic and may lack elaborate design details or intricate workmanship which add to the fashion's cost. **Classics** are basic styles that have received acceptance for a long time, and often by many differing social groups (indeed massive social acceptance is common). These styles are often simple in design and reflect a basic, strong, and widely adopted trend in fashion. Examples of classics include the traditional tailored blazer, trenchcoat, button-down oxford shirt, penny loafers, and Levi "501" jeans. Even classics can be dated, however, if design details depart from what is customary. For example, a blazer can easily be dated by wide or narrow lapels or by the fabric (polyester knit versus wool flannel).

A specialized jargon is also used by professionals in the fashion business. Some of this jargon occasionally spreads to the general public when used by fashion writers. Typical of this jargon are terms for specific styles, frequently coined by the fashion industry or its media. Well known terms developed in this nature include "mini," "midi," "maxi," "A-line," "New Look," "Mod," and "punk." Jargon is often used to publicize and glamorize the newest styles offered; terms like "fashion forward," "prophetic," and "hot number" are examples. Current usage can be found in fashion trade publications, and meanings can often be inferred from the context.

THE FASHION PROCESS—HOW FASHIONS DEVELOP AND SPREAD

Fundamental to understanding fashions is to view the evolution of new fashions as a process of collective human behavior over a period of time. This we term the **fashion process.** The fashion process is defined as a dynamic mechanism of change through which a potential new fashion is created and transmitted from its point of creation to public introduction, discernible public acceptance, and eventual obsolescence. In this process, a potential new fashion is invented, adopted by certain leading consumers,

High fashion includes expensive designer labels (top left).

(*WWD,* Fairchild Publications)

Classics reflect widely adopted trends in fashion (top right).

(THE BETTMANN ARCHIVE)

Mass fashions are the most popular ready-to-wear (bottom).

(K-Mart)

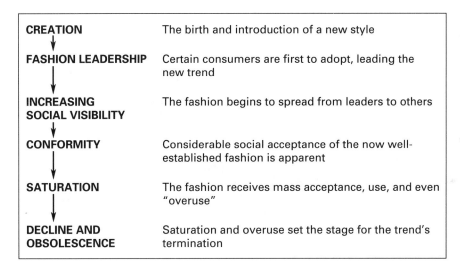

CREATION	The birth and introduction of a new style
↓	
FASHION LEADERSHIP	Certain consumers are first to adopt, leading the new trend
↓	
INCREASING SOCIAL VISIBILITY	The fashion begins to spread from leaders to others
↓	
CONFORMITY	Considerable social acceptance of the now well-established fashion is apparent
↓	
SATURATION	The fashion receives mass acceptance, use, and even "overuse"
↓	
DECLINE AND OBSOLESCENCE	Saturation and overuse set the stage for the trend's termination

FIGURE 1.1 Stages in the Fashion Process

spread to other consumers until it reaches a maximum level of acceptance for a period of time, and terminated as an accepted fashion.

The fashion process can be conceptually broken down and analyzed as a series of six sequential stages. These are identified as creation, fashion leadership, increasing social visibility, conformity to the style within and across social groups, saturation of the style, and decline and obsolescence (fig.1.1).[3] These stages are introduced here and developed in depth as the book progresses.

Stage 1: Creation   First a new style different from *current* fashions is invented and introduced to consumers. Numerous "inventors" provide this creative inspiration—obviously high fashion designers are influential, but creative consumers, the "beautiful people," celebrities (like popular singers) and subcultures are often sources of creative new styles. New fashions originate and are shaped by a wide variety of cultural, social, historical, and economic forces as described in chapter 2.

Stage 2: Fashion Leadership   The fashion process really begins when the potential fashion is introduced to the market and adopted by certain leading consumers. These first consumers are referred to by a variety of terms: fashion leaders, fashion innovators, fashion innovative communicators, fashion change agents, or fashion-conscious consumers. They initiate the fashion process by being the first to adopt and display a new style within their social groups. However, if their choices are too innovative or contrasting with the currently accepted fashions, the style could easily receive no further acceptance by other consumers and quickly become obsolete. Who are these fashion leaders? Different analysts have identified them as members of the most prestigious social classes, wealthy consumers, public celebrities, individuals noted for their good taste, social groups noted for good taste, members of specific subcultures, or simply consumers who are especially responsive to change. So the fashion leadership phase of the fashion process may begin in differing segments of the consumer population.

Stage 3: Increasing Social Visibility   In this stage, the new fashion is adopted and worn by a growing number of fashion leaders and other early adopters within many social groups. However, the style is still characterized by newness and novelty. Therefore, it is still a highly visible and noticeable style, and its growing adoption gives it even greater social visibility. With this high social visibility, the new style captures widespread attention and interest among many consumers. Not only is it worn by an increasing number of consumers, but it may also receive greater publicity, promotion, and availability in retail stores. These influences lay the groundwork for widespread, even mass acceptance.

Stage 4: Conformity   Having passed the introductory phases, the fashion usually gains a larger amount of social acceptance and social legitimation as it is adopted in differing social groups. By this time, the object has become a well-established fashion, but it may still continue to spread within social groups and from one group to another. A key underlying influence on this continued acceptance is social conformity. As the fashion increasingly becomes the socially appropriate style of dress, more and more consumers will feel compelled to adopt the style and conform to the trend.

Stage 5: Saturation   In this phase, the fashion reaches its highest level of social acceptance. During this time, nearly all consumers have become aware of the fashion, and have made a decision to either accept or reject it. Acceptance of the fashion is widespread, and the mass conformity to the fashion creates a form of social saturation, since it is in constant use by a large number of people. In other words, social saturation is a condition in which the fashion is overused. It is being worn on a daily basis, and it may now be socially appropriate in many contexts. The fashion is no longer new or novel, and to many it may even seem dull and boring. Its exclusivity has been lost. This loss sets the stage for termination of the fashion process.

Stage 6: Decline and Obsolescence   Social saturation of the fashion becomes an ultimate force in its decline and final obsolescence. At this stage, the fashion has lost all its appeal as a novel or preferred taste, largely because of the mass conformity to the style that has been perpetuated. Decline in use occurs as new styles are introduced and accepted as replacements for the socially saturated fashion. Eventually the old fashion becomes obsolete when its acceptance and use decreases to a negligible number of consumers.

The introduction and acceptance of a new fashion often has great impact on the decline and obsolescence of the previously existing fashion, because for an existing fashion to die, there must be a more desirable replacement for it. When certain fashion leaders introduce such an object, this leads the way for initiation and propagation of a new fashion process, which turns consumers' attention away from the old object while generating enthusiasm for the new.

FASHION AND THE INDIVIDUAL

As the preceding introduction implies, the fashion process is the result of many *individuals* making the decision to adopt—purchase and wear—a new style of appearance. This is frequently termed the **adoption process,** or the consumer decision-making process. The actual process by which a consumer adopts **innovations** such as new fashions involves many learning processes and mental stages. Everett Rogers, an expert on the diffusion (acceptance) of innovations, has suggested five basic stages of this process: awareness, interest, evaluation, trial, and adoption (Rogers 1962, fig. 3.1, p.75).[4] As with other innovations in our society (e.g., technological innovations), new fashions are adopted only after the consumer is aware of and interested in the fashion and has had a chance to evaluate and try out the fashion. During this process of learning about a new fashion, consumers often receive information and influence from various sources. This leads to formation of attitudes, both positive and negative, which determine if the consumer will adopt the style. The fashion to be adopted must be perceived as having some advantage over existing fashions. While sometimes this relative advantage is based on functional attributes of the fashion, such as a new and improved fabric or fabric finish, more often than not the relative advantage is that the fashion is simply perceived as being "more fashionable," "more consistent with my self-concept," "more prestigious," "individualistic," or "similar to what my friends are wearing." In addition, other characteristics of a new fashion, such as its

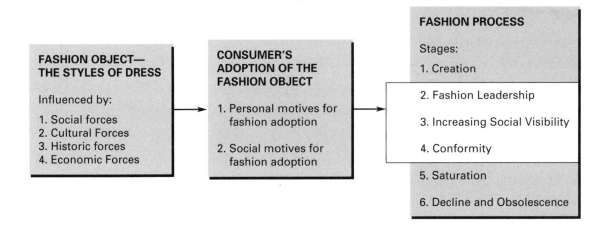

FIGURE 1.2 Framework for Understanding Fashion in Contemporary Society

compatibility with the consumer's life-style (activities, roles) determine its ultimate acceptance and use.

Both personal and social motives underlie a consumer's adoption of a particular fashion. For example, a person may adopt a fashion due to the perceived consistency between what the fashion symbolizes and his or her self-concept, or due to perceived similarity between the fashion and the clothing being worn by some comparison group. Choices are also made consciously for purposes of impression management, that is, controlling one's self-presentation to impress and influence others. These and other psychological and social forces that shape fashions are investigated in several later chapters. Figure 1.2 shows the relationships among the fashion object, consumers' adoption of the fashion object, and the stages of the fashion process. This framework lays the foundation for this book by focusing on the evolvement of the fashion object itself, the motives underlying a consumer's decision to adopt a specific fashion object, and the overall process by which the fashion is first adopted and eventually spread within and between groups.

THE FUNDAMENTAL PRINCIPLES OF FASHION

Fashions are governed and shaped by an exceedingly complex interplay of forces from within and external to the fashions' adopters. Our goal is to derive fundamental principles for systematizing and understanding these complex processes. The concepts of the **fashion process** and the individual's **adoption process,** just introduced, offer such principles as foundations. There are several other powerful and fundamental principles that we have implied and now make explicit. These are introduced now as a preview of what is to come as the book progresses.

1. *New fashions are invented by many sources, not just fashion designers.* The origination of new fashions is influenced by many forces: past fashion designs, cross-cultural contact, art movements, and life-style activities are among these dominant forces. By drawing inspiration from these factors, apparel manufacturers, fashion retailers, and consumers themselves, as well as fashion designers, create fashion in our contemporary society.

2. *New fashions evolve from past fashions, and are not dramatically different from them.* Fashion is said to have *historical continuity,* or to gradually change from year to year in small increments. For example, jacket designs or skirt lengths change only fractionally in most years. In some instances, historical fashions are resurrected and updated, and become modernized fashion trends as well.

3. *Fashions are determined by external forces: our culture, society, lifestyle, history, economy, and marketing system, and therefore serve as a reflection of their time and place.* Fashions vividly express the culture and society from which they are created and therefore reflect the zeitgeist—spirit and life-style—of a society. Our appearances equally reflect the daily activities and roles we pursue.

4. *Many different fashion trends exist simultaneously, in different groups of the consumer population.* Under the umbrella of what is considered fashionable at any given time, numerous "fashionable" styles exist and are adopted by different consumers and social groups, depending upon the consumer's own personal and social motives for adopting a specific fashion.

5. *Individuality and conformity are opposing forces that join together to influence fashion creation and adoption.* While fashion adoption results in similarity in appearances among many people, there is much individuality possible in each fashion as well. The adoption of a fashion by a consumer can satisfy the consumer's need for expressing individuality and the consumer's need for security obtained by being similar to others. This is made possible by the large number of styles and combinations of styles that are considered fashionable at any given time. Thus an individual can wear a fashion that is not only unique to him or herself, but which is also similar to what others are wearing.

6. *Fashions have life cycles.* Much like living things, fashions are born and they ultimately grow, mature, decline and pass away. Like living things, their content and character changes over the life cycle as well.

7. *All fashions end.* Passing fashions, even our favorites, must inevitably give way to the new. Some end because they are socially saturated—overused and overly visible. They lose their novelty, uniqueness, status, prestige, or power to enable us to express ourselves as individuals, and thus are terminated. Some end because they reach the extreme of that particular styling. For example, in the 1960s skirt lengths rose from the miniskirt to the micro-miniskirt and then could get no shorter without being immodest. Reaching such an extreme forces the end of many trends.

Fashion reflects the spirit and lifestyle of any time period. For example here in 1924 two smartly attired young women were photographed in the Easter Sunday procession along the boardwalk at Atlantic City, New Jersey.

(UPI / BETTMANN)

Fashions allow consumers to conform and to show individuality at the same time.
(*WWD*, Fairchild Publications)

WHY IS FASHION IMPORTANT?

We conclude with the question "Why is fashion important?" As a start toward answering this vital question, consider this basic, all-encompassing fact: **fashion adoption is a fundamental part of human behavior.** Our fashions are integral props to our lifestyles, intimate parts of our personal identity, and reflections of the society and culture in which we live. Fashions help set the stage for our daily lives and relations with others. Particular fashions give us *identity kits*, giving us a stylistic way to manage our appearances, express our psychological selves, present our self-images, personalities, moods, changing roles, and make impressions on others (**impression management**) (Kaiser 1990, chap. 6). We use fashion as a form of nonverbal communication that may declare, among other things, our age, sex, status, occupation, and fashion interest (Lurie 1981). To understand these fundamental aspects of fashion is to understand one of the most basic and necessary parts of everyday life in contemporary society.

Changing fashions are just as important. Just as the fashions of any given time represent the **zeitgeist** or "spirit of the times"—the life-styles of people and the current social climate—changing fashions represent changing times and new life-styles. Fashions reflect the basic social and cultural forces of the society in which they exist. In fact, new fashions may even signal forthcoming social changes, as is often implied by fashion writers (e.g., Banner 1983; Johnston 1972). Did the dress of the increasingly independent woman of the 1950s and 1960s, such as casual wear, pants, career apparel and minis, signify the coming of the liberated and professional woman of the 1970s, 1980s and 1990s? But perhaps the very best justification for us to see changing fashions as important is so simply stated: "Fashion . . . permits us to live in a world of freshly cut blooms where without it we should suffer from an over supply of artificial flowers." (Robinson, in Sproles 1981, 68). New fashions bring excitement, newness, variety, and novelty in life, stimulating human living and interactions perhaps with greater power than most forms of human behavior.

Fashion is also important because the creation of a fashionable appearance has become *the central force* determining the appearances consumers accept. Consumers choose different appearances for many reasons, and fundamental ones such as comfort and functionality are obviously important, but through this century changing styles and changing tastes have dominated consumers' choices. This has been encouraged by the tremendous growth of mass-produced, "ready-made" fashions in all prices and designs (Daves 1967; Kidwell and Christman 1974). Changing styles in all their forms, colors, materials, designs, details and silhouettes have also

Interior of Galeries Lafayette, a fashionable Paris store.
(*WWD*, Fairchild Publications)

been stimulated by newer and better textile and apparel technologies. The increased wealth and leisure, so well documented as the hallmark of the twentieth century, have provided consumers the wherewithal to continually demand novelty, innovation, and change in styles. And through years of social evolution, specific fashions have become attached to our specific roles and activities in life; for example, professional suit styles, leisurewear, sportswear, and many others have evolved as uniquely identified fashion trends, so making fashion the driving force in consumers' behavior toward appearances in general.

The study of fashion becomes of even greater consequence when we realize that fashion adoption is a *world phenomenon,* not just something pervading the United States, Canada, Western Europe and other western societies. Contemporary fashions of this century are sweeping the world, integrating themselves into the social cultures and life-styles of Asian nations, Eastern Europe, the former Soviet Union and now even the Third World. The 1990s spread of democracy and open markets in Europe and the former Soviet Union will accelerate this. Thus fashion change is increasingly a key variable to understanding *world dress,* the dress of all countries and cultures. Furthermore, international trade of fashion is big business in the world economy. Just as United States and European fashions have spread over the globe, we as Westerners admire the arts and cultures of other peoples, and display this admiration by adopting their culturally based styles as our own.

Finally, understanding fashion is vital to the entrepreneurial and business world. The obvious case in point is those entering careers in the fashion business, especially the design and marketing of changing fashions. For them, understanding the many ways new fashions originate, the human motivations behind fashion adoption, the processes by which fashion trends spread, and how to forecast the emergence of new fashions is indispensable. Successful fashion marketers demand such skills, but knowing the human science of fashion adoption is no less important to the manufacturers of textiles and apparel, for *understanding fashion* is the crucial ingredient which, if absent, guarantees failure to all businesses where fashionable changes are ever-present.

SUMMARY

A **fashion** may be defined generally as a style of consumer product or way of behaving temporarily adopted by a discernible proportion of members of a social group because that chosen behavior is perceived to be socially appropriate for the time and situation. Fashions may occur in many differing classes of objects, including different classes of consumer products and social forms of human behavior.

Clothing is the classic and most obvious object of fashionable behavior. Using the general definition of fashion as a guide, we may specifically define a clothing fashion as a style of dress that is temporarily adopted by a discernible proportion of members of a social group because that chosen style is perceived to be socially appropriate for the time and situation.

The **fashion process** is a dynamic mechanism of change through which a potential fashion object is created and transmitted from its point of creation to public introduction, discernible public acceptance, and eventual obsolescence. Consumer behavior in the process may be conceptualized as a continuous sequence of six stages. The start of a fashion's life, stage one, begins when it is created and introduced to consumers. In stage two, the new object (the potential fashion) is introduced and adopted by certain leading consumers, or fashion leaders. During stage three, the new object becomes highly visible and communicable to a wider audience of consumers, as it is now adopted by a large number of fashion leaders and other early adopters. Stage four occurs as the fashion becomes widely accepted by many different social groups; a major influence on this continued diffusion is social conformity. Stage five is reached when the fashion achieves widespread and massive acceptance and becomes socially saturated from overuse. This sets the stage for the final stage, decline and obsolescence of the fashion.

The fashion process is the result of many individuals making the decisions to adopt (purchase, wear) a style. This **adoption process** is a mental learning process of five stages: awareness, interest, evaluation, trial, and adoption. It is influenced by information sources and a variety of personal and social motives, such as self-image and impression management. Individuality versus conformity are among the principal motivations here.

From these perspectives of fashion, several fundamental principles of fashion are identified: (1) new fashions are invented by many sources, not just fashion designers; (2) new fashions evolve from past fashions and are not dramatically different from them; (3) fashions are determined by external forces (our culture, society, lifestyle, history, economy, and marketing system) and therefore serve as a reflection of their time and place; (4) many different fashion trends exist simultaneously in different groups of the consumer population; (5) individuality and conformity are opposing forces that join together to influence fashion creation and adoption; (6) fashions have life cycles; and (7) all fashions inevitably must end (even our favorites).

Why is fashion important? We have indicated fashion is a significant and fundamental phenomenon of human behavior, related to our lifestyles, personal identity, and our social culture. Changing fashions are also significant, both as reflections of a changing society and to bring newness and excitement into life continuously. Fashion adoption is also important because it has become the central force shaping our appearances. Fashion is of even greater consequence when we consider that fashion adoption has become a world phenomenon. And finally, fashion is a significant product, important to the success of business and the economy of our world.

NOTES

1. See the Appendix to this chapter for a more complete presentation of these and other varying definitions of fashion.
2. Conceptualizations of fashion as a general phenomenon of human behavior have been offered by many analysts (Simmel 1904; Sapir 1931; Blumer 1969; Sproles 1979). Some particularly unique treatments of this subject include fashions in arts and crafts (Elliot 1937), fashions in literature (Warner 1902), fashions in the printed page (Gress 1931), fashions in educational practices (The Association of Princeton Graduate Alumni 1957), and fashions in science (Crane 1969).
3. This and the following conception of the fashion process are derived from the general theory of adoption and diffusion of innovations (Rogers 1962; Rogers and Shoemaker 1971; Rogers 1983; Robertson 1971). Also, for some relevant theoretical works on fashion which have influenced this and the following conceptualization of the fashion process, see Simmel (1904), Veblen (1912), Nystrom (1928), Sapir (1931), Robinson (1961), Lang and Lang (1961), King (1963), Blumer (1968, 1969), Sproles and King (1973), and Sproles (1974, 1979, 1981, 1985). Many of these earlier works are classics in the development of fashion theory. It should be noted that the transition from one phase to the next may not be clearly defined, but it is still useful to think of phases as a conceptual framework for fashion analysis.
4. This concept of the adoption process is modified in Rogers' later work (1983), and slightly modified models are also suggested by consumer analysts (Wilkie 1990). However, the original concept suggested by Rogers is appropriate to introduce for its simplicity and conceptual clarity. Refinements are suggested in later chapters.

DISCUSSION QUESTIONS AND PROJECTS

1. What definition(s) of fashion do you find most appropriate? How would you define fashion?
2. What makes a fashion *object* different from other "objects" (products) that consumers buy and use?
3. Fashion is very important to the acceptance of new styles of appearance. How is fashion also important to the acceptance of other consumer products such as automobiles, furniture, houses, and stereos? Does fashion play a role in acceptance of services such as new restaurants, entertainment (e.g., rock stars), movies, dance steps, social activities?
4. Describe the steps that took place in the growth of any current fashion you are now wearing. How did you learn about it? How many people in your network of friends dress in similar styles? When do you think this style will go out of fashion?
5. Some critics suggest that consumers' adoption of fashions is an example of human vanity, frivolity and waste. Others suggest it is a very important core attribute of our society and life-style, something of serious importance and consequence. Which view did you hold as you began this chapter? In what ways do you see your adoption of fashions as important to yourself as an individual and to our society and economy?

SUGGESTED READINGS

Blumer, Herbert. "Fashion." *International Encyclopedia of the Social Sciences* New York: The Macmillan Company, 1968.
Calisibetta, Charlotte. *Fairchild's Dictionary of Fashion.* 2d ed. 1988.
Sapir, Edward. "Fashion." *Encyclopedia of the Social Sciences.* 1931.
Webster's Unabridged Dictionary (look up the word fashion and see its many meanings as suggested by this authoritative source of the English language).

APPENDIX:
SELECTED DEFINITIONS OF FASHION

This is a compendium of historical and recent definitions of fashion, to help readers appreciate the subtle and varied meanings of fashion. The 1901

Oxford English Dictionary, a basic source of the English language, offers twenty definitions of fashion. Here are some representative selections:

- "To give fashion or shape to; to form, mould, shape (either a 'material' or 'immaterial object')."
- Fashion is "the mode of dress, etiquette, furniture, style of speech, etc., adopted in society for the time being."
- Fashion is a ". . . mode of action, hearing, behavior, demeanor, 'air.'" Fashion is ". . . conventional usage in dress, mode of life, etc., especially as observed in the upper circles of society; conformity to this usage."

Psychologist Ross, quoted by Hurlock (1929, 4), defined fashion as ". . . a series of recurring changes in the choices of a group of people, which, though they may be accompanied by utility, are not determined by it."

Economist and marketing professor Nystrom (1928, 4), suggests "Fashion is nothing more or less than the prevailing style at any given time."

Fashion merchant Daniels (1951, 51) states, "Fashion is a conception of what is currently appropriate."

Sociologists Barber and Lobel (1952, 126) suggest "Fashion in clothes has to do with the styles of cut, color, silhouette, stuffs, etc., that are socially prescribed and socially accepted as appropriate for certain roles, and especially with the recurring changes in these styles."

The Fashion Dictionary (Picken 1973, 138) offers two definitions:

- Fashion is the "prevailing or accepted style; often embracing many styles at one time."
- Fashion is the "particular line or construction, as of a garment."

Fairchild's Dictionary of Fashion (Calasibetta 1988, 205) defines fashion as "the contemporary mode in wearing apparel or accessories as interpreted in textiles, fur, leather, and other materials. In the broader sense it also involves the designing, manufacturing, promotion, and selling of such items."

Sociologists Lang and Lang (1961, 323) treat fashion as "an elementary form of collective behavior, whose compelling power lies in the implicit judgment of an anonymous multitude."

Economist Robinson offers two fashion definitions:

- "Fashion, defined in its most general sense, is the pursuit of novelty for its own sake." (Robinson 1958, 127)

◆ Fashion is ". . . change in the design of things for decorative purposes." (Robinson 1961, 376)

Marketing professor King (1964, 324) writes: "Fashion adoption is a process of social contagion by which a new style or product is adopted by the consumer after commercial introduction by the designer or manufacturer."

Fashion industry analysts Jarnow and Guerriero (1991, 546) suggest fashion is "A continuing process of change in the styles of dress that are accepted and followed by a large segment of the public at any particular time."

Home economists Horn and Gurel (1981, 497) define fashion as the "the popular, accepted, and prevailing style at any given time and place."

The 1966 (Third) Edition of *Webster's Unabridged Dictionary* offers a variety of definitions, including:

◆ Fashion is "the form of something or the way it is constructed: appearance or mode of structure."
◆ Fashion is "the prevailing or accepted style or group of styles in dress or personal decoration established or adopted during a particular time or season."
◆ Fashion is "a way of dressing, behaving, dancing, decorating, or an interest (as in a recreation) that is considered especially up-to-date or noticeably following the contemporary trend in such activities."

From a differing perspective, Sapir (1931, 139) compares and contrasts the meaning of fashion to other related concepts:

The meaning of the term fashion may be clarified by pointing out how it differs in connotation from a number of other terms whose meaning it approaches. A particular fashion differs from a given taste in suggesting some measure of compulsion on the part of the group as contrasted with individual choice from among a number of possibilities . . . . Particular people or coteries have their fads, while fashions are the property of larger and more representative groups. A taste which asserts itself in spite of fashion and which may therefore be suspected of having something obsessive about it may be referred to as an individual fad . . . . Just as the weakness of fashion leads to fads, so its strength comes from custom. Customs differ from fashions in being relatively permanent types of social behavior.

2

The Birth and Evolution of New Fashions

OBJECTIVES

◆ To examine the historical continuity of fashion.
◆ To examine fashion as a reflection of social and cultural change.
◆ To describe the forces instrumental in shaping the fashion objects in contemporary society.
◆ To identify the origins of new fashions.

Changes in styles and appearances are a modern fact of life. Indeed, the regular innovation and change in fashions have been observed and documented in fashion history for hundreds of years. First and foremost a phenomenon of Western cultures and societies, the forces of innovation and change now sweep new fashions across cities, states, international borders and continents. So many forces, some obvious and some exceedingly subtle, are credited for this: the general pervasiveness of our change-oriented culture, the consumer-oriented growth of wealthy industrial nations, the power of the seductive fashion production and marketing system, the easily imitated glamour and occasional creativity of celebrities, and inexorable powers of social and cultural change. To understand the forces that direct and inspire our changing appearances is to understand the vast complexities and inner-workings of our total social, cultural, economic and historical milieu.

Our starting place, then, is to delineate the broad forces of our society that shape changing appearances. To gain this understanding requires a fundamental appreciation of the social and cultural contexts of change, the roles of the fashion marketing system as producer of change, the special powers of extraordinary events as inspirations to change, the creative roles of consumers as agents of change, and the unique historical context in which change evolves from year to year.

HISTORICAL CONTINUITY IN FASHION CHANGE

To begin our discussion on the birth of new fashions, it is necessary to look at fashion change in its historical context. New fashion objects are seldom revolutionary in nature. Instead they follow a trend of relatively small design changes. Fashion is said to have **historical continuity,** that is, fashion is an evolutionary outgrowth and elaboration of previously existing fashions. For example, changes in dress lengths (from shorter to longer and vice versa) have occurred over long periods of years. A dramatic change in dress lengths, perhaps from knee to floor length, would constitute a revolutionary rather than evolutionary change. The principle of historical continuity in change would predict that such a dramatic change would be unlikely to occur over a short period. One major reason is that a radical departure from styles of the immediate past would probably be too innovative to be accepted immediately by most consumers.

Thus the historical continuity of fashion constrains the degree of fashion change. Very few times in history has fashion changed dramatically, violating the principle of historical continuity. Such changes typically have occurred immediately after major wars, thus reflecting the dramatic sociopolitical changes which were occurring at the time. For example, a drastic change in fashion came immediately after the French Revolution. In the decade between 1789 and 1799 men's and women's fashion went from a rococo style dress with five-foot wide skirts, ornate vests, powdered wigs, and luxurious fabrics to a sober and simplified fashion which included wool frock coats and ankle length trousers for men and narrow skirts and dull colors for women. These dramatic fashion changes reflected changes in the political attitudes of the country.

A second dramatic change in fashion came immediately after World War II. Between 1946 and 1947 fashionable skirt lengths for women fell up to twelve inches. Christian Dior's "New Look" epitomized the radical change from the masculine war-time fashions to feminine dresses and suits that had rounded shoulders, slim waists, and full sweeping skirts. These fashions reflected the social desire to forget the past war strife and to move toward prosperity. However, if wartime restrictions had not been in place,

skirts may have cycled into the "New Look" by 1946-47 in the typical evolutionary pattern.

The radical fashion changes shown in Dior's "New Look" were objected to by the "Little Below-the-Knee Club," 1947.

(UPI / BETTMANN)

From a historical perspective, it appears that the silhouettes and dimensions of fashion objects progress along repeating cycles of change. The cyclical nature of fashion objects has been studied by several researchers in an effort to understand the forces of fashion change over long periods of time, spanning the past three centuries of changing dress. Alfred L. Kroeber (1919), an anthropologist, was the first to investigate cyclical changes in fashion. Using fashion illustrations from three important fashion magazines of the time, Kroeber tabulated changes in the width measurements and length measurements of women's dresses from 1844 to 1919. He found that similar skirt length recurred every 35 years, similar skirt width recurred at the rate of once every 100 years (50 years in each direction), neckline width also recurred at the rate of once every 100 years, neckline length rose in one-third of the time required for its descent, the diameter of the waist fluctuated irregularly, and skirt length changed three times faster than skirt width. In a later study of the period from 1605 to 1936, Richardson and Kroeber (1940), using similar measurements, found women's skirts alternating from broad to narrow and from long to short with some regularity, completing the full cycle in about a century.

In another investigation which suggests the validity of the cyclical nature of fashion, Young (1937) noted that, "when the typical annual fashions are arranged chronologically in unbroken series over a long term of years, their changes appear to follow rather definite laws of modification and development within an almost unchanging pattern of evolution" (p. 107). To support her hypotheses, Young examined representative pictures of skirts for 1760 to 1937. She found that the three classifications of skirts styles, bell-shaped, back fullness type, and tubular-shaped, each had a cycle of 30 to 40 years resulting in three cycles per century. Her sweeping conclusion was that

> *fashion is by no means ruled by a comparatively small group of designers in Paris and elsewhere, who are commonly regarded as being the arbiters of style. Rather, it must be that the arbiters, unknown to themselves, are in actuality ruled and restricted within somewhat narrow limits by the unsuspected working of a fundamental principle of change.* (P. 123)

Probably one of the most adamant believers in the notion that fashion changes are cyclical and move in a pattern of continuity was economist and fashion analyst Dwight E. Robinson. In studying style changes of skirt width for women and facial hair for men for a hundred-year period, Robinson (1975) concluded that: (1) "fashions run an inexorable cycle" (p. 122), and (2) "fashion cycles display a regularity that puts them effectively outside the influence of external events" (p. 126). In essence, this reinforces the view that broad fashion trends, once started, must inevitably evolve and run their course.

Although historical evidence has pointed to the cyclical nature of fashion, John and Elizabeth Lowe (1982, 1984, 1985) extended Richardson and Kroeber's work to determine if the same conclusions could be made about twentieth century fashion. Their model of fashion change was developed based upon four assumptions (1984, 731):

1. *Inertia operates.* Because of inertia, a fashion trend set into motion will continue its direction until an extreme is reached. For example, if skirts have been progressively getting narrower, they will continue to do so until they become very snug-fitting.

2. *Resistance to that motion occurs.* There is a tendency for fashion not to change too fast. There appear to be cultural forces and aesthetic rules which slow the rate of fashion change.
3. *Dress dimensions are not independent.* Rather they affect one another in ways which follow the principles of design (i.e., proportion, emphasis, form) to create aesthetically pleasing designs. They found correlations between some of the dress dimensions. For example, when skirts were short and emphasis was on the legs, the neckline was neither wide nor deep.
4. *Some fashions are totally unpredictable.* Some innovations which are adopted cannot be predicted.

Using similar methods as Richardson and Kroeber, the Lowes used historical data from 1789 to 1936 (1982) and from 1932 to 1980 (1984, 1985). They came to the conclusion that fashion change is, in part, a result of historical stylistic development and that the transformation of dress dimensions through time is predictable. However, they noted that stylistic changes in fashion were not a closed system, but were affected by external forces, especially socio-political unrest. They also discovered that the historic consistency of current fashions may not fit the deterministic models and assumptions of the past. As indicated by the Lowes:

The deterministic cycles they espoused are not well realized in the period from 1937 to 1980. Skirts do not balloon outward to Civil War proportions in the mid-twentieth century as Richardson and Kroeber suggest they should. Likewise the bustle has failed to return in the 1970s as Young's model would have predicted (1985, 204).

In addition, the Lowes found that the rate of fashion change was not accelerating despite the advancements in production and distribution of fashion. They also discovered increased within-year variance in style changes. This result they attributed to the increased participation in the fashion process by a greater variety of consumers.

It appears that historical continuity is primarily seen in the most basic and broad fashion trends, but that these trends are not necessarily cyclical in nature. While basic trends in dimensions and silhouettes may change little from year to year, smaller design details of fashion are affected by current social forces and are easily subject to dramatic changes. Details such as ornamentation, color, and fabric designs may exhibit distinct yearly changes. Variation in these elements of design provides variety and individualism in styling, and design changes of these types are infrequently resisted by consumers. For changes in the most basic elements of styling, however, historical continuity is apparent in the longer-running, basic fashion trends.

FASHION AS A REFLECTION OF SOCIAL CHANGE

Social change is "a succession of events which produce over time a modification or replacement of particular patterns or units by other novel ones" (Smith 1976, 13). Social change is an exceedingly powerful and pervasive feature of our twentieth century. Theories of social change are used to explain and predict the events of a society that result in socio-economic, political, or cultural change within that society. Although primarily stemming from the basic discipline of sociology, the study of social change integrates areas such as economics, political science, anthropology, philosophy, and the humanities in an effort to better understand changing patterns within a society.

There are several fundamental characteristics of contemporary social change:

1. Rapid change is occurring frequently and even constantly;
2. Change occurs as sequential chains of events which reverberate throughout many segments of a society;
3. Change is frequently planned, or is a result of deliberate innovation;
4. The material, technology, and social strategies for creating change are rapidly expanding;
5. Change is a normal occurrence affecting a larger number of individual experiences and functional aspects of society, and few aspects of life are exempt from the influences of change (Moore 1974, 2).

Social change, in recent decades, has modified such social institutions as the class structure, social lifestyles, roles of men and women, and the structure and function of families. Many fashion theorists contend that fashion is a reflection of these socio-economic, political, and cultural changes (Behling 1985; Bush and London 1960; Lauer and Lauer 1981; Robenstine and Kelley 1981; Wilson 1985). These theorists recognize that social, cultural, historical, and economic forces all influence what fashion objects will emerge and be adopted by consumers. This phenomenon has led analysts to offer a general observation that fashions always evolve to be modern, or to symbolize the "spirit of the times" (Flugel 1930; Blumer 1969). James Laver (1937), a fashion historian, notes the social appropriateness of fashion at specific times in history:

Designer Willi Smith's (1948-87) unisex clothing is a reflection of changing roles of men and women, 1985.
(THE BETTMANN ARCHIVE)

In every period costume has some essential line, and when we look back over the fashions of the past we can see quite clearly what it is, and can see what is surely very strange, that the forms of dresses, apparently so haphazard, so dependent on the whim of the designer, have an extraordinary relevance to the spirit of the age. (For example) The aristocratic stiffness of the old regime in France is completely mirrored in the brocaded gowns of the eighteenth century . . . . Victorian modesty expressed itself in the multitude of petticoats, the emancipation of the post-War flapper in short hair and short skirts. We touch here something very mysterious, as if the Time Spirit were a reality, clothing itself ever in the most suitable garments and rejecting all others. (P. 250)

Indeed, Robert and Jeanette Lauer (1981) note that "If clothes express the spirit of the age, it follows that we can use changing fashions as an indication of a changing society" (p. 18). As it relates to fashion change, other changes occurring within a society create an environment that stimulates a societal need for innovations in clothing. If so, then the acceptance or failure of each innovation satisfies the need created by social change. *Table 2.1* presents a summary of examples of the link between social change and the emergence of new fashions in the twentieth century.

TABLE 2.1   LINKS BETWEEN EVOLVING FASHIONS AND SOCIAL CHANGE

Decade / Evolving Fashions	Social Environment and Social Change
1900 (Start of Century)	
◆ Fashion begins twentieth century with styles carried over from past century. Women's styles are lavishly designed, emphasizing bust, hips, waist. Men's business suits have become a symbol of industrial progress (Harris and Johnston 1971).	◆ Women are primarily in traditional home roles, though a number of women's activist movements seeking reform have occurred in the past decades. Women are dependent on men. Status symbolism is a major fashion function.
1900s	
◆ Women at work in male styles—shirtwaist and skirt similar to man's "sober suit and white collared shirt" (Roach 1974).	◆ Typewriter used in offices. Women at work in basically clerical jobs. Five million women in the labor force.
◆ Ready-made, mass produced clothing industry continues major growth started in late 1800s. Shirtwaist dress is first ready-to-wear fashion. New York becoming a major fashion center, and an American style of dress is emerging (Daves 1967).	◆ Beginnings of mass manufacturing, communications, and retailing. Women working in fashion and textile industries. Beginning of the century of "expressionism, activism, dynamism, and new technology" (Pistolese and Horsting 1970).
1910s	
◆ Hobble skirts—tight and close fitting. Fuller and more mobile skirts begin to replace the hobble skirts about 1915 (Lester and Kerr 1967). World War I begins, imposing economy and simplicity on clothing.	◆ Automobiles emerge late in the decade, beginning to change women's patterns of life-styles, freedom, and mobility.
◆ Movie clothes became an emerging influence which will "crystallize in the 1920s" (Hollander 1974).	◆ Movies provide "glimpses of fantasy-elegance" rather than real world style. Idealized fashion images from movies a new influence on dress and grooming. Movies as influence to spread established rather than new styles.
◆ European art trends, Cubism and Futurism, as fashion influences (Pistolese and Horstring 1970).	
1920s	
◆ Clothing fitted to body shape, but in an increasingly loose and unrestrictive way. Skirt lengths getting shorter. Style variety becoming more apparent.	◆ Increasing interests in sports, avant garde life-styles, women's rights. Women's interest in activity and freedom increases. The Roaring Twenties, jazz, night club life.
1930s	
◆ Increased emphasis on careful and precise grooming (Squire 1974). Daytime, evening, street dresses—variety of dress lengths.	◆ Movie influence on styles increases. New fibers—rayon, acetate, and later nylon—appearing in fabrics. Effects of the Depression being felt as a moderating influence on change.
1940s	
◆ Fabric rationing and fashion simplicity forced by World War II.	◆ Women working in factories during war.
◆ The "New Look" of 1947, longer and fuller skirts, a Dior designer influence. Fashion interest and rate of fashion change increase.	◆ Women ready for a change from wartime austerity.

Decade / Evolving Fashions	Social Environment and Social Change

1950s

◆ Increasing youth interest in fashion. California youth-fashion influences. Male fashion interest increasing. "Unisex" fashion trend begins. Women wearing pants. Diversity in clothing styles, colors, and fabrics. Abstract and modern art influences. Many well-known designers in Europe and United States.

◆ Young people have financial ability to pursue fashion interests (Squire 1974). Families becoming child-centered. Interest in fashion by age groups begins to displace traditional status symbolism functions. New roles for men and women emerging. Man-made fibers becoming an important clothing functional component. Growing influences of the mass marketing and retailing economy. Rates of social and technological change increasing. New occupations, inventions, communications (television), population mobility, entertainment, sports interests.

1960s

◆ Continuing trends toward unisex styles. Youth ("hippie") styles emphasize comfort and practicality rather than status symbolism (Reich 1970; Harris and Johnston 1971). Fashion emphasis on young styling in general. Pants become an important woman's fashion. Miniskirt lengths grown in acceptance. Durable press clothing arrives.

◆ Changing roles in society. Youth challenges to traditional values and symbols of adult society. Feminism becomes a contemporary active movement. Increasing emphasis on individualism. Communal living in certain population sub-segments. Generally, a decade of social reforms.

1970s

◆ Increasing fashion interest among men (McQuade 1971). Future of business suit challenged (Johnston 1972). Diversity in women's styles is the greatest in fashion history—pants suits, many dress lengths, variety in color and fabric choice. Men's leisure suits and sportswear trends.

◆ Relaxing of social and sexual norms, greater belief in individuality and freedom of choice. Changing marriage and family patterns. Highly developed mass marketing and communication system. New concerns with environment and conservation of resources. Thirty-eight million women in the labor force.

1980s

◆ A wide range of fashion trends is prominent. "Dress for success" reaches new heights of acceptance.

◆ Growth in designer label and private label goods. Birth of new design houses (e.g., Donna Karan, Michael Kors). Rock stars and "supermodels" become new fashion leaders. Off-shore production and importing of apparel and accessories increases rapidly (imports accounting for half of the domestic market), stimulating mass diffusion of fashion trends. Quick Response technology creates "pull" system within the industry.

◆ Diversity—in lifestyles and cultural groups— becomes a central feature of society. Individualism and acceptance of difference is widely promoted. Career advancement for women becomes a norm.

◆ U.S. trade deficit increases as global manufacturing and marketing increase. Growth in mass merchandisers and off-price retailers. Merging companies within the fashion industry. MTV starts. Purchase and use of VCRs leads to increased use of video technology.

1990s

◆ Variety in fashion trends and powerful influences from the 1980s carry over to the early 1990s.

◆ Environmental concerns lead to new technology and "green marketing" of environmentally safe apparel lines. Cultural diversity spurs growth in ethnic goods.

◆ Will fashion changes be influenced by growing economic conservatism and lower materialism among consumers?

◆ Collapse of the Soviet Union and emergence of European Economic Community creates avenues for export or expansion of companies overseas. Economic recession creates caution among consumers, a potential influence on fashion change.

The process of social change can be examined on several levels: the type of change occurring, the origins of the change, and the channels within a society which facilitate the change (Smith 1976). Fashion as a reflection of social change will be discussed in terms of each of these levels. The first level in the process of social change is the type or form of change that emerges. Within any society there are three types of patterns or units that undergo change: socio-economic patterns, political patterns, and cultural patterns (Smith 1976). Changes may occur in the socio-economic patterns of resource allocation and production within social groups. Political change occurs when there are changes in the distribution of power and authority, in the formulation of law, and in the institutions of a society. Changes may also occur in the cultural patterns of a society. This involves change in knowledge, artistic and literary styles, ideas and beliefs, and modes of behavior. As part of a society's material culture, fashion can effectively be studied as an example of cultural change.

Fashion change exists within a broad cultural context. Cultural influences not only affect the form which changing fashion objects take, but also affect the speed of fashion change within a society. **Culture** is viewed as the distinctive way of life of a group of people. Hall (1959) describes three separate levels of culture: formal traditions, informal traditions, and technical capabilities. Each level contributes a different strength to the emotional resistance to change by the members of a society and are based on sanctions associated with the cultural precepts.

Formal traditions are fundamental and unquestioned customs and behaviors. They are learned as political laws or strict cultural norms. Violations for going against formal traditions can range from arrests to social shock. Formal traditions are passed from one generation to another with little resistance, and, therefore, they are very slow to change. An example of a formal tradition would be the social norm of morality in Western society of wearing clothing in public. This social norm is regulated by laws of indecent exposure and violation of these laws can result in an individual being fined or arrested.

Formal traditions also include clothing **customs.** A custom is based upon traditional patterns of behavior. Often clothing customs are associated with religious ceremonies, rituals, and rites of passage. Examples of clothing customs include a traditional graduation gown and mortar board, special clothing worn by individuals when they are baptized, and traditional wedding gowns. One clothing custom seen in virtually every society is that of sex differentiation in clothing. In most

cultures males wear different clothing than do females. This particular clothing custom mirrors overriding formal traditions of sex role behavior and status.

Informal traditions are behaviors learned by imitating models within a society. As the models change, so do the informal traditions. Social meanings associated with clothing and changing fashions can be considered informal traditions. Most basic of the informal traditions surrounding fashion is that of cultural ideals of attractiveness. Cultural ideals of attractiveness define what is socially considered physically handsome or beautiful. Fashion objects often reflect cultural definitions of attractiveness. Consequently, through the use of fashion objects, males and females strive to achieve this culturally defined ideal of attractiveness.

As informal traditions are culture specific, ideals of attractiveness often vary among cultures. For example, anthropologists Clelland Ford and Frank Beach (1951) studied over two hundred primitive societies in search of universal definitions of female beauty. However, they found no universal standards of beauty. In fact, even when societies agreed on what parts

Clothing customs, such as graduation gowns, resist the influences of fashion (top left).
(*WWD*, Fairchild Publications)

Wedding attire represents formal traditions of a society (top right).
(*WWD*, Fairchild Publications)

of the body were important to physical attractiveness for females, they very seldom agreed on what characteristics of that body part were considered attractive.

In Western society, standards of attractiveness are often communicated through the media and reflected in fashion objects. However, even within a society, standards of attractiveness change over time. Social psychologists Elaine Hatfield and Susan Sprecher (1986) describe changing standards of female beauty:

> Standards of beauty are never static. They are forever changing—especially for women. At the turn of the century, the Gibson Girl was the ideal. She was tall and full-breasted. In the 1920s, the "flapper" sped into view. Women cut their hair, removed the scarves and other stuffing from their bodices, and began to bind their breasts. (The brassiere was originally invented to hide breasts.) From the 1920s on, ideals of beauty flickered from movie screens. In the 1950s, the leading Hollywood queen was Marilyn Monroe. She was the sex symbol of the era; once again beauty equaled voluptuousness. In the 1960s, Twiggy brought in the beanpole look, which did not last long. In the 1970s the shapely, sensuous look with legs returned with Raquel Welch. What about the 1980s? Today we admire a variety of beauty models. There are the Brooke Shieldses (all-American look), and the Dolly Partons (with abundance). (P. 17)

According to a 1982 *Time* cover story, the new ideal of female beauty is "taut, toned and coming on strong." Because of the fitness craze, muscles, once a symbol of masculinity, have become the status symbol of fitness, health, and sexiness for both sexes. Along with this new ideal have come the "jock chic" fashions that best reflect it: tights and leotards, jogging and bicycling shorts, and running shoes. Cultural ideals of attractiveness and the fashion objects that reflect these ideals are informal traditions and therefore develop and change within an overall cultural context.

Technical abilities, the abilities to produce goods, are also fundamental forces on styles of dress and amount of change a culture may develop. The basic ingredients for development of fashion are the availability of resources and the technical as well as artistic skills of the designer and manufacturer. To translate these ingredients into the desired form requires a certain level of technological sophistication in fabricating clothing. At a basic level, a relatively simple technology can suffice to convert leaves or reeds into items of apparel (grass skirts, for example), to remove animal skins for furs to drape over the body, or to sew fabrics into garments.

Ideals of beauty focused on women's legs in the 1920s ("flapper"; top left), 1960s (Twiggy; top right), and 1980s (Norma Kamali's design, 1982; left).

(Top left, THE BETTMANN ARCHIVE; top right, UPI / BETTMANN; left, *WWD*, Fairchild Publications)

But to produce complex fabrics demands a more sophisticated technology: the abilities to harvest fibers, to spin fibers into yarns, and to interlock yarns into fabrics by processes like weaving, knitting, and felting. In a yet more advanced technology, synthetic fibers and dyes have emerged as technological inventions for producing a range of complex fabrics.

The simple invention of the eyed sewing needle is perhaps one of the most significant events in the technology of clothing construction. Anthropological evidence indicates that the needle existed at least thirty to forty thousand years ago (Crawford 1940). The needle was invented to sew animal skins, and later fabrics, into body-contoured apparel. Today, use of the needle remains (with the aid of mechanical sewing machines) the primary technology for construction of clothing.

In Western civilization, advanced technologies as well as the basic sewing machine, have made possible the development of numerous styles and forms of dress. Nonetheless, many technologies that open the door to fashion changes have emerged only within the past two centuries, after thousands of years of limited technological innovation. Today's technology for producing clothing is a recent invention in the history of humankind, but it has made possible an almost infinite range of colors, fabric designs, and styling concepts to create fashion changes.

Thus, the changes in fashion over time within a society are affected by that society's formal traditions, informal traditions, and technical abilities. Formal traditions of moral clothing behavior, informal traditions such as ideals of attractiveness, and technical abilities of fabric and apparel production affect the styles that will be adopted by the consumers and the rates of change the culture can accommodate. A new color trend such as neon may be accommodated by ideals of attractiveness and technical skills for production; skimpy swimwear may not emerge as a viable fashion object in a morally conservative culture.

ORIGINS AND CHANNELS OF FASHION CHANGE

As we have suggested so far, fashion change takes place within a cultural context and as a reflection of social change. The second and third levels to be examined in the process of social change, the origins of change and the channels within a society which facilitate the change, will be discussed together as they apply to fashion change. Many broad, amorphous, and sometimes difficult to identity forces shape the processes of change. Let us now take a more precise look at the instigators and channels of specific changes in fashion. Three strong forces bring about changes: planned changes which are initiated and propagated by the fashion industry, unplanned changes where new fashions become an outgrowth of major or extraordinary events in society, and changes inspired by creative consumers ranging from public celebrities to average consumers.

Creators of Fashion within the Fashion Industry

The fashion industry obviously plays an important role in the creation and initiation of fashions. Fashion designers, fashion manufacturers, fashion retailers, and individuals in auxiliary industries such as fashion advertising or display may all contribute to the initiation and proliferation of many novel, innovative, exciting and even seductive new styles each year. The temptations to consumers are ever-present and pervasive. Individuals within each segment have the opportunity to create new silhouettes, details, or fabric combinations. For example, a visual merchandiser in a fashion retail store may create a new fashion by bringing together separate designs of several manufacturers and displaying them in new and unique combinations that were not thought of by the separate manufacturers.

Fashion designers, by virtue of their profession, are the primary creators of fashion within the fashion industry. Their charge is to adapt existing styles into perceivably new forms which will be accepted by consumers. When strolling through a store or flipping through the pages of a fashion magazine, one may notice the similarities in styling among the fashion objects hanging on the racks or being advertised. One may wonder why fashion designers create and manufacture such similar designs when they have virtually thousands of styles from which to choose. All fashion objects originate, evolve from, and are influenced by the designer's social milieu. It is because of these social influences that designers, apart from one another, create such similar designs. As Herbert Blumer (1969) notes in his observations of the fashion industry,

The designers were attuned to an impressive degree to modern developments and were seeking to capture and express in dress design the spirit of such developments. I think that this explains why the dress designers—again a competitive and secretive group, working apart from each other in a large number of different fashion houses—create independently of each other such remarkably similar designs. (P. 279-80)

Designers get their inspiration for new designs from all areas of society: art, technological advancements, the environment, the clothing worn by the

Examples of couture
fashion include: Elsa
Schiaparell adjusting
the hat of one of her
innovative designs,
1953 (near left). André
Courrèges' leather
miniskirt and boots
designed in 1967 (top
left). This unique
design of fur and
denim is by Karl
Lagerfeld for Fendi,
1992 (top right).

(Near left, Robert Capa /
MAGNUM PHOTOS, Inc.;
top left, Texas Fashion Collection;
top right, *WWD*, Fairchild
Publications)

peoples of other cultures, as well as designs of the near and distant past. For example, technological advancements in fibers and fabric construction often serve as a source of inspiration to fashion designers. French fashion designer Elsa Schiaparelli was renowned for her innovative use of fabrics made of the new manufactured fibers of the 1930s. In the early 1960s Courrèges and Pierre Cardin used innovative plastics and vinyl for apparel. Norma Kamali was instrumental in the experimentation and use of knitted fleece in designs. And Karl Lagerfeld, in his fur designs for Fendi, has utilized advancement in fur processing to create nontraditional fur apparel. Developments and advancements in fiber and fabric manufacturing provides designers with new design options which would otherwise not exist.

Within our society, the fashion marketing channel facilitates the emergence and distribution of changing fashion objects. The fashion marketing system includes thousands of specialized design houses, large manufacturers, small manufacturers, specialists in accessories, importers, media, consultants, service organizations, and retail outlets. The core of this marketing system has five components: fiber production, fabric production, fashion production, marketing services, and retail sales. Figure 2.1 shows the relation among these components and the flow of production and marketing activities among the components.

The marketing of products at each stage is active and competitive. In the first stage of the process, producers of natural and manufactured fibers sell their products directly to fabric-producing mills. Many manufactured fibers are engineered and marketed for specific kinds of apparel, and producers' pricing of fibers is often extremely competitive. Some fiber producers also devote considerable advertising and promotion to make consumers aware of their brands and styles, thus exerting a subtle influence on the entire marketing system. The second stage of the process involves fabric production and marketing. At this stage the fashionability of fabrics, in light of design and color trends, becomes crucial to the marketing process. Producers must predict trends in fashion as much as several years in advance, and select styles of fabrics consistent with these trends for each segment of the apparel market. Samples of these designs are marketed to apparel producers, and price competition among producers is usually aggressive for nearly all but the most innovative or limited-supply fabrics.

Worldwide apparel manufacturing firms design and market fashions, and competition can be especially keen at this level of the business. Most firms are relatively small, and most specialize in apparel for specific homogeneous groups of consumers, termed **target markets** or **market segments.** Smaller companies are often the most creative, as they have to be in order to survive. Large and well-known companies such as Esprit and Levi Strauss also play dominant roles in the industry and occasionally influence major fashion trends. Perhaps most unique in this industry is the

The garment district in New York City is the home of designers and manufacturers.
(*WWD*, Fairchild Publications)

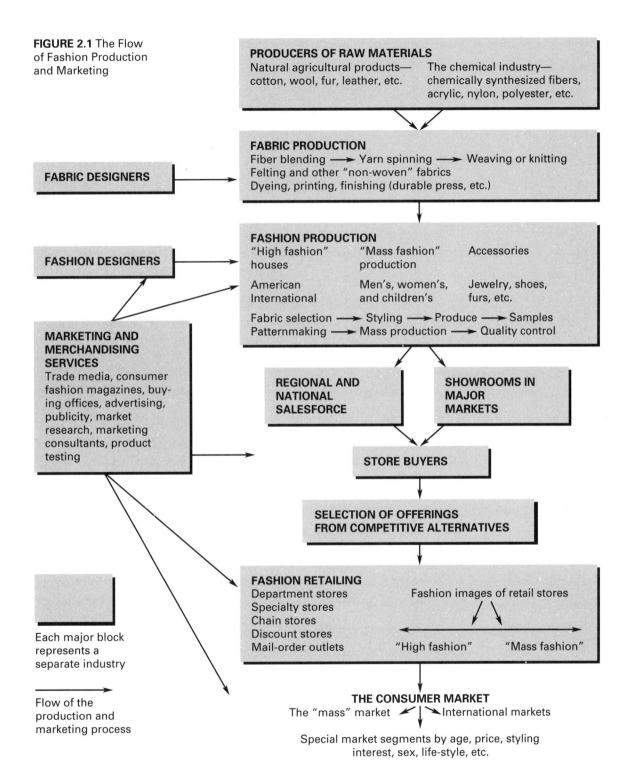

FIGURE 2.1 The Flow of Fashion Production and Marketing

PRODUCERS OF RAW MATERIALS
Natural agricultural products—cotton, wool, fur, leather, etc.
The chemical industry—chemically synthesized fibers, acrylic, nylon, polyester, etc.

FABRIC DESIGNERS

FABRIC PRODUCTION
Fiber blending ⟶ Yarn spinning ⟶ Weaving or knitting
Felting and other "non-woven" fabrics
Dyeing, printing, finishing (durable press, etc.)

FASHION DESIGNERS

FASHION PRODUCTION
"High fashion" houses | "Mass fashion" production | Accessories
American International | Men's, women's, and children's | Jewelry, shoes, furs, etc.
Fabric selection ⟶ Styling ⟶ Produce ⟶ Samples
Patternmaking ⟶ Mass production ⟶ Quality control

MARKETING AND MERCHANDISING SERVICES
Trade media, consumer fashion magazines, buying offices, advertising, publicity, market research, marketing consultants, product testing

REGIONAL AND NATIONAL SALESFORCE

SHOWROOMS IN MAJOR MARKETS

STORE BUYERS

SELECTION OF OFFERINGS FROM COMPETITIVE ALTERNATIVES

FASHION RETAILING
Department stores
Specialty stores
Chain stores
Discount stores
Mail-order outlets

Fashion images of retail stores
"High fashion"   "Mass fashion"

THE CONSUMER MARKET
The "mass" market ⟵ | ⟶ International markets
Special market segments by age, price, styling interest, sex, life-style, etc.

Each major block represents a separate industry

⟶ Flow of the production and marketing process

phenomenon of style piracy or "knock-off" copying. This occurs when one company copies and markets the designs of another more successful, prestigious or innovative company. Many firms "knock-off" the high fashion designs in less expensive (and less elaborate) copies, and thus spread new styles throughout the mass market in all price ranges.

Apparel is produced both domestically (within the United States) and "off shore" (outside the United States). In some cases, the apparel is designed and cut within the United States and constructed off shore. Because apparel production is very labor intensive, apparel companies often have their goods manufactured in countries which have low wages, in order to keep the cost of apparel competitively low.

Apparel producers aggressively compete to sell their styles directly to retailers by using traveling sales representatives who visit retail stores, and by locating merchandise showrooms in important markets like New York, Chicago, Atlanta, Dallas, and Los Angeles. Professional buyers employed by retail stores regularly visit these markets to evaluate current styles and make purchases for their stores. Buyers base their selections on the characteristics of consumers in the target market, or market segment of the store, and the buyers' knowledge of trends in purchasing preferences of the store's customers.

This is the stage of fashion marketing which is most risky from the fashion industry's point of view. Apparel producers must often forecast trends in fashion six months or more in advance and plan for production accordingly. Similarly, retailers must forecast their customers' preferences three or more months in advance and make purchases. If either the manufacturer or retailer makes serious mistakes in these forecasts, the results can be lost sales, markdowns on merchandise, and significant financial loss.

In some cases, the distinction between the apparel manufacturer and the retailer has become blurred. Many apparel manufacturers now own and operate their own retail stores (e.g., NIKE, Esprit, Liz Claiborne, and Ralph Lauren). In addition, many retailers are having products produced specifically for their stores. This growing segment of the industry is referred to as "private label" apparel for retailers. For private label apparel, store buyers or product development specialists work directly with apparel producers to manufacture apparel to their specifications. Thus the apparel is unique to a particular store or group of stores.

Retail stores are the main link between the fashion industry and consumers. The classification of stores has become increasingly complex as stores have evolved in structure and organization. However, four basic kinds of retailing outlets dominate the fashion business: department stores, specialty stores, mass merchandisers, and discount stores. Each of these has a different marketing strategy, with the major differences being in fashionability, prices, services, and store image. Consumers will patronize differing outlets depending on their particular preferences for fashionability as well as the store image perceived by the consumer (Sproles 1978).

Traditional **department stores** such as Bloomingdale's, Dillard's, and Macy's offer a wide variety of merchandise—apparel, home furnishings, appliances, jewelry, sporting goods, toys, and cosmetics. Other large departmentalized stores such as Nordstrom and Saks Fifth Avenue offer only apparel, accessories, and limited housewares. Most department stores emphasize the newer, higher-quality, higher-priced, brand-name fashions, and their target market is primarily middle- to upper-income consumers. Department stores also attempt to develop strong fashion-oriented images within their local consumer markets. A variety of advertising and promotional activities, combined with extensive displays, stimulate consumers' patronage of these stores. Personal salesmanship and customer services are also used in selling products to consumers.

Specialty stores focus exclusively on marketing a specific group of related apparel products to relatively narrow target markets such as young professionals or high-income consumers. Specialty stores may be small single-unit stores or large multi-unit chains such as The Limited, The Gap, and Zale Jewelry. Their marketing strategy involves the most current

The Atlanta Apparel Mart (left) houses more than 2,000 apparel showrooms with over 11,000 apparel lines represented. In the Dallas Market Center, the Hall of Nations (right) is the central atrium for approximately 3.1 million square feet devoted to wholesale merchandising.

Department stores offer a wide variety of merchandise to consumers (top right). The Gap, as a specialty store, focuses on a relatively narrow target market (directly below). J.C. Penney's mass merchandises fashion goods on a nationwide basis (bottom left). Discount stores, such as K-Mart, emphasize lower than average prices (bottom right).

(All photos: *WWD*, Fairchild Publications)

trends in fashions. Often a specialty store will develop its marketing activities around a very narrow line of products, such as expensive high-fashion apparel, professional and career apparel, leather goods, or sport shoes. Promotional strategies will aim at the tastes of the store's particular market segment and emphasize the store's fashion image and quality of products.

Mass merchandisers such as JC Penney and Sears are centrally organized and operated groups of stores similar to one another in marketing practices and lines of merchandise. The marketing strategy of these stores focuses on moderately priced apparel of well-established fashionability. Most offer private brand names in addition to nationally advertised brands. Recently, some such as JC Penney have actively promoted an increasing fashion image, but have continued to emphasize basic styles sold in large volume to lower-and middle-income consumers.

Discount stores, most well-known of which are Kmart and Wal-Mart, sell a large variety of merchandise with the marketing emphasis on lower-than-average prices. Many analysts increasingly think of such stores as mass merchandisers, but clearly the approach of these stores is "brands at a discount." Relative newcomers to discounting during the 1980s were "off-price" retailers like Fashion Gal, Marshall's, Ross, and "outlet stores" for national brand merchandise. To achieve low prices, such stores minimize their services and other expensive promotional activities. Merchandise is selected by customers on a self-service basis, and costs of departmentalizing the store are kept to a minimum. Discounters sometimes carry the store's own brand names, but nationally known brands are preferred by many. Though discounters do not strongly attempt to create a fashion image, the lure of profits from emphasizing current fashions has encouraged some to increase fashion advertising and promotions. This strategy has emphasized both the low prices and fashionability of the discounter's offerings.

At all stages of fashion marketing, people in the industry get information needed to make marketing plans and decisions from marketing services. Larger firms do marketing research to analyze consumer demand and predict fashion trends. The **trade publications,** such as *Stores Magazine, Chain Store Age, Women's Wear Daily,* and *Daily News Record* provide a constant stream of market information and analysis of current trends. Industry research services also monitor trends in the market. Nationwide panels of consumers are surveyed by cooperating companies and the Market Research Corporation of America to measure trends in consumer purchases. **Trade associations** such as the American Textile Manufacturers Institute, the American Apparel Manufacturers Association, and the National Retail Federation provide their members with statistical reports of industry trends from regular industry surveys. These and many other services for market monitoring provide a substantial base of data which can increase professionals' effectiveness in predicting fashion trends and planning market strategy. Predicting consumer preferences is at best tricky, even with good research, but increasingly the large firms are using such scientific methods to determine new trends and to influence consumers' acceptance of these trends.

Extraordinary Events as Makers of Fashions

As a reflection of social change, fashions may have their beginnings in Hollywood, on the street, on Broadway, on TV, or at a major sporting event. Many such "extraordinary" or special social events, political forces, and arts and leisure activities serve as a sort of spawning ground of unplanned fashion changes. In each case aspects of the social environment have affected the specific fashion object that emerged by means of legitimizing and increasing the social visibility of the fashion.

Social Events   Social events such as national celebrations, World's Fairs, Olympics and other sporting events often serve as facilitators for fads or showcases for new fashions. For example, fad items often commemorate a national event (e.g., Statue of Liberty birthday sweatshirts), a sporting event (e.g., Superbowl hats or attire celebrating the Olympics), a scientific discovery (e.g., the discovery of King Tut's tomb in the 1920s which set off an Egyptian craze) or a scientific phenomenon (e.g., Haley's Comet garb). The timeliness of these fashion objects are their unique quality, and they often become "old hat" soon after the event but may eventually become collectors' items years after the event.

Ever since the East German women's swimming team in 1973 replaced their nylon swimsuits with a second-skin style in nylon and spandex, crushing everyone by saving precious seconds with the resistance-free suits, the Olympics has served as a showplace and laboratory for new fashions and technological advancements in sports clothing (Adler 1980). Because of the social visibility of these events, the sports clothing worn by the athletes has influenced the clothing worn by professional and amateur athletes in the sport as well as on nonsports clothing which draws its inspiration from sports apparel. New designs have highlighted the Olympics for such sports as swimming, skiing, figure skating, gymnastics, and track and field events. For example, in the 1988 Summer Olympics in Seoul, Korea, Florence Griffith-Joyner made headlines not only with her world record-breaking sprinting but also with her unique fashion statements, including her long colorfully painted fingernails and colorful one-legged and hooded suits.

Florence Griffith-Joyner wearing one of her innovative original designs, 1988 (above).
(REUTERS / BETTMANN)

Gertrude "Gussie" Moran shows her lace panties at Wimbledon, 1949 (top right).
(AP / WIDE WORLD PHOTOS)

Andre Agassi has influenced fashion worn by tennis players, 1990 (bottom right).
(THE BETTMANN ARCHIVE)

Wimbledon has long been known as the showcase of tennis wear much like the Olympics is known as a showcase for other sports clothing. Wimbledon has served as the legitimizing event for many tennis fashions. Women were admitted to Wimbledon in 1884. The winner that year, Maud Watson, wore a then sensible long-sleeved white dress with a straw boater hat. Because tennis was a summer game, white was adopted by both men and women as the appropriate color to wear on the courts, a tradition that has only recently been broken. Over the past century, Californians have been notorious for breaking Wimbledon's stiff dress code and in the process setting precedents for tennis fashions. For example, May Sutton, a seventeen-year-old Californian who captured a title in 1905, shocked the English when she rolled up the sleeves of her dress to fight the heat. In 1919, twenty-year-old Suzanne Lenglen from the French Riviera revolutionized tennis fashion when she won Wimbledon wearing a simple calf-length cotton dress, obviously without corset or petticoats. In 1931, Mrs. Fernley-Whittingstall appeared stockingless on court and in 1933 Alice Marble wore shorts on court. On June 21, 1949, the *New York Times* wrote "the tennis set at fashionable Wimbledon was buzzing today about the panties with the lace fringe. The panties belong to Gertrude Moran, United States Women's indoor titleholder, whose well-proportioned sun-tanned figure has gained her considerable space in the London press." The new fashion which made such a stir was designed by British fashion designer Ted Tinling, and included a short feminine dress with matching lace-fringed panties. The panties could be seen each time "Gorgeous Gussie" served or hit the ball, and international photographers caught all that could be seen to print on the front page of newspapers' sports pages (Adler 1980). In 1979, eighteen-year-old Linda Siegel made front-page news when she wore a low-cut backless tennis dress (Adler 1980) and in 1985, Anne White was the first to wear a skin-tight one-piece spandex and nylon bodysuit (Kirkpatrick 1985). This attire was consequently banned by Wimbledon officials. Thus the courts at Wimbledon have been important stages for prominent tennis figures, by virtue of their wearing a new tennis fashion, increasing the social visibility and legitimizing the use of a fashion.

Socio-Political Events Political events throughout the world often influence the form of fashion objects because they are highly covered by the media and they provide a vehicle for cross-cultural awareness. For example, television coverage of the political unrest in the Middle East in the late 1980s resulted in the popularity of kaffiyehs (the large, brightly checked square of cotton worn around the neck, over the shoulders, or wrapped around the head) which are commonly worn by Palestinians. However, once

**Sonny and Cher wear
Op-Art inspired
fashions, 1966.**
(THE BETTMANN ARCHIVE)

considered a political statement, the wearing of kaffiyehs became simply a
fashion statement after its widespread acceptance (Cocks 1988).

In July 1986, *Elle* fashion magazine announced "Soviet Chic" as the latest fashion look. This came after (then) Soviet Prime Minister Gorbachev's
wife, Raisa, stunned the French and American public with her high-fashion
designer clothing, which she wore during her trips with her husband to
Europe and the United States. That same year French fashion designers
showed traditional Russian designs, including suits and dresses inspired by
Soviet army uniforms, cossack pants, and Russian fur coats. Meanwhile
the Soviets were negotiating contracts with French fashion manufacturers
and designers (Duka 1986). Thus political events often nurture cross-cultural exchange and provide fashion creators with inspiration for new and
unique fashion objects. The media coverage of such events also contributes
to the social visibility and acceptance of such objects. At times, fashion
becomes preoccupied with a particular culture due to the perceived intrigue
associated with the culture. For example, in the mid-1980s African and
Australian cultures influenced fashion due to the perceived excitement and
adventure associated with Africa and Australia.

Arts and Leisure Activities   Leisure activities also provide avenues for fashions to obtain social visibility. Leisure activities such as sports, movies, television, and music are often part of the "popular culture" which influences the form of fashions. Fashions are often a reflection of the popular art forms and art movements of a specific period. Examples of styles being influenced by art movements include those of the late 1700s when the Neoclassicism movement was reflected in the softly draped Greek-inspired women's apparel. In the late nineteenth and early twentieth century, the Art Nouveau movement, with its simple, fluid, nature-inspired lines and decoration, was seen in the designs of Paul Poiret, one of the leading couture fashion designers of the time. Fashion and fabric design were often used as a medium for artists involved in the Surrealist movement of the 1920s and 1930s (Martin 1987). In the 1960s, Pop Art and Op Art were evident in many of the fabric designs popular at that time. For example, fabrics were printed to create optical illusions or to serve as a canvas for Andy Warhol-style designs (Howell 1975). The post-modern art movement of the 1980s was often seen in Memphis-inspired fabrications and architectural silhouettes.

At any given time, functional clothing specifically designed for a popular sport which receives social visibility in the media influences the onset of these functional designs as fashion objects. However, such sport-inspired fashions may or may not retain the functional qualities of the original designs. In the late 1800s and early 1900s, clothing was designed specifically for the social sports of the day: croquet, tennis, golf, roller skating, archery, and riding. Although these first sportswear costumes were somewhat functional in nature, they still came under the jurisdiction of the fashion dictates of the time. It was not until bicycling became popular at the turn of the century that a sports costume, in this case "bloomers," became popular. Throughout the century as sports have become more popular, fashion has been influenced more and more by sports costumes, and active sportswear looks have highlighted the covers of *Vogue* since 1910 (Lee-Potter 1984).

In addition, many American designers have achieved international status based upon active sportswear styles. The first American designer to achieve such notoriety was Claire McCardell in the 1930s. Claire McCardell designed innovative active sportswear, including her famous wrap swim suit known as the "diaper suit," and cotton and wool "play clothes" (Lee-Potter 1984; Martin 1985). Since then American fashion designers such as Bonnie Cashin, Rudi Gernreich, Norma Kamali, and Geoffrey Beene have made fashion statements with their sports-inspired fashions (Martin 1985).

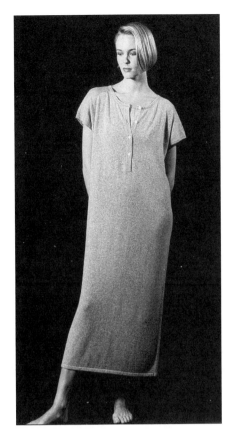

American designers have a tradition of casual, wearable fashions. Bonnie Cashin's layered looks were essentially functional, but also very decorative. Calvin Klein in 1984 was inspired by the classic T-shirt.

(Left, *WWD*, Fairchild Publications; top, Bonnie Cashin)

Because movies are seen by large groups of people and performers are often fashion leaders, costuming in movies often becomes inspiration for the fashion industry and is desired by consumers. According to costume designer Bob Ringwood, in order for costumes in films to become fashion statements, the costumes must be reflective of what is going on at the time. "It's important to be a chameleon, and to do that I must be aware of the current trends. I do a lot of research in order to give every film I do, even the period pieces, a modern slant. If I design something too far out, the public won't understand it. I can't be a slave to fashion. The costumes have to work . . . . Film and fashion are very close to one another. It's the whole idea of fantasy that comes out a great deal." (Neuhauser 1988, 8) Examples of the influence of film on fashion span the past 70 years. In the Roaring Twenties, movie queen Gloria Swanson ". . . drew legions of women to movie houses to watch her parade in fashion orgies that were more erotic than the films' handsome leading men." (Davis 1983, 25) In 1934, when Clark Gable removed his shirt in the movie *It Happened One*

Night to show his bare chest, sales of men's undershirts fell dramatically. Conversely, Elizabeth Taylor created a sensation when she wore a satin and lace slip in the 1960 movie *Butterfield Eight.* In the 1950s, both Marlon Brando in *On the Waterfront* and James Dean in *Rebel Without a Cause* did much to popularize the white T-shirt for men. The 1967 movie *Bonnie and Clyde* brought pinstripe suits back into style. In 1974, *The Great Gatsby* catapulted its costume designer, Ralph Lauren, into the limelight and started him on his way. The 1977 film *Annie Hall* started a fashion craze of floppy hats, baggy pants, and oversized vests. John Travolta popularized the white, three-piece kingpin suit in the 1977 disco movie *Saturday Night Fever* and the modern western look in *Urban Cowboy,* released in 1980. The movie *Flashdance,* reflecting the dance craze of the early 1980s, created a consumer desire for ripped sweatshirts and leg warmers. After *Top Gun* came out, the whole flight trend took off. In 1981, *Raiders of the Lost Ark* popularized the worn leather bomber jacket and "Indiana Jones" hat (Davis 1985). *Out of Africa* highlighted the "safari look" popular in 1986, which included African prints, safari camp shirts, khaki shorts and pants, pith helmets, and African-inspired jewelry. *The Untouchables,* released in the summer of 1987, signaled a resurgence of 1930s men's tailored clothing. Giorgio Armani designed the wardrobe for this movie, which introduced fashion trends such as five-button vests,

The "Annie Hall look" is often cited as a movie-influenced fashion trend. Many movies have been similarly recognized for roles in stimulating fashion diffusion.
(The KOBAL Collection)

Throughout the 1960s, the Beatles served as fashion leaders (left and above).

(Left, THE BETTMANN ARCHIVE; right, UPI/BETTMANN)

creaseless seam-to-seam pants, and three-piece suits (DeCaro 1987). In the summer of 1988, when Susan Sarandon showed off black lace garters in the movie, *Bull Durham,* sales of garter belts shot up (New Snap 1988). The horizontally striped shirt with white collar and cuffs (known as the "gekko" after the movie's character) became a symbol of status after Michael Douglas wore the shirt as Gordon Gekko in the movie *Wall Street* (Wise 1988). Thus film and fashion do go together. However, in order for the costuming to become a fashion statement, it must also be a reflection of current ideas and ideals.

Although the influence of music on fashion is complex, it primarily stems from the fact that musical performers often serve as fashion change agents. For example, Elvis Presley prompted the rock 'n' roll look of peg jeans, white socks, and pointed black shoes; the Beach Boys popularized Hawaiian and surfer shorts; and the Beatles instantaneously made mop hairstyles fashionable. However, the Beatles copied the design of their "Beatle jacket" from Pierre Cardin, who originated it. Hosted by Dick Clark, "American Bandstand" debuted on August 5, 1957 and provided teenagers with the opportunity to see rock stars on television. In recent years, the music video has spurred the fashion influence of rock stars such as Michael Jackson, Madonna, Cyndi Lauper, Sting, David Bowie, George

Michael and Tina Turner, to name a few. Rock stars' clothing are what's copied and the new looks change as new fashion videos are released. In fact, in 1988 the Council of Fashion Designers of America gave an award to MTV (Music Television) for its influence on fashion. Music also serves as an inspiration for fashion designers. As designer Jean-Paul Gaultier says, "We live in a world of noise, sound, music. I take this into consideration when I design, as music is so much a part of the contemporary scene. And of course I am delighted if I see musicians wearing my clothes." (Beckett 1985, 474)

Along with MTV, other television programming has influenced fashion. Nolan Miller, costume designer for the television show "Dynasty," launched a Dynasty Collection ready-to-wear line based upon the designs seen weekly by consumers. The show also launched a women's perfume, Forever Krystle, and a men's cologne, Carrington, named after characters in the series. "Miami Vice" served as a showplace for men's fashions and popularized looks such as T-shirts worn under unconstructed jackets and the finely groomed stubble-beard. The situation comedy "Murphy Brown" has done much to popularize designer Donna Karan, whose ready-to-wear lines are worn by star Candice Bergen on the show. The costumes worn by stars of soap-operas also do much to legitimize and popularize current fashion trends. As with other media, television serves as a stage on which new designs can gain social visibility.

Consumers as Creators of Fashion

Consumers often play the role of fashion change agents, those who initiate and propagate the acceptance of **fashion innovations** (Rogers and Shoemaker 1971). These individuals are sometimes called fashion innovators, although the term is also used for those individuals who are the first to wear a new fashion that was initiated by designers or others in the fashion industry.

Throughout history, individuals have drawn attention to themselves and have often gained notoriety for their unique fashion looks—looks that were not created by the fashion industry, but were created by the consumer him- or herself. For example, in the early 1800s George "Beau" Brummell and other aristocratic men initiated a fashion look for men commonly called "dandyism," which included very tight-fitting breeches, perfectly cut coats, upright collars, and knotted or bowed cravats (Laver 1969).

In 1850 Mrs. Amelia Bloomer and other early feminists attempted to reform women's fashions (which at the time included restrictive corsets and crinoline petticoats) by wearing a more "rational dress." This fashion, which at the time was considered very radical, included a simple but

This engraving of a meeting of the "bloomer" committee for rational dress was published in the "Lady's Newspaper," 1851.
(THE BETTMANN ARCHIVE)

fashionable bodice, a full skirt that reached below the knee, and baggy trousers known as "bloomers," which reached to the ankle, that were worn under the skirt. This dramatic attempt to change fashion was a complete failure due to wealthy women's resistance to such "unfeminine" attire. However, fifty years later the look was adopted for the purpose of bicycling (Laver 1969).

Subcultures, such as the "hippie" movement, often create their own styles (1967).
(UPI / BETTMANN)

Many subcultures developed their own styles, which became trends. Bohemians in the 1950s and the counterculture "hippie" movement of the 1960s are examples. In the mid-1970s, the punk look was initiated by English youth in the streets of London and has shaped trends in the U.S. In its beginnings, the style included safety pins pierced through a cheek or ear, cheap fabrics such as plastic, and "vile" designs and colors. By the early 1980s this look also included pink or green hair worn in short spikes, several ear or nose rings, and slashed clothing (Rhodes and Knight 1984; Wilson 1985). Because of its shock value it took high fashion designers such as Zandra Rhodes, known as the "High Priestess of Punk," to legitimize the look and make it acceptable to the public.

In the mid-1980s, entertainers such as Madonna, Cyndi Lauper, and Prince served as fashion innovators. Because of their popularity and social visibility, the fashion industry copied their looks for ready-to-wear clothing. Many other celebrities and entertainers have also had similar if less publicized influences, offering a sort of "consumer" influence on trends.

Thus consumers themselves, broadly defined as average people to creative celebrities, can initiate fashion. However, for a particular fashion look to be accepted by the mass public, the look must receive social attention and visibility and be legitimized by the fashion industry or by respected or prestigious individuals in society. Thus well-known public figures are having a "consumer impact" on today's trends.

SUMMARY

This chapter focused on inspirations to changing fashions. At the most basic level, fashions are shaped by social change and cultural context. Within any society, social change can be found in socio-economic patterns, political patterns, and cultural patterns. As an aspect of a society's material culture, fashion change falls into the cultural social change category. Fashion changes within a society are affected by formal traditions, informal traditions, and technical abilities. For example, formal traditions related to morality in clothing, informal traditions of ideals of attractiveness, and technical abilities of fabric and apparel production affect what fashion objects will emerge and be adopted by members of a society.

Specific changes in fashions are initiated and propagated by the fashion industry, extraordinary or special events in society, and by creative consumers. Fashions are created by designers and other creative individuals in the fashion industry as well as by creative consumers who design and initiate new fashions. The fashion marketing system facilitates the emergence and distribution of changing fashions. The system is made up of fiber producers, fabric producers, apparel manufacturers, apparel retailers, and service industries to each of these components. This channel provides a means for fashion change to develop and occur, and the system can have an important and even seductive influence in promoting change. Unplanned fashion change occurs when special social events, political forces, and arts and leisure activities provide a vehicle for social visibility of a new fashion object.

There is a historical continuity in major changes in fashions, such as trends in basic silhouettes and skirt dimensions such as length. The principle of historical continuity suggests that fashion change is evolutionary, not revolutionary: it takes place in small steps year after year. Thus historical continuity is like a guiding and organizing force that sets limits on the direction of change and amount of change taking place at a given time. Consumers will accept small amounts of change year-to-year, but major and rapid changes are rare and occur only under extraordinary conditions or events.

DISCUSSION QUESTIONS

1. What is meant by historical continuity in fashion? Give examples of fashions that have exhibited historical continuity and examples of fashions that have not. What forces contribute to fashions exhibiting historical continuity?
2. Describe the cultural and social influences that helped to shape the origination and emergence of a fashion object you are wearing.
3. Follow a selected fashion object throughout its origination, production and marketing. Describe each stage in the process and the influence of the segment of the industry at each stage in the evolution of the fashion object.
4. Identify current celebrities, athletes, film and music stars, and other socially visible consumers who influence fashion adoption. What characteristics do these individuals possess that provides them with such influence?

SUGGESTED READINGS

Blumer, Herbert. "Fashion: From Class Differentiation to Collective Selection." *Sociological Quarterly* 10 (1969): 275-91.
Lauer, Robert and Jeanette Lauer. *Fashion Power: The Meaning of Fashion In American Society.* Englewood Cliffs, NJ: Prentice-Hall, 1981.

Lowe, Elizabeth D. and John W. G. Lowe. "Quantitative Analysis of Women's Dress." *The Psychology of Fashion,* edited by Michael R. Solomon (1985): 193-206.

Lowe, John W. G., and Elizabeth D. Lowe. "Stylistic Change and Fashion in Women's Dress: Regularity or Randomness?" *Advances in Consumer Research* 11 (1984): 731-34.

3

A Theory of the Fashion Process

OBJECTIVES

♦ To introduce the diffusion of innovations theory, a general theory of how change (including changing fashions) takes place.
♦ To apply this diffusion of innovations theory to the case of how new fashions start and are accepted by consumers.

We now turn our attention to the central focus of this book, understanding consumer behavior during the course of the fashion process. To begin the analysis of consumer behavior in the fashion process, we will examine a general theory of human behavior in the acceptance of innovations such as fashions. Developed by Everett M. Rogers (Rogers 1962; Rogers and Shoemaker 1971; Rogers 1983), it is known as the **diffusion of innovations** theory. The theory systematically describes:

♦ the concept of an innovation
♦ the *characteristics* of the innovation that influence its acceptance among potential adopters
♦ the mental *process* involved in a person's decision-making to adopt the innovation
♦ the *diffusion* or spread of the innovation to many adopters
♦ the role of *leaders* and *change agents* in influencing the acceptance of the innovation.

This chapter describes Rogers' theory and shows how the theory can be applied to better understand the specific case of innovation in fashion and the evolution of the fashion process. Although this theory was not originally developed to explain and predict adoption of fashion innovations, diffusion theory has been applied in many investigations of clothing and fashion (Beal and Rogers 1957; King 1963, 1964, 1965; Reynolds and Darden 1972; Sproles and King 1973; Polegato and Wall 1980; Solomon 1985).

THE CONCEPT OF A FASHION INNOVATION

Diffusion theory begins with the concept of an **innovation,** defined by Rogers (1983, 11) as "an idea, practice, or object perceived as new by an individual." Broadly speaking, innovations range from new social movements to a change in child-rearing practices, to a new method of birth control, to any sort of new consumer product, especially new fashions. A contrasting definition (Barnett 1953, 7) states that an innovation is "any thought, behavior, or thing that is new because it is qualitatively different from existing forms." Under this definition, an innovation would qualify as new only at the time of its invention. Thus, when the innovation is communicated to some population several years after invention, it might be perceived as new (as in Rogers' conception), but it would not be purely new, having existed for several years.

Notice that, according to Rogers, the innovation need not be new in an absolute sense. What is important is the individual's *perception* of an object as new. A product may have been available for some time, but to someone just learning about it, the item is indeed new. Nor is the item necessarily new only at the time a person first learns about it. It remains new until the potential adopter has learned about the innovation and has had the opportunity to form attitudes concerning the innovation's value or "functionality" for his or her particular situation.

An explanation using fashion will help clarify this important principle. Consider a new fashion that first emerges in Europe, New York, or California. At this point, the fashion is indeed new and different from existing fashions. However, the fashion may spread to other parts of the world later. As the fashion spreads to each new place, it is seen as new by those it reaches, even though the style has existed elsewhere for some time and is no longer thought of as new in those places. In short, newness is determined by one's perceptions and one's environment.

Following Rogers, we can view a **fashion innovation** as a style or design perceived as new by an individual. In each fashion season, the fashion industry offers new styles to consumers. How different these styles are from the preceding season's offerings, and how different they are from an individual's current wardrobe and the clothes of people around him/her, determine the extent of newness the individual perceives. In practice, each fashion season offers something new in colors, fabrics and design details. So although there may not be any radical change in fashion from season to season, such as a major change in silhouette, generally something new each year confronts consumers, who learn about it and form preferences. Adoption of fashion innovations, then, is a continuous process for both the fashion industry and consumers.

CHARACTERISTICS GOVERNING ACCEPTANCE OF AN INNOVATION

Rogers (1983) has identified five characteristics of an innovation which may be considered by an individual when an innovation, such as a new fashion, is introduced: relative advantage, compatibility, complexity, trialability, and observability. Consumers' perceptions of these characteristics influence the acceptance or rejection of an innovation and the rate at which the innovation will be accepted by the members of a population.

Relative advantage refers to the degree to which the innovation is seen as more satisfactory than previous alternatives. The relative advantage of a new product when compared to existing products might lie in lower cost, greater utility, newer or more satisfying aesthetics, or increased social prestige. For fashions, an important measure of relative advantage may be

Fashion shows expose consumers to fashion innovations.

the degree to which a new style is differentiated from previous fashions. In other words simply because one style is perceived as newer or more fashionable, it may be considered to have relative advantage over another item that is perceived as less fashionable. Another aspect of relative advantage is the prestige or perceived exclusivity it offers the adopter. For example, an expensive fur coat may be perceived as having advantage over a fabric coat, not necessarily for its warmth but more for its high social status and prestige. On a more utilitarian level, the introduction of a new easy-care fabric used as the material for a fashion object may offer a relative advantage over previous fabrics in the product's performance and convenience of care. In this example, consumers would be evaluating the relative advantage of the advanced technology as well as the fashionability of the product.

Compatibility is the degree to which an innovation is consistent with the existing norms and values held by potential adopters. An innovation reasonably consistent with norms and values has a greater probability of acceptance than one that violates prevailing norms and values. For example, in the mid-1960s fashion designer Rudi Gernreich introduced the monokini or topless swimsuit in the United States. While this style was considered acceptable in places such as the French Riviera, it violated the social norms or standards of public decency among the majority of U.S. women and was not accepted by many. Another example of a failure in social compatibility with life-styles is the case of mid-length dresses introduced in 1969 and 1970. This style failed to be adopted when first introduced in part because people perceived it as too different to fit their more informal life-styles, which were emphasizing mini-lengths and pants. Similarly, in the 1980s, designers attempted to introduce skirts for men. Although the kilt-like styling was adopted by a few daring consumers, the image of the "look" was incompatible with the majority of men's self-concepts. These examples point out that if a new style is too novel or unique in design, it is likely to receive slow and possibly negligible acceptance among consumers.

Complexity refers to the difficulty a person may have in understanding and learning to use an innovation. A new style may be complex in several ways. The style may be introduced but be rejected by consumers because they cannot visualize how they could use it appropriately in their lives. Or, consumers might find it difficult to coordinate the new item with other clothing and accessories into a total fashion look and therefore reject the new style. The adoption of each new style requires a learning experience, and if this learning experience is quick and easy, the innovation may have a greater chance of acceptance. Experts in the fashion business are so

Super MICROFT®, super water repellency. air-capsules keep water effectively out.

Teijin has developed the new textile fabrics in the world called Super MICROFT®, the construction of Lotus leaf.

"Super-water repellency" Air pushes out water.

"Excellent water repellency durability" Long-lived function.

"Comfortability" Resists wind yet releases humidity.

"Natural feel" Cotton-like natural touch.

"Easy-care property" Neither laminated nor coated.

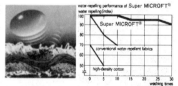

Super MICROFT®

TEIJIN AMERICA, INC.:
10 Rockefeller Plaza Suite 1001, New York, N.Y. 10020 U.S.A.
Phone: (212)307-1130 Cable Address: NYTEIJIN NEWYORK
Telex: 421091(TEIJIN 421091) Facsimile: (212)307-6042

TEIJIN LIMITED Osaka Head Office:
11, Minami-honmachi 1-chome,
Higashi-ku,
Osaka 541, JAPAN

TEIJIN

Innovative fabrics are promoted by highlighting their relative advantage over existing fabrics.

aware of this problem of complexity that many types of advertising and promotion attempt to show consumers how easy it is to put together looks. For example, displays frequently show complete looks with all appropriate accessories, and even may suggest the life-style events where the look would be appropriate. Similarly fashion shows and advertisements frequently present a complete look, not just individual items, with comments on where it would be appropriate. All of these marketing techniques educate consumers and reduce the complexity of decision-making.

Trialability is the extent to which the costs and benefits of adopting the innovation are quantitatively and qualitatively evaluated. It also refers to how easily the innovation may be tested on a small scale with a limited commitment before the individual makes the final decision to adopt or reject. New and inexpensive innovations in products like cosmetics and packaged foods can be easily tried, and if the consumer's experience is satisfactory, they can buy more. But some new styles are not so easily tried without risks. Of course, the consumer can make a preliminary trial of clothing in the store's fitting room, but the real trial begins when the item is bought and worn. When a new style is expensive or different from current fashions, the risks are substantial and trialability is reduced. However, if the consumer takes these risks and receives personal satisfaction or social approval for the decision, the style has passed the test of trialability and more purchases and use of the style may follow.

Observability constitutes the degree to which an innovation is visible and communicable to others. Rogers (1962) also refers to this characteristic as *communicability*. Easily communicated or observed innovations have the greatest opportunity for adoption. Perhaps no innovations are so visibly communicable as new fashions, and this observability influences their adoption and diffusion. But by virtue of this communicability, many styles will simultaneously compete for attention, and only those that are observable and have other favorable characteristics will be endorsed by consumers and emerge as fashions.

Experts in consumer behavior often add a sixth characteristic, perceived risk (Robertson, Zielinski, and Ward 1984; Wilkie 1990). **Perceived risk** refers to negative results a consumer imagines may come from adopting an innovation. Some of these risks are implied by other characteristics as well. New fashions may have economic, social and technological risks associated with them. From the economic viewpoint, consumers may wonder whether a new style is worth the money, or if they will get enough use (wearings) to get their money's worth. Social risks may also be consequential, as when the consumer wonders whether friends will approve of or be impressed favorably by the new style. And technological risks are always present, as when the individual worries whether a style will maintain its attractive appearance through multiple wearings and cleanings (i.e., will it retain its color, shape, and other design qualities). For these reasons, new fashions can be very risky purchases, and this constrains the individual's decision to purchase.

THE INDIVIDUAL'S DECISION-MAKING PROCESS

In deciding to adopt or reject an innovation, a person goes through a decision-making process that involves information seeking and learning. This is sometimes referred to as the innovation-decision process, although the term **adoption process** is more prevalent in a consumer and fashion literature. In the original theory of the adoption process, Rogers (1962) identified five sequential stages:

1. Awareness, or first knowledge of an innovation
2. Interest, the seeking and obtaining of further information
3. Evaluation, or the formation of attitudes toward the innovation and its characteristics based on information received
4. Trial, or a limited testing of the innovation when possible
5. Adoption, or rejection, deciding whether or not to continue the use of the innovation (fig. 3.1)

In the current literature, this five-stage model has been revised to include these stages (Rogers 1983):

1. Knowledge, or one's first learning of an innovation and some of its characteristics
2. Persuasion, the formation of favorable or unfavorable attitudes toward the innovation

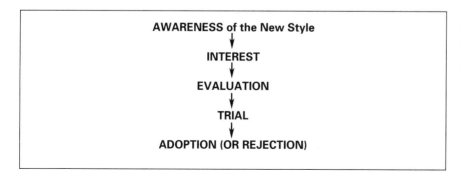

AWARENESS of the New Style
↓
INTEREST
↓
EVALUATION
↓
TRIAL
↓
ADOPTION (OR REJECTION)

FIGURE 3.1 The Consumer's Decision-Making Process in Accepting a New Style (Rogers' Model)

3. Decision, or the activities that lead to either adopting or rejecting the innovation
4. Implementation, or putting the innovation into use
5. Confirmation, a seeking of further support to assure the decision made was the correct one

These alternative concepts help us understand the basic mental processes that might occur when consumers are confronted with fashion innovations. Investigators of consumer behavior have also proposed models of the adoption process that embody these and additional stages as well. For example, Robertson (1971) proposed a mental model of consumer decision-making that involves cognitive (thinking) activities, affective (feeling) activities, and behavioral (doing) activities. The stages of this model are shown in figure 3.2. Each stage of Robertson's model can be described as follows. At the first stage of problem perception, a person sees a need for a product before the innovation is actually offered. A consumer may become dissatisfied or bored with his or her existing wardrobe and thus feel a need for new purchases. At the awareness stage, the consumer learns about a new product filling that need. Awareness is stimulated by many everyday sources of information—newspapers, fashion magazines and TV, or simply watching what others are wearing and shopping the stores. At the comprehension stage, one learns the product's characteristics and functions, perhaps by seeking more information such as talking with friends. Evaluation of the product and formation of attitudes then begin. If attitudes are positive, the consumer may either proceed directly to trial, or seek further legitimation of the decision by obtaining more information.

Assuming the trial stage is reached, the consumer may proceed to further adoption, or continued wearing of the style and perhaps purchases of additional items in that style. Finally, the individual may experience dissonance, which may lead to concern as to whether a correct decision has been made. The theory of cognitive dissonance, when applied to consumer behavior, suggests that after the purchase is made, consumers may seek further information by reading advertisements or talking with friends, to become assured the right decision was made. Advertisers often give this confirmation when they emphasize the style is "as seen in Vogue," is endorsed by a noted designer, or is seen in fashionable cities and resorts. This positive reinforcement can determine whether or not the consumer continues to use the product.

Robertson's model suggests that consumers may skip stages of the process, return to previous stages, or reject the innovation at any time. Two forms of nonrational decision-making are also provided for, the

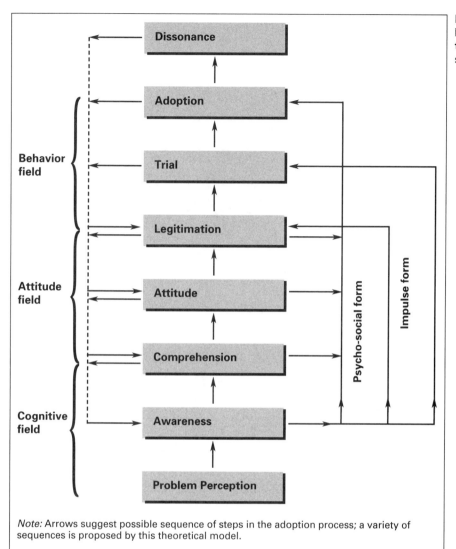

Figure 3.2
**Robertson's Model of
the Adoption Process**
Source: Robertson (1971, 75)

Note: Arrows suggest possible sequence of steps in the adoption process; a variety of sequences is proposed by this theoretical model.

psycho-social form and the impulse form. The psycho-social form is a decision influenced by the consumer's desire to conform or to create favorable impressions among others. For example, a teenage boy may purchase a style of athletic shoe simply because his friends have purchased that style of athletic shoe. The impulse form results when an immediately favorable impression of an innovation leads to purchase before the implications of purchase are systematically analyzed. A consumer may impulsively purchase an accessory on display in a store. For both of these situations,

**Fashion innovations
such as these by Rudi
Gernreich, which are
not consistent with
existing norms and
values, are seldom
accepted in mass by
consumers.**
(UPI/Bettman)

several stages of the decision-making process may be brief or even skipped entirely. This model is persuasive, since fashions can sometimes be adopted by just such casual and limited decision-making processes.

These are not the only models that have been proposed on the adoption process. One other model suggested by Wilkie (1990) should be noted because it is based on the famous "hierarchy of effects" model of consumer behavior that is used extensively in marketing to explain how consumers decide to purchase new brands. Similar to the preceding models, this one suggests a relatively organized, ordered series of steps in consumers' learning and decision-making: unawareness, awareness, knowledge, liking, trial, use evaluation (a reevaluation following the trial stage), and adoption (continued use). Consumer researchers have made considerable use of this model, and it appears to be a helpful one in explaining many but not all consumer decisions.

Awareness of fashion innovations is stimulated by fashion shown in fashion magazines

DIFFUSION OF INNOVATIONS

Diffusion is the spread of an innovation within and across social systems. Whereas the adoption process focuses on individual decision-making, the diffusion process centers on the decisions of many people to adopt an innovation. How fast and how far an innovation diffuses are influenced by formal communications from the mass media, personal communications among adopters and potential adopters, the persuasive influence of consumer leaders and other change agents, and the degree to which the innovation is communicated and transferred from one social system to another. Diffusion theorists point out that these communications become the vital element in the functioning of the diffusion process (Rogers 1983).

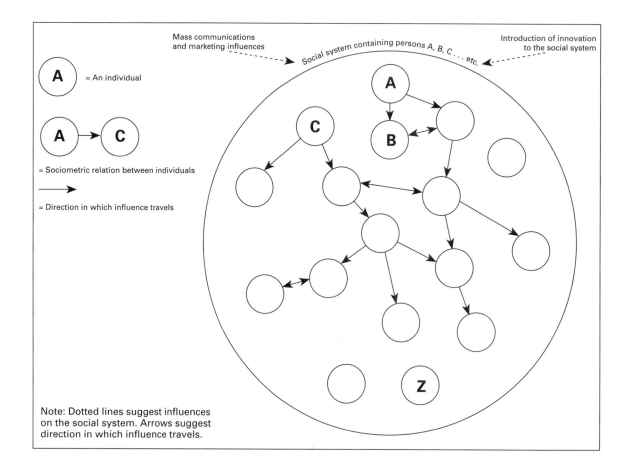

Figure 3.3 Diffusion of Innovation Within a Social System.

Diffusion within a Social System

Diffusion theory seeks to explain how an innovation is adopted by many people within a social system. A social system might be the residents of a city, the students of a school, a group of friends, or any other group of individuals who regularly interact. One way of looking at diffusion within a social system is to construct a sociogram, as exemplified in figure 3.3. The sociogram describes the interactions of individuals within the social system, and represents both verbal and visual interactions between individuals. Each interaction can be considered an act of communication through which information and influence concerning an innovation can be spread. Communications can also enter the social system from outside: from the mass media, the marketing system, or contact with other social systems. Ultimately, awareness of the innovation is diffused to most members of the social system through the combined influence of external

The adoption of styles depicting cultural roots spurs the fashion diffusion process. Here, dancers in Kwanzaa honor the past and look to the future.

(© Catherine Smith/Impact Visuals)

sources and interpersonal communications within the system. Early research demonstrates the importance of personal communications in diffusion of fashions and other consumer products. For example, Robertson (1971) found interpersonal communications were influential in the acceptance of clothing, appliances, and foods. He found both one-way and two-way discussions between group members were influential. The classic fashion leadership studies of Katz and Lazarsfeld (1955) and King (1963) also have demonstrated the significance of interpersonal communications and opinion leadership to diffusion of fashions. Each person begins the adoption process at the time he or she first becomes aware of the innovation.

This is an important model of consumer behavior in the fashion process. Later we will pay particular attention to the two main parts of this process, the influences of communications and social interactions.

Diffusion across Social Systems

As time passes, innovations diffuse or spread from person to person and from place to place across communities and countries. The basic nature of this process can be seen in figure 3.4. In this figure each circle represents a separate social system to which an innovation will eventually be diffused. The innovation may be invented and diffused first in modern social systems and, as time passes, the innovation will be

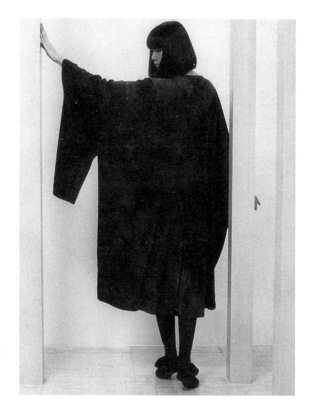

Fashion designs such as this one by Rei Kawakubo for Comme les Garçons, promote the diffusion of styles across cultural groups.
(*WWD*, Fairchild Publications)

introduced and diffused to traditional or less innovative social systems. Communications and contracts between social systems will play central roles in this process.

Several factors can enter into this process of diffusion. These are:

- *Geographic Location* Modern experts in diffusion point to geographic accessibility to innovations as being crucial to diffusion (Brown 1981) since geographically accessible areas will receive innovations earlier than will those that are isolated from contact with the outside world. However, isolated subcultures may develop fashions unique to their own groups.
- *Mobility* Social systems whose members are mobile, or who travel and have other types of contacts with outside social systems, are likely to receive early exposure to an innovation. When the mobile individual becomes aware of an innovation adopted by another social system, the innovation is likely to be transferred to his or her home social system. Likewise, mobile individuals in innovative social systems will transfer their innovations to members of other social systems.

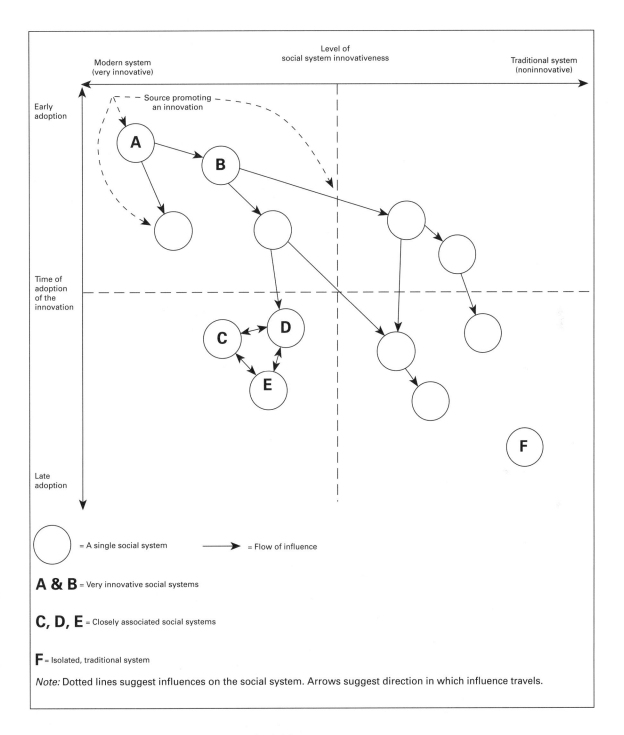

Figure 3.4   Diffusion of Innovation across Social Systems

Madonna, fashion innovator, in a perfomance at Chiba marine station on April 13, 1990.
(Reuters, Bettman Newsphotos)

- ◆ *Norms Governing Innovativeness* Social norms must favor innovative behavior if acceptance of an innovation is to occur. Even if a social system receives early word of an innovation, adoption and diffusion may still occur slowly and later in time if norms do not favor change.
- ◆ *The Marketing System* In the diffusion of consumer products, a marketing environment composed of many retailing outlets offering many choices is likely to stimulate diffusion of innovations. Innovations will be offered early, and marketing communications (e.g., advertising) are likely to promote interest in innovative behavior. However, in less competitive local markets, retailers may be reluctant to take the risk of promoting innovations until they have become established successes in larger and more competitive markets.

In the diffusion of fashions across a large heterogeneous society such as the United States, the process of diffusion across social systems can be very complex. Ideally one might consider the United States as a single social system in which diffusion occurs. However, the United States should be realistically viewed as a composite of many social systems, each having a different process of diffusion. To describe such diversity within a society, anthropologists use the term subculture. From a consumer behavior perspective, subculture may be defined as "any cultural patterning that preserves important features of the dominant society but provides values and life-styles of its own" (Berkman and Gilson 1986, 156). Thus each ethnic group, religion, social class, race, age, or geographic region constitutes a **subculture** or separate social system where diffusion occurs. Further, each subculture may have its own demographic and life-style groups where widely differing fashions are accepted or rejected. Thus the transfer of different fashions among social systems might follow a variety of mechanisms, depending on what kind of social system leads in the diffusion process.

The diffusion of fashions is affected by mass marketing, mass communications, and retail availability of styles in different areas of the country. Often the mechanism and rate at which diffusion occurs is more importantly influenced by these factors than by the transfer of innovations among subcultures. Diffusion of fashion is also stimulated by the high level of social and physical mobility of the population, which transmits and legitimizes new styles within and across subcultures or social systems. Finally, since the fashion industry and a large part of its clientele are concentrated in Europe and in large cities of the East and West coasts of the United States, these have become important starting points for fashion trends which then diffuse to the rest of the country. These are among the factors that must be considered when the diffusion of a specific style is analyzed.

THE INFLUENTIAL LEADERS OF DIFFUSION

The diffusion of innovations theory proposes that several kinds of leaders play crucial roles in initiating and propagating the acceptance of innovations, and that the activities of these leaders determine whether an innovation will be adopted or rejected. One important type of leader, industry change agents, perform business-oriented roles as professional promoters of an innovation on behalf of their employers or other advocating clients. Clearly fashion designers and marketers who sponsor new styles are such change agents. These individuals have obvious interests in regularly introducing innovations in dress and promoting rapid acceptance of each new style to their markets of buyers and consumers.

However, fashion designers and marketers cannot dictate what fashion innovations will be accepted. Consumers themselves become important leaders in the actual process of fashion acceptance. That is, as discussed in chapter 2, within the consumer population certain *consumer leaders*

The Kennedys in the early 1960s and "Princess Di" in the 1980s were influential fashion leaders.

(Top: UPI/Bettman Newsphotos; Bottom: *WWD,* Fairchild Publications)

influence the initiation and acceptance (or rejection) of new styles. Three specific kinds of consumer leaders may be identified: the innovator, the opinion leader, and the innovative communicator. **Innovators** adopt an innovation first. They are the first to display a new product, thereby bringing attention to it, and they play leading roles in the early history of an innovation's acceptance. Fashion innovators may simply be the first to wear new styles of the fashion industry but often they are creative consumers who invent new looks themselves. This may come from many sources: mixing and matching styles currently on the market, shopping second-hand stores (a fashion phenomenon of the 1980s and 1990s), or even creative home sewing. Those in the fashion business watch closely for this "street fashion" pioneered by innovative consumers, for although often it is avant garde or bizarre, some of it sets the direction for significant fashion trends that spread to the mass population.

Equally if not more important are **opinion leaders,** those who influence adoption and diffusion through interpersonal communications and contact with others. Their influence occurs in face-to-face interactions with others, such as during informal conversations with friends or coworkers, where they can socially legitimize the acceptance of an innovation. They may have especially powerful influence as visual communicators of styles—what they wear will be noticed by peers and other consumers as well—and this may ultimately be their most powerful role as influentials. How much opinion leaders actually influence the diffusion of an innovation depends on many things, such as the extent to which they are respected as leaders, their credibility as knowledgeable people, personal prestige or charisma, and how much they reflect the norms of groups of which they are members.[1]

The **innovative communicator** simultaneously performs the roles of innovator and opinion leader. That is, the innovative communicator is both an early buyer of a new product and an interpersonal communicator of information and influence concerning the product. Such a person is of obvious importance to fashion diffusion, since the wearer of a new style can both visually and verbally communicate information about it.[2]

Popularly referred to as fashion leaders, fashion-conscious consumers, contemporary consumers, trendsetters, and other indicative terms, these fashion innovators, opinion leaders and innovative communicators are crucial to the fashion process. Their preferences establish the basis for new fashion trends. While the professional change agent may only offer products for acceptance, the buying and wearing choices of consumers ultimately establish fashion leadership. Consumer change agents are models of behavior whose tastes set the standard of excellence that others follow.

Who are the consumer leaders of fashion? This is a point of much discussion and debate—and it is so important that chapter 5 is devoted solely to this subject. Presently it suffices to say that fashions are influenced by many types of people. People who are public celebrities or who frequently are topics in the mass media are obvious candidates. A good example in recent years is Diana, Princess of Wales (or Princess Di, as she is commonly known). During the 1980s she helped popularize small hats (especially with veils), sailor suits with wide collars (the "nautical look"), pearl chokers, and blue sapphire engagement rings. According to Hanmer and Graham (1984):

> *When the Princess comes into a room for a formal dinner or some other function, there is almost always a gasp of surprise and pleasure. Fashion writers hurry to record her new tastes in clothes and before long the clothes she likes are initiated and reinterpreted in a thousand stores across the country. (P. 7)*

Other celebrities such as rock stars, particularly very popular ones like Michael Jackson, Cyndi Lauper, Madonna, Bruce Springsteen, and Tina Turner have had looks imitated (television and especially MTV and rock videos of the 1980s and 1990s have given these influences an additional stimulus). Thus it is easy to conclude that people in the public's eye have great opportunity to start new fashion trends. But as we shall come to appreciate later in chapter 5 the leadership of fashion trends comes from all walks of life—from the well-to-do to the average person-on-the-street, from youths, and from many subcultures. In short, fashion leadership by consumers is a widespread and diversified form of innovative human behavior.

The personal characteristics of leaders in fashion trends are varied (Sproles 1979; Rogers 1983). Those who are innovative are venturesome, risk-taking, and novelty-seeking when compared to other consumers. This position entails substantial social risks, but it also carries rewards of social prestige, recognition for originality, and even social notoriety. Some may be wealthy, and thus able to consume new styles lavishly, but many of the less well-to-do find affordable yet very innovative and attractive styles as well. Many are found in the younger, better-educated segments of the population, and they often live in urban areas. They are socially gregarious and have active lifestyles in general. Those who play strong roles as opinion leaders appear to be particularly well integrated into social groups and reflect the social norms of their groups. Thus they tend to have special credibility to their peers or social acquaintances, thereby enhancing their impact on adoption of fashions. In total, the leaders of fashion have the special attributes—psychologically, socially, and economically—to perform their important roles initiating and spreading the acceptance of new fashion trends.

SUMMARY

The diffusion of innovations theory provides a basic explanation of the process by which consumers accept new styles of dress. The theory describes the concept of an innovation, the characteristics of the innovation that influence its acceptance among potential adopters, the mental decision-making process the consumer goes through in adopting the innovation, the diffusion of the innovation to many adopters, and the role of leaders in the diffusion process.

An innovation is "an idea, practice, or object perceived as new by an individual" (Rogers 1983, 11). Six characteristics of an innovation influence its adoption: relative advantage over previously accepted styles, compatibility with existing norms or values, complexity of use, trialability, observability or communicability, and perceived risk in adoption.

In deciding to adopt or reject an innovation, consumers go through a decision-making process of learning known as the adoption process. The five stages of this process are individual awareness of the innovation, interest in obtaining more information about it, evaluation of the innovation accompanied by formation of attitudes, trial of the innovation, and finally, the decision to adopt or reject the innovation. Another five-stage model proposes that adoption has these stages: knowledge, persuasion, decision, implementation, and confirmation. Other models with similar stages have been proposed as appropriate explanations of the adoption process for consumer decisions.

Diffusion is the spread of an innovation within and across social systems. How far and how fast an innovation diffuses depends on communications together with the influences exerted by consumer leaders and change agents. Industry change agents such as fashion designers and manufacturers promote the adoption and diffusion of an innovation on behalf of their employers. Consumer leaders, including fashion innovators, opinion leaders, and innovative communicators, also are crucial in initiating and propagating the process of adoption and diffusion.

NOTES

1. Rogers (1983) and Gatignon and Robertson (1985) provide useful reviews of basic concepts and research findings concerning innovators, opinion leaders, and the adoption and diffusion processes.
2. See Baumgarten (1975) for development of the concept of the innovative communicator in the context of fashion. The related concept of the fashion-conscious consumer is suggested in Sproles and King (1973).

DISCUSSION QUESTIONS AND PROJECTS

1. What is an "innovation?" What makes a fashion innovation new (different) from the previous fashions it is to replace?
2. Consider a new style which you think is coming out this year, and may become fashionable (e.g., a new jacket style, skirt length, color, hairstyle). Analyze the characteristics of this innovation as suggested in the diffusion theory, and assess the style's chances of acceptance based on your analysis.
3. Think about some item of new clothing you bought recently. How did you go about deciding to buy this style? What things did you think about? Write a narrative indicating these various thought processes and steps leading to your choice.
4. Taking your narrative from question 3 above, analyze your adoption process in terms of the models suggested by Rogers and Robertson in this chapter. Did you go through all the steps suggested in these models? In the order suggested? Did you skip steps?
5. Diffusion theory attempts to explain, in general terms, how a fashion may spread within social systems (groups) and across social systems (from group to group, and place to place). Taking this general idea, how do fashions spread in the United States? Where do they start (e.g., places, groups)? What stimulates their spread? Do you think these processes differ in other parts of the world, for example, in Canada, Europe, Asia, and in less developed (Third World) countries?
6. Using the idea of a sociogram (fig. 3.2), diagram how fashions typically spread in your network of personal friends, acquaintances and casual contacts. Are there certain leaders, followers, late adopters, nonadopters? Identify those you would consider the innovators and opinion leaders (only a few will qualify!). What does the sociogram,

and your identification of the leaders, tell you about the process of fashion diffusion?

SUGGESTED READINGS

Gatignon, Hubert, and Thomas S. Robertson. "A Propositional Inventory for New Diffusion Research." *Journal of Consumer Research* 11 (1985): 849-67.

Katz, Elihu, and Paul Lazarsfeld. *Personal Influence*. Glencoe, Illinois: The Free Press, 1955.

Robertson, Thomas S. *Innovative Behavior and Communication*. New York: Holt, Rinehart and Winston, 1971.

Rogers, Everett M. *Diffusion of Innovations*. Glencoe, Illinois: The Free Press, 1962.

Rogers, Everett M. *Diffusion of Innovations*. 3d ed. New York: The Free Press, 1983.

4

Fashion Life Cycles

OBJECTIVES

◆ To introduce the concept of the fashion life-cycle and the use of curves (graphs) to describe the life-cycle of fashions.

◆ To show varied applications of the life-cycle concept in analyzing each stage of the fashion life-cycle, from the birth of the fashion through its acceptance and decline.

T he adoption and diffusion of a fashion can be portrayed and analyzed using the concept of the fashion life-cycle. This chapter develops principles and applications of fashion life-cycles, building on the foundation of diffusion theory introduced in chapter 3. We will focus on the development of fashion life-cycle curves, sometimes called diffusion curves, which visually show the pattern of consumers' adoption of a fashion.

PRINCIPLES OF LIFE-CYCLE CURVES

The life-cycle curve for a fashion is a graphical representation of a frequency distribution showing consumers' acceptance of a specific style—a new skirt length, jacket style, type of fabric, type of sportswear, or any other innovation in dress (or other fashion objects). The life-cycle curve for a specific style shows several key variables:

1. The length of time diffusion takes. A fashion trend might last from as little as several months up to a full decade, although most trends average several years.

2. The rate of speed at which consumers adopt the object as time passes. Some styles are rapidly adopted, while others may meet with strong resistance and slow adoption.
3. The level of acceptance of the object at each point in time. Certain fashions are accepted by a vast majority of the population, whereas others diffuse only to a small number of consumers.

A life-cycle curve is constructed by counting the number of consumers who adopt the style at each point in time and drawing a graph of this acceptance. In figure 4.1, the dotted line represents such a fashion count at each period; this dotted line indicates that adoption by consumers may be somewhat irregular: spurts of purchasing may precede brief declines. However, fitting a smooth curve to the overall trend of adoption, the solid dark line in figure 4.1 provides a theoretical representation of the frequency distribution, which is shaped like a bell. This theoretical curve is a fundamental representation of consumer behavior in the acceptance of a fashion, and is used throughout this chapter.[1]

In the diffusion of a specific fashion, Nystrom (1928) suggested that two diffusion curves may be graphed, an acquisition or purchasing curve and a use curve (fig. 4.2). An acquisition curve shows the total number of people who have purchased, received as a gift, or sewn the style at each stage. The use curve represents the actual number of people wearing the style at each time. The two curves parallel each other early in the diffusion process; later, the use curve accelerates as cumulative adoption increases. Finally, the period of consumer use may continue for some time after acquisitions have ended, with wearings tapering off as items are worn out or replaced by newly emerging fashions.

A fashion-life cycle curve depicts the rate and duration of the diffusion process. An example of this is shown in figure 4.3, which compares the rate and duration of diffusion for a fad, fashion, and classic. Typically a fad will have a rapid rate of early growth, indicated by the steepness of the curve, a low level of adoption, and an early and precipitous decline in use. By comparison, a fashion may show a more gradual growth rate, a higher peak of acceptance, and a prolonged period of decline. The classic may show a pattern beginning with a slow period of initial growth followed with a higher and longer peak of acceptance and a very long period of gradual decline. Although shown that the acceptance of classics is greater than for fads, it may that for some fads the curve may be very high and for some classics the curve may be relatively low.

Data from a life-cycle curve can be used to calculate the cumulative level of acceptance for a fashion at each period. This level can be

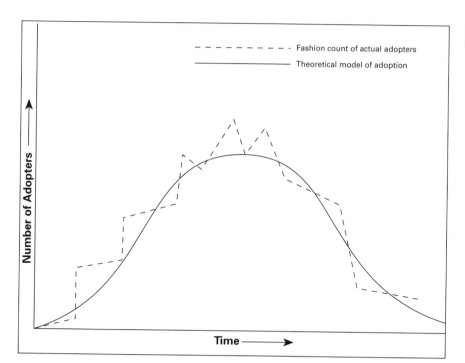

Figure 4.1   Theoretical Diffusion of a Fashion

- - - - - Fashion count of actual adopters
———— Theoretical model of adoption

Number of Adopters

Time ——→

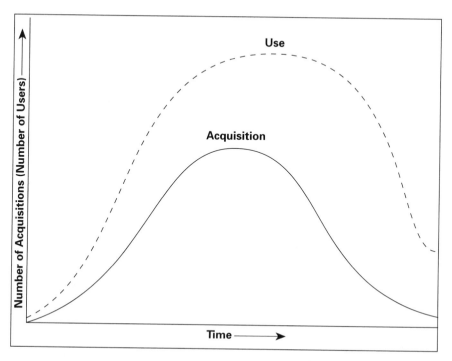

Figure 4.2   Consumers' Acquisition and Use of a Fashion

Use

Acquisition

Number of Acquisitions (Number of Users)

Time ——→

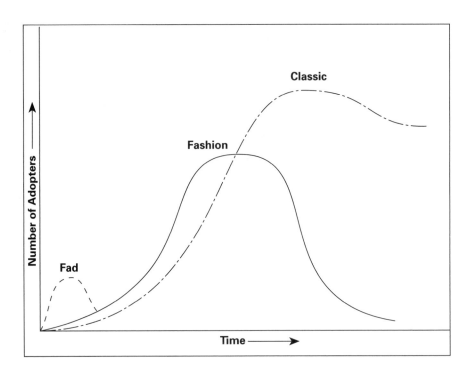

Figure 4.3   Diffusion of a Fad, Fashion, and Classic

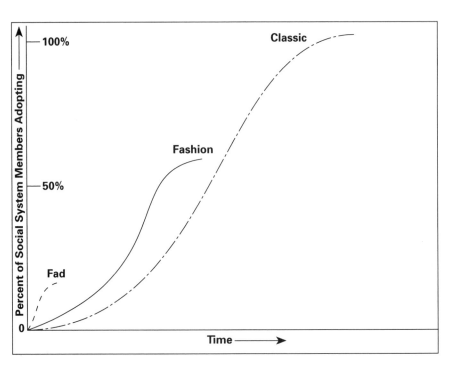

Figure 4.4   Cumulative Level of Acceptance

expressed as the percentage of members within a social system who have actually adopted the style at each time. When curves such as those shown in figure 4.3 are graphed in this manner, the S-shaped curves shown in figure 4.4 will result. This figure illustrates the principle that fads are adopted only by a small percentage of all possible adopters, while fashions are accepted by a large part of a social system. Classics may be viewed as the most successful fashions, since total or nearly total adoption by a social system may eventually occur.

DETAILED ANALYSIS OF FASHION LIFE-CYCLES

A fashion life-cycle can be divided into a series of subperiods of time for more detailed analysis of adoption and diffusion. For example, one can identify categories of consumer adopters and coordinated stages of fashion marketing based on the style's level of acceptance. Life-cycle curves may also be subdivided by fashion seasons and by the diffusion processes occurring within separate social systems. These subanalyses are important because consumer behavior at each stage of diffusion changes, and one should know these changes and the transitions from one stage to the next.

Categories of Consumer Adopters

Consumers fall into groups of adopters depending on when they adopt a fashion.[2] In figure 4.5, the life-cycle is divided into five adopter categories by time of adoption. The first two categories include fashion innovators and opinion leaders described in the previous chapter. Additionally, the second category may include a kind of consumer termed an early conformist, who may not necessarily qualify as a fashion leader but who is still an early adopter in the fashion trend.

As diffusion accelerates, the fashion process moves into a third stage dominated by a category of mass-market consumers. During this time, the style becomes a well-accepted fashion as it becomes widely available in retail stores and is adopted by the largest number of consumers. Eventually, adoptions level off and the diffusion curve begins to descend. Consumers adopting after this time can properly be categorized as fashion followers, since the fashion trend has been firmly established by mass-market consumers. Finally, as the fashion declines, certain late adopters known as "laggards" and "isolates" will still make their first decisions to adopt the fashion. Fashion laggards may be viewed as consumers who almost grudgingly adopt the style, perhaps as a result of social pressure or because of its availability at low prices. Fashion isolates are those consumers who become late adopters because they are isolated from communications and social influences (e.g., some rural consumers, home-bound consumers) that would normally encourage them to be earlier adopters. In some cases, consumers who would normally be early adopters are forced into late adoption of a style because the style was not available to them (e.g., low income, physically challenged).

We must also consider, as a separate category of consumers, the nonadopters. These consumers, for whatever reason, never acquire the fashion. Nonadopters might include such groups as low-income consumers, some elderly consumers, people who cannot get a good fit in clothing or accessories, those who resist the pressures to conform, geographically isolated consumers, or consumers living where the style is not available. Some subcultures in the United States do not conform for religious or moral reasons. For example, the Amish of Pennsylvania and the Old Russian Believers of Oregon maintain their traditional way of dressing based on such influences.

Stages of Fashion Marketing

From the marketer's viewpoint, the fashion life-cycle can be divided into marketing stages. The marketing life-cycle of a product extends from its commercial design and introduction, through various marketing processes, to its ultimate decline and obsolescence. Figure 4.6 divides this life-cycle into four stages: commercial introduction, inventory accumulation and promotion, mass merchandising, and clearance and obsolescence.[3] At each of these stages, marketing activities may be focused on the particular category of consumers who adopted at that time.

At commercial introduction, the product is new and typically merchandised as high fashion, often at a premium price through exclusive retail stores. Closely following this introductory stage is that of inventory accumulation and promotion where less fashionable stores begin stocking and promoting the style. During this stage of diffusion, the highest level of promotion may be expected in trade channels, directed primarily at buyers for retail stores. As the style is purchased by store buyers and offered to consumers, diffusion into the mass market accelerates. This promotional stage is critical to retailers, for it separates the successful and profitable styles from those rejected by consumers and sold at a markdown.

Marketers watch the behavior of consumers closely during these introductory and promotional stages, for the volume of sales determines whether the mass merchandising stage will be reached. If acceptance of

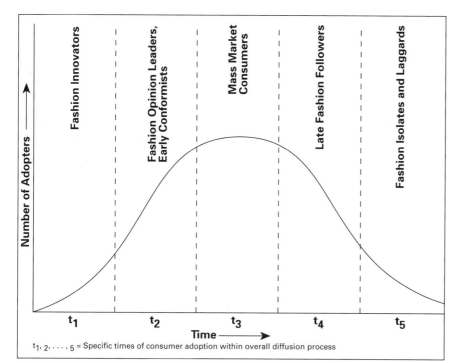

Figure 4.5 Categories of Consumer Adopters

(Figure 4.5 labels, left to right:)

Fashion Innovators

Fashion Opinion Leaders, Early Conformists

Mass Market Consumers

Late Fashion Followers

Fashion Isolates and Laggards

Number of Adopters →

t_1 t_2 t_3 t_4 t_5

Time →

$t_{1, 2, \ldots, 5}$ = Specific times of consumer adoption within overall diffusion process

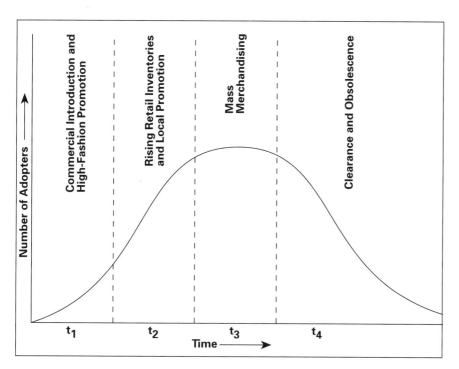

Figure 4.6 Stages of Fashion Marketing

(Figure 4.6 labels, left to right:)

Commercial Introduction and High-Fashion Promotion

Rising Retail Inventories and Local Promotion

Mass Merchandising

Clearance and Obsolescence

Number of Adopters →

t_1 t_2 t_3 t_4

Time →

the style accelerates, the mass merchandising stage begins. The style is copied by mass production and made available in nearly all retail stores and price ranges. Eventually consumer demand for the style tapers off and the stage of clearance and obsolescence begins. At this time, clearance sales become the principal means for stimulating further demand for the fashion. The fashion finally reaches marketing obsolescence when it cannot be sold at any price, except possibly to a minority of isolates and laggards.

Fashion Seasons

It may take several years for a fashion to completely diffuse through a population. When this happens, consumers' acceptance of the style can be further broken down into mini-processes of diffusion, in which the overall diffusion of the fashion takes place over several consecutive fashion seasons.

There are a variety of fashion seasons in each year, and regional variations in seasons with the typical season lasting from two to six months (fig. 4.7). For most fashion apparel, the fashion seasons include Fall I, Fall II, Holiday, Resort, Spring, and Summer. However, not all apparel producers will manufacturer lines for all seasons. Traditionally, the largest fashion seasons (in terms of number of companies participating and the number of lines) are spring and fall. There are also specialized seasons which center around holidays or peak periods for consumer demand (e.g., Christmas, wedding, and back-to-school seasons). A synthetic season, not related to the fashion seasons or traditional periods of consumer demand, is typified by sales. Sale seasons such as preseason specials and end-of-season clearance sales are used by marketers to reduce inventory. In some cases preseason sales may also be used to test consumer demand before the actual season begins.

As figure 4.7 suggests, a complete process of diffusion can occur in a single fashion season. For example, early in a spring season, a new style may be introduced; as several months pass, consumer acceptance will peak. Late in the season, a decline in adoption may take place, though there could be another mini-diffusion process at the season's end, encouraged by sales and followed by termination. However, often a successful spring style will be carried over to the summer season, and a new diffusion process begins. In this manner a dominant fashion trend becomes established as the fashion achieves expanded acceptance in each successive season. An overall diffusion curve for the fashion can then be constructed by summing up the style's individual diffusion curves for each season.

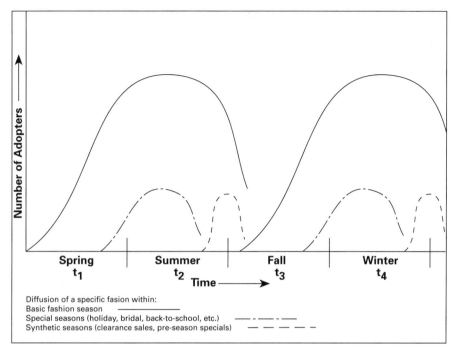

Figure 4.7 Diffusion in Annual Fashion Seasons

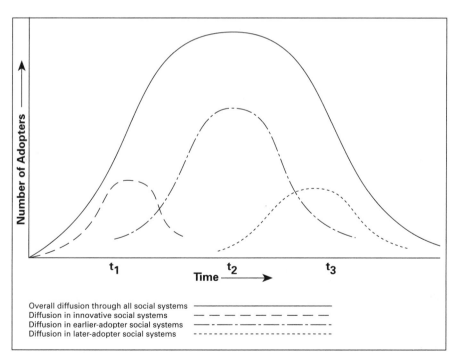

Figure 4.8 Variation in Fashion Diffusion across Social Systems

Diffusion across Social Systems

Separate life cycles can be graphed for each social system where a fashion diffuses. For example, figure 4.8 portrays the diffusion of a fashion within three types of social systems of differing innovativeness. In the first season that a new style is introduced, diffusion may occur largely in the most innovative social systems. After the fashion successfully diffuses there, the diffusion process may begin to occur in other social systems of the population. The fashion finally begins to penetrate later-adopting social systems after it has already reached a peak of acceptance throughout the mass population. The overall diffusion curve for the fashion becomes a simple addition of the diffusion in each of these separate social systems.

This analysis raises an issue in identifying adopter categories. Each social system theoretically will have its own fashion innovators, opinion leaders, mass market consumers, fashion followers and laggards. Note, however, that a person categorized as a fashion follower or laggard within a very innovative social system would still be an innovator in later-adopting systems. Therefore, the individual's adopter category depends on his or her own social environment, and even the most laggard social system may have innovators of a sort.

Simultaneous Trends in Diffusion

A variety of fashion trends may diffuse simultaneously. For instance, the dominant fashion trends might vary in different classifications of merchandise. Rates of diffusion may also vary. In classifications such as sportswear and leisure styles, diffusion may be rapid. For basic merchandise such as occupational dress, trends may be stable and of longer duration. In certain classifications, fashion changes may even be extremely rapid, perhaps even faddish.

There are also dominant trends in basic styling features that touch all classes of merchandise. This can happen in such features as color, fabric patterns, garment dimensions such as dress lengths, and design details such as jacket lapels and pants cuffs. For example, when a single styling feature such as tapered pants legs, pink shirts, or a specific dress length becomes fashionable, that styling feature will be offered in sportswear, occupational dress, and formalwear.

To exemplify these principles, simultaneous trends are graphed in figure 4.9. If one examines any specific time, one might observe some trends beginning their diffusion, others peaking, and some declining. Each of these trends may have different levels, rates, and lengths of acceptance, and occasionally a brief fad may appear among the dominant trends.

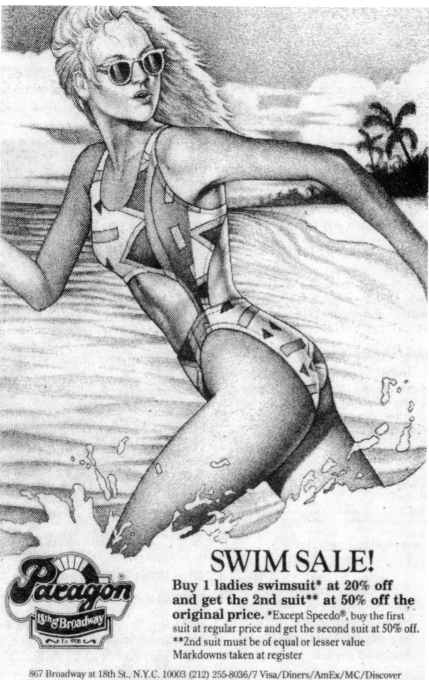

SWIM SALE!

Buy 1 ladies swimsuit* at 20% off and get the 2nd suit** at 50% off the original price. *Except Speedo®, buy the first suit at regular price and get the second suit at 50% off. **2nd suit must be of equal or lesser value Markdowns taken at register

867 Broadway at 18th St., N.Y.C. 10003 (212) 255-8036/7 Visa/Diners/AmEx/MC/Discover
Mon.-Fri. 10:00-8:00 Sat. 10:00-7:00 Sun. 11:00-6:00
Mail and Phone Orders Add $5.00 Shipping. N.Y. Residents Add Local Sales Tax

Synthetic seasons are created by retail stores through publicized sales.

**Figure 4.9
Simultaneous Diffusion
of Several Fashion
Trends**

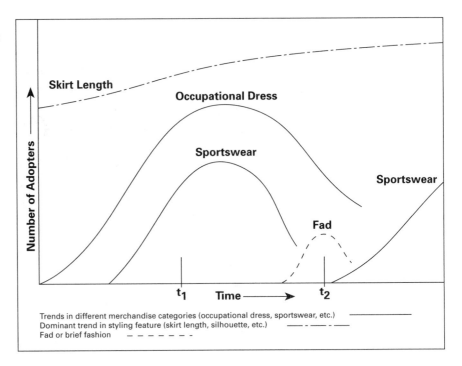

In analyzing simultaneous fashion trends, it is also important to recognize that existing trends compete with emerging trends. For instance, focusing on time t1 in figure 4.9, we see several trends that have become well established. One might expect high resistance to fashion change at this time, although brief fads could gain a temporary position. However, at the later time, t2, the termination of the previously dominant trends signals the opportunity for introduction of innovations and the emergence of new trends.

SUMMARY

A fashion life-cycle curve, sometimes called a diffusion curve, graphically represents consumers' acceptance of a specific style over a period of time. The curve portrays several key variables, including the total length of time over which diffusion occurs, the speed at which consumers adopt the object, and the level of acceptance of the object at each point in time. Several detailed analyses of a fashion life-cycle curve may be made. The curve can be subdivided into the five adopter categories of fashion innovators, opinion leaders and early conformists, mass-market consumers, fashion followers, and fashion laggards and isolates. Four sequential stages of fashion marketing may also be identified: commercial introduction of a new style, inventory accumulation and promotion, mass merchandising, and clearance and obsolescence of the fashion. When diffusion occurs over a period of years, the process may also be broken down into mini-processes of diffusion within each consecutive fashion season. Finally, separate diffusion curves may be graphed for diffusion of a fashion within each social system, and these curves may be added together to form an overall diffusion curve for the fashion.

At any time there may be a variety of simultaneous trends in fashion diffusion. These may occur in different categories of merchandise—sportswear, say, or occupational dress—and for specific styling features like garment dimensions and design details. The life-cycles for each trend may be simultaneously graphed to portray the status of currently existing trends and the competitive situation between established and emerging trends.

NOTES

1. The bell-shaped curve is a general model for the diffusion of an innovation (Rogers 1983; Wilkie 1990). The use of the bell curve as an ideal model describing fashion diffusion is also accepted among clothing analysts (Horn and Gurel 1981; Kaiser 1990). However, it should be noted that the bell curve is an ideal representation of what can be a relatively irregular pattern of diffusion. For example, some styles (especially fads) may grow exponentially or in other abnormal patterns.
2. This represents an adaptation of the classic model of five adopter categories in diffusion theory. The five adopter categories are innovators, early adopters, early majority, late majority, and laggards (Rogers 1983). The dividing line between categories is established by subdividing the diffusion curve by the number of standard deviations away from the mean on the normal (bell-shaped) curve. For fashion adopter categories, no such division has been validated through research.
3. Some fashion analysts specify a five-stage marketing life-cycle including introduction, rise, culmination, decline, and obsolescence. The difference between such approaches and the present one is minor, but our model of four stages appears appropriate both for simplification and to clearly identify the major stages of marketing activity in fashion trends.

DISCUSSION QUESTIONS AND PROJECTS

1. What is the purpose and value of a diffusion curve?
2. Draw your best estimate of the diffusion curve (acceptance) of a fashion which has been popular in your social system (school, city, network, or friends) during the past year or more. Label both axes of your graph, showing the months the diffusion has taken place and the level of acceptance at each month.
3. To get accurate measures of actual acceptance of new styles requires actual counts of tangible evidence like sales figures (retail stores and marketing services often have such figures). Another way of approximating this measure is by taking fashion counts. Form a group and take such a count of people actually wearing a particular style every day for at least one week. Draw a daily diffusion curve for this observed behavior.
4. Why are the acquisition (buying) and use curves different? What does this suggest about the value and use of fashion counts and sales data in plotting the trend of fashion diffusion?
5. Divide the life-cycle into stages of fashion marketing. What kinds of consumers are adopting (buying) at each stage? What does this suggest for planning your strategy for marketing at each stage (e.g., variety of assortments, total amount in inventory, advertising, in-store promotions, pricing, markdowns, clearances, obsolescence of the style)?
6. How do fads, fashions and classics differ in life-cycle? List fads, fashions and classics you know and draw approximate graphs of their life-cycles (total months/years of diffusion, total levels of acceptance at each stage).
7. Many different fashion trends may be spreading at the same time. Taking the separate graphs you have done in question 6 above, combine these into a single graph showing simultaneous trends in diffusions (see fig. 4.9). This may help you realize the complexity of analyzing many differing trends of varied length and acceptance simultaneously, which is the major challenge of fashion analysts in all levels of the fashion business.

SUGGESTED READINGS

Rogers, Everett M. *Diffusion of Innovations*. Glencoe, Illinois: The Free Press, 1962.

Rogers, Everett M. *Diffusion of Innovations*. 3d ed. Glencoe, Illinois: The Free Press, 1983.

Wilkie, William L. *Consumer Behavior*. 2d ed. New York: John Wiley, 1990.

5

Fashion Leadership

OBJECTIVES

◆ To survey four major theories of how consumers start and spread new fashion trends.

◆ To assess the appropriateness of each theory for explaining the acceptance of new styles in today's society and economy.

Who are the leaders in the adoption and diffusion of new fashions? To many observers, fashion leadership is synonymous with the role of the fashion designer, because designers originate many new styles and some become fashion trends. Some observers point to people with personal style as the true leaders of fashion. Those with personal style have creativity, individuality, and resourcefulness in dressing—skills of good taste admired and imitated by others. Other observers have pointed to the historical significance of fashion leadership among upper-class consumers. And contemporary analysts have persuasively argued that innovative leadership can come from nearly any segment of the consumer population. In short, there are sharply contrasting perspectives on how fashion leadership occurs.

This chapter examines theories proposed to explain how different groups of *consumers* lead and initiate the fashion process. Each theory identifies consumers who are first to adopt a style and how the style spreads from these leaders to other consumers. Four theories predominate:

◆ **The Upper-Class Leadership Theory** Popularly referred to as the "trickle-down" theory, this theory suggests that fashion is an elitist phenomenon initiated by the highest socioeconomic classes and copied later by lower classes.

- **The Mass-Market Theory** Sometimes referred to as the horizontal flow or the "trickle-across" theory, this theory suggests that, due to mass marketing, new styles are simultaneously available to all social classes, and that new fashions simultaneously spread across each social class.
- **The Subcultural Innovation Theory** Referred to as the "bottom-up," status float, or "trickle-up" theory, proponents of this theory suggest that new styles originate from lower-status segments or subcultures of the population, and then diffuse upward into the mass population.
- **The Innovativeness and Collective Selection Theory** This theory suggests that nearly any type of consumer can be the innovator leading fashion trends if the style can pass the test of collective selection in the mass population.

THE UPPER-CLASS LEADERSHIP THEORY

The theory of upper-class leadership offers the oldest and most established perspective on the fashion process. One of the most precise statements of this theory has been offered by the German social philosopher Georg Simmel (1957):

> *Social forms, apparel, aesthetic judgement, the whole style of human expression are constantly transformed by fashion, in such a way, however, that fashion . . .in all these things affects only the upper classes. Just as soon as the lower classes begin to copy their style, thereby crossing the line of demarcation the upper classes have drawn and destroying the uniformity of their coherence, the upper classes turn away from this style and adopt a new one, which in its turn differentiates them from the masses; and thus the game goes merrily on. Naturally, the lower classes look and strive toward the upper, and they encounter least resistance in those fields which are subject to the whims of fashion; for it is here that mere external imitation is most readily applied. The same process is at work as between the different sets within the upper classes, although it is not always as visible as here. (P. 545)*

This is often referred to as the trickle-down theory, since it proposes that fashions are first adopted in the upper class, and then are imitated by each succeeding lower class until they trickle down to the lowest social class. The theory also implies that the upper classes adopt new fashions as symbols of exclusiveness and differentiation from their social inferiors:

The fashions of the upper stratum of society are never identical with those of the lower; in fact, they are abandoned by the former as soon as the latter prepare to appropriate them (Simmel 1957, 543).

This form of class competition for symbols breeds new fashions. The upper class adopts a new fashion to symbolize its superior position, the lower classes show their social equality by adopting the fashion, and the upper class then discards the fashion and adopts a new one to reassert its superior position.

Fashion leadership from the upper classes is also thought of as a phenomenon of wealth. In his classic book *The Theory of Leisure Class,* Thorstein Veblen (1912) pointed out that the increasing wealth of the leisure class gave rise to what he termed "conspicuous consumption" of products symbolizing wealth:

No line of consumption affords a more apt illustration than expenditure on dress. . . . Other methods of putting one's pecuniary standing in evidence serve their end effectually, and other methods are in vogue always and everywhere; but expenditure on dress has this advantage over most other methods, that our apparel is always in evidence and affords an indication of our pecuniary standing to all observers at the first glance. . . . No one finds difficulty in assenting to the commonplace that the greater part of the expenditure incurred by all classes for apparel is incurred for the sake of a respectable appearance rather than for protection of the person (Veblen 1912, 167, 168).

Veblen goes on to say that the pacesetter in standards of conspicuous consumption of apparel will be the leisure class.

Historical Basis for the Theory

The theory of upper-class leadership has a long tradition of historical support. Nearly all books of fashion history and museum collections of costumes have served as chronicles of exclusive and aristocratic fashions. Based on such historical evidence, it is easy to conclude that fashion has traditionally been the province of wealthy people, landowners, and the ruling classes. But the degree to which fashions trickled to the lower classes is difficult to document, for there is little record of lower-class fashions either in the historical collections or in art from different periods. Only the fashions of the upper classes are preserved to any appreciable degree in historical records.

In the United States, fashion as an upper-class phenomenon can be documented from records of the seventeenth and eighteenth centuries. During this time, fashions identified a person's wealth and position in society. However, with the Industrial Revolution in the eighteenth and nineteenth centuries, the development of technology for manufacturing clothing and factories for mass production made fashionable clothing available to a larger part of the population. Developments in mass marketing and communications in the twentieth century have further increased the variety of fashions available to virtually the entire population (Kidwell and Christman 1974; Daves 1967).

Therefore, although upper-class leaders undoubtedly played important roles in early fashion history, many authorities argue that their role in the fashion process has diminished in modern society. In the changing social and economic environment of the twentieth century, many new influences on consumer behavior have emerged. These changes have not necessarily made the trickle-down theory obsolete, but the theory has been substantially modified. These modifications prepare for a transition to new theories of fashion leadership for contemporary society.

Transitions to New Theories

As early as 1928, economist and marketing professor Paul Nystrom observed a shifting of leadership away from the upper class to "fashion-conscious social groups":

To find the earliest indications of new fashions and fashion trends one must find groups of people who have wealth, at least enough to make it possible for them to buy freely beyond the boundaries of absolute necessities, leisure in which to plan for and make use of fashion goods, freedom from dominating restraint of custom or habit, courage to try new things, intelligence, shrewd appreciation of the social significance of the events and affairs of the world, good taste with a real basis in artistic sense and, last but not least, a keen desire to compete with other people for preeminence in style and fashion . . .

So, paradoxical as it may seem, resorts, restaurants and other social meeting places made exclusive by high prices and charges, as a rule, mean nothing to fashion movements. The very wealthy who alone can patronize these places may wear bizarre, exotic, queer, strange apparel today and throw it away tomorrow. What they wear from day to day may be style of a sort, but it is not fashion. The custom of such wealthy people may be very lucrative for a new specialty shops, but doesn't mean a thing from the standpoint of large-scale production and marketing in the fashion field. The business student must look for beginnings of fashion trends in localities, meeting places and groups in which there is distinct fashion sense (Nystrom 1928, 33-35).

Though Nystrom's argument may imply a modest role for wealth and higher social class in fashion leadership, it strongly suggests that leadership of major fashion trends is far from concentrated in the upper echelons of society.

Well-known and respected individuals are in natural positions to influence others.
(*WWD*, Fairchild Publications)

Writing in 1951, fashion merchant Daniels elaborated on some significant changes in the modern fashion process:

Fashion no longer refers to price. Students of marketing used to talk about the fashion cycle as having three phases . . . with different price characteristics for each phase. By contrast, the fact today is that the fashion cycle moves so quickly that it is a blur. Almost everyone instantaneously wants the same thing. The differential price characteristic has virtually disappeared. Radio, TV, the theater, and the press can be thanked for this (Daniels 1951, 52).

Daniels does suggest that social leaders or the "international set" may be the first to adopt new styles, thereby initiating a trickle-down process. But he goes on to state that such a "distinguished group" cannot start a new trend unless the roots of that general trend are already established (Daniels 1951, 52). The implication is that distinguished leaders will successfully initiate new trends only if the new styles they adopt are relatively consistent with the dominant trends already established in society. If these new styles are too innovative, the chances are the style will not diffuse.

These two analysts also point out major changes in the fashion process brought about by modern mass production, marketing, and communications. Daniels particularly stresses the idea that mass communications encourage almost everyone to want the same new styles instantaneously, and how the industrial capabilities of mass production and marketing fulfill this demand. The effect is to accelerate greatly the rate at which the fashion process occurs, which can subvert a slowly staged trickle-down process.[1]

Upward mobility, achieving a higher social position in society, has also changed our view of the trickle-down theory. The motivation to achieve a higher and better status in life has historically been strong in American society, and the opportunity to achieve has been widespread. When people achieve upward mobility, say through occupational advancement, they may adopt new patterns of consumption to symbolize their new social position (Barber and Lobel 1952). A restatement of the trickle-down theory then becomes feasible:

To the degree that status is defined in terms of consumption of goods and services one should perhaps say, not that such an individual has only the illusion of mobility, but rather that the entire population has been upwardly mobile. From this point of view, status-symbolic goods and services do not "trickle-down" but rather remain in fixed positions; the population moves up through the hierarchy of status-symbolic consumption patterns (Fallers 1954, 317).

In other words, consumers' tastes are upgraded as they achieve higher social positions and new life-styles. Their adoption of new products, including fashions, may then represent their willingness and ability to assume a new standard of living rather than mere imitation of standards set by a higher class.

Public figures or the "nouveau riche" can represent a special situation where upward social mobility can lead to a new type of elitist fashion leadership. For example, celebrities, movie stars, political figures, and business persons can gain social prominence. With public exposure and publicity, these people can become centers of public admiration, and their tastes in dress become symbols for emulation. The public figure can thus become a new kind of upper-class fashion leader. Not all public figures come to serve as models for fashionable behavior, but a few, such as the President, the First Lady, or a movie star, receive the necessary public attention to have at least an indirect influence on general fashion trends.

Calvin and Kelly Klein are members of the new upper-class fashion leadership.
(*WWD*, Fairchild Publications)

Another view of changing patterns in fashion leadership is colorfully described by Steiner and Weiss (1951):

> *[There are] . . . three levels of sophistication in matters of taste. At the bottom of the heap is to be found the innocent who naively considers ostentation and conspicuous display to be in the highest good taste even though, and perhaps because, he cannot afford such pretension. On the middle rung are the newly arrived whom we may now call the snobs. These make use of straightforward Vebleian technique to exert their hegemony over the mass of innocents. Still retaining their position at the top of the social hierarchy are the elite who . . . may be termed the counter-snobs (Steiner and Weiss 1951, 264-65).*

Steiner and Weiss suggest that snobs, the "nouveau riche" or newly arrived upper middle class, may actually take temporary roles as fashion leaders as a result of their conspicuous consumption. Meanwhile, the true upper class may quietly engage in "counter-snobbish" behavior by expressing simple but expensive tastes. But in the end, the tastes of the upper class are recognized, and these become the standard of leadership. Then a balance of power in exercising leadership might shift back and forth between snobs and counter-snobs as they compete for new symbols of "elitehood."

The interesting feature of this view is that it distinguishes between traditional upper-class leaders and a new elite of upper middle-class leaders who have recently attained status through upward mobility. The analysis suggests that fashion leadership has largely moved from the most elite classes, who prefer anonymity and private socializing among peers, to a new and larger middle and upper middle class who are more visibly part of the mass population. There is, however, a strong implication in this reasoning that the elite still retain a role of leadership as suggested by the traditional trickle-down theory.

One final view of the trickle-down theory is particularly significant in relation to a new theory of fashion leadership. In 1961, economist Robinson reaffirmed the trickle-down theory, but added the implication of a simultaneous horizontal flow of fashions within social classes:

> *. . . any group (or cluster of groups forming a class) will tend to take cues from those contiguous with it. Horizontally fashions will spread outward from central loci; and vertically—the more important consideration—any given group will tend to adopt as its mentor not the highest distinguishable group, but, rather, those immediately above it. In consequence of the vertical contiguity of class groupings, new fashions*

tend to filter down by stages through the levels of affluence. The process of discarding any fashion will be a mere reflex of its proliferation. For an object of fashion to lose its meaning for the topmost class, it is only necessary for it to be taken up by the second most and so on down the line (Robinson, 1961, 383).

This speaks in clear support of the trickle-down theory. Nonetheless, the proposition that fashion leadership flows from "central loci" of adopters within a single social class to contiguous members of the same class is important to the development of a new, mass-market theory of fashion to be discussed shortly.

In conclusion, a number of factors encourage a modification of the trickle-down theory, and a transition to more modern theories of leadership. Nevertheless, the traditional theory of upper-class leadership has a long history of support, and there are obvious contemporary examples of class leadership, as recently exemplified by the influences of Diana, Princess of Wales, and the widespread "class-celebrity" influence of the 1980s and 1990s. But the theories presented in the remainder of this chapter offer new explanations of contemporary fashion leadership, most of which are strongly and persuasively advocated by fashion analysts today.

THE MASS-MARKET THEORY

The mass-market theory of fashion leadership has emerged as a logical alternative to the trickle-down theory. Essentially, the theory proposes that the system of mass production in the fashion industry, combined with mass communication of fashion information through many different media, makes new styles and information about new styles available simultaneously to all socioeconomic classes of the population. This makes it possible for diffusion to occur simultaneously in each class, and the trickle-down process is effectively eliminated. Given the social-class orientation of the theory, it is frequently referred to as the horizontal-flow or trickle-across theory. However, the terminology of mass-market theory seems more descriptive, since the theory presupposes mass diffusion throughout the population largely as a result of mass marketing and mass communication.

At the center of the mass-market theory lies the hypothesis that real leadership of fashion comes from within a person's own social class, and especially from peer groups. Instead of looking to higher-status persons for leadership, people look to certain individuals from their own station in life:

When most people speak of fashion leaders, they mean the glamorous women who first display the expensive fashions. However true this may be, we are interested in another type of fashion leader: the woman who is influential face to face. In such relationships, we may be sure, the fashion leader is not necessarily the most glamorous woman, but rather a woman known personally to the advice-seeker, a woman to whom she can feel free to turn for advice. Thus, the two women, the adviser and the one advised, are not likely to be separated from each other by a wide gap in their social standing. They are, rather, more likely to move in generally similar social circles. (Katz and Lazarsfeld 1955, 263-64)

This theory suggests that each class or social group generates its own cadre of respected leaders who have greater influence than some unknown person from a higher social class.

A large variety of styles are created by mass production of fashion.

(© Robert Fox, Impact Visuals)

Key Dimensions of the Theory

In the first formal statement of the theory, King (1963) presented four arguments for the mass-market theory:

1. During a fashion season, the fashion industry's marketing strategy virtually assures simultaneous adoption of new styles by consumers in all socioeconomic groups. The new styles, including silhouette, fabric, color, and detail changes, are usually available to all consumers at the same time.
2. Consumers may freely choose from a large variety of existing and new styles in each new season, and can freely satisfy their personal tastes and needs rather than follow the lead of an upper class.
3. Each social class has its own fashion innovators and opinion leaders, who play key roles in starting new fashions within their peer social networks.
4. Fashion information and personal influence "trickle across" each social class, with fashion influence between social equals predominating over the vertical flow of fashion from upper to lower classes.

Modern marketing creates conditions favorable to the process of mass fashion-acceptance. Fashions can be mass-produced quickly and inexpensively for the ready-to-wear market. Rapid communication about new styles through the mass media and merchandising programs of retail stores increases consumers' awareness of new styles. Mass diffusion is further stimulated by the sew-at-home industry, because pattern companies and fabric producers feature the most popular mass fashions. A multiplicity of styles are thereby available in the mass market, serving nearly every functional need and life-style within a heterogeneous population.

The modern social structure also favors a mass-market perspective of leadership. Increasingly, society is becoming a vast and heterogeneous middle class, with varied life-styles and vaguely defined subclasses within it. Upper and lower classes remain, but they are a small part of the population. With this contemporary class structure in mind, it is plausible to reason that diffusion takes place in one great mass of social equals.

Furthermore, in such a social environment it can be argued that the traditional trickle-down process of fashion leadership might have less chance to occur. The highest classes may continue to patronize the most exclusive designers and retail stores, but their life-styles and constantly changing wardrobes are mostly invisible and anonymous to the mass population at large. Only the publicity-prone minority receive the widespread exposure necessary for leadership. The styles of such celebrities may be noticed by the more curious of the general public, but for the most part consumers are forced to look among their own social peers for fashion leaders.

Shopping centers and malls represent mass distribution of fashion. There is a stark comparison between the Northgate Mall in Seattle built in 1953 and "The Mall" at Rockingham Park with its center court and musical stair from the 1990s.

(International Council of Shopping Centers)

Therefore, the mass market theory focuses attention on the behavior of fashion innovators and opinion leaders in all segments of the population. When a new style is introduced to the mass market, these change agents will simultaneously play their influential roles in initiating diffusion within their social groups. Selective acceptance of the style then becomes an informal process of social influence, rather than a choice dictated by some higher authority.

Research Supporting the Theory

Several studies have provided research-based support of fundamental propositions of the mass-market theory. The Katz and Lazarsfeld study (1955), the first of several classics, focused on the existence of fashion opinion leaders in different social classes. From interviews conducted with 690 women in Decatur, Illinois, they found an equal percentage, 26 percent, of opinion leaders in both middle- and high-status groups; only among low-status groups was the concentration of opinion leaders smaller, 16 percent (Katz and Lazarsfeld 1955, 265). They also found that 57 percent of all influential relations were between women of equal status. Only those in the lower class went outside their class for fashion information to any degree, and then only to the adjacent middle class. These findings indicate substantial concentrations of opinion leaders in all major social classes, and most relations involving fashion opinion leadership are among people of similar status.

Mass retailing shapes the diffusion of all trends.
(*WWD*, Fairchild Publications)

King's classic Boston study (1963) expanded on the Katz and Lazarsfeld study by examining several socioeconomic characteristics of fashion innovators and opinion leaders. Innovators were defined as people who bought fashions early in the fashion season—August and September of the fall season. His findings indicate that many early buyers in a fashion season are average rather than elite in social position. The majority of early buyers were of modest or lower incomes, most were middle class or lower as measured by occupational status, and most thought of themselves as middle class or lower. Opinion leaders were also found at each income level of the early buyers, and the vast majority of their leadership-oriented interactions were among people of similar social status. These findings suggest that fashion leadership is dispersed across social classes and income groups, rather than concentrated in the upper classes.

King states that these findings cast serious doubt on the trickle-down theory. However, in defense of the trickle-down theory he notes that elite designers and their clientele are watched closely by the rest of the fashion industry, and styles adopted at that level are frequently copied by less well-known manufacturers. When this occurs, the mass-marketed styles are at least "partially distillations of upper class taste" (King 1963, 115). However, this does not mean consumers consciously follow fashions from the upper classes; rather, it merely indicates that the styles available in the market have previously been offered by exclusive designers to an elite clientele.

Research by Grindereng (1967) supports another key proposition of the mass-market theory. The research was conducted in a large Midwestern department store with an established fashion image. In the first step of the research, Grindereng analyzed the silhouettes and design details of styles available in the store's custom, moderate, budget, and basement departments. This survey indicated that similar silhouettes and design details were available in each department, except that the basement department had only a limited selection of basic silhouettes. Then she analyzed the fashion orientations and demographic characteristics of customers purchasing items in each department, using questionnaires mailed to charge-account customers. Findings indicated "the same basic silhouettes and design details selling to all classes during the same time period" (Grindereng 1967, 172).

The preceding investigations offer varied evidence favoring the fundamental propositions of a mass-market theory. Although a trickle-down process of fashion can be inferred from some data, it appears in each study that diffusion simultaneously across social classes is far more prevalent. Therefore, in situations where the marketing system makes a new style immediately and widely available in all price ranges, the mass-market theory appears as an extremely persuasive explanation of fashion leadership.

THE SUBCULTURAL LEADERSHIP THEORY

The subcultural leadership theory, one of the newest theories of leadership, had its birth in the 1960s and early 1970s. During this time, many **subcultures** of American and European societies—youths, African Americans, hippies, Hell's Angels, and others—became highly visible parts of society. Such subcultures created changing forms of status symbolism that evolved into new fashions:

> *In recent years, many standards in fashion have been set, not so much by the upper or even the middle classes, as by the declasse, anti-class youth, and counterculture. Long hair, head bands, beads, pretie-dyed apparel, vests, miscellaneous leather and suede, carefully faded and neglected dungarees, and all the other paraphernalia of the counterculture costume, not only mock the materialistic status symbols of the established classes, but have successfully spread into the enemy camp, Fifth Avenue and Main Street, where they have caught on and been copied; and American capitalism, once more demonstrating its incredible adaptability, turns the "revolution" and the revolutionary costume to good profit (Blumberg 1974, 493).*

Subcultural fashion leadership, 1992.

(© 1992 Brian Palmer/Impact Visuals)

Fashion trends have been initiated by many subcultural groups including youths, blue-collar workers, and ethnic minorities such as African-Americans and Native Americans (Field 1970). Taking all of these perspectives into account, a wholly new pattern of fashion leadership can be generated by these or other segments of the population. For present purposes and as indicated in chapter 4, a subcultural group may be considered to be any subgroup of people who exist within a dominant and larger population, and who share a uniquely identified pattern of values and life-style which may be clearly differentiated from those prevailing in the larger population. Many subgroups such as social classes, ethnic groups, religions, and communities could be identified as subcultures.

Like the previously discussed theories, the subcultural innovation theory has a distinct social class orientation, but with a different flavor. Specifically, the theory suggests that a major form of fashion leadership can originate from the lower classes, or from lower-status segments of the population. Given this emphasis, various versions of the theory have been termed "upward diffusion", the "bottom up" effect, "percolating up," and the "status-float phenomenon" (Blumberg 1974; Field 1970; Troxell and Judelle 1971).

Subcultural Leadership

A subculture becomes a leader of fashions by its ability to invent new styles. In some subcultures these innovations may be no more than customary artifacts from their cultural heritage. Eventually the unique style of a subculture, whether new or customary, may be noticed by the larger population and admired for its creativity, artistic excellence, or appropriateness to current life-styles. At that point, the style can emerge from its subcultural origin and diffuse into the larger population. This diffusion could occur by a trickle-down process: the style might skip from the originating subculture to the upper class and then trickle down. Or, the mass-market mechanism may take control, as mass production makes the object available throughout consumer markets. Of course, members of the subculture may not intend or even wish for diffusion to occur; like the upper class, the subculture may take exclusive pride in its styles. Nevertheless, the admired symbols of subcultural identity become selectively assimilated into the dominant culture.

"Gapbridgers" aid the diffusion of a style by linking a subculture to the mass population (Troxell and Judelle 1971). Since the subculture may not possess a natural position of leadership recognized by the larger population, it is necessary for these influential persons from other social systems to introduce and legitimize the style to the larger population. Gapbridgers could be prestigious persons, celebrities, youths, opinion leaders or even average persons having regular contact with subcultures or special appreciation of their styles. Such people are actually innovators within their social systems, and without these innovators a subcultural style may have little chance to diffuse into the larger population.

Several features of modern society favor subcultural leadership. Perhaps most significant is the increased visibility and influence of minority and youth subcultures. Many of their ideals of social equality, anti-materialism, environmental concern, and practicality rather than status symbolism have been communicated to the mass population.[2] This increased subcultural visibility has encouraged the imitation of their styles of living.

The Principal Leaders

Subcultural leadership can come from many quarters—ethnic groups, racial groups, the youth culture, and perhaps the lower class. In general, the larger and more visible subcultures have the greatest chance of being recognized as centers of leadership.

The fashion industry often gives credit to minority cultures for inspiring fashions in the larger mass market. Particularly the colorful fabrics and dress of African Americans and the crafts of Native Americans have started fashion trends. African Americans have expressed pride in their heritage, and the media and marketers have reinforced these styles as desirable. Although minority subcultures as consumer groups have been studied, the majority of research focuses on members' general consumption patterns and media exposure rather than examining the subculture's influence as a fashion leader.

The youth culture has long been identified as a distinct cultural segment of American society. The young, a market segment extremely conscious of their dress, are a big market segment. None of us would argue whether teenagers are frequently creative (perhaps faddish as well as fashionable) in dress. More recently young adults, especially "yuppies" (young urban professionals) have commanded center stage for fashionable behavior in general among the younger population.

The fashion-conscious young are often active adopters and leaders of some mass-marketed fashion trends. However, they often create their own styles, mixing various existing garments, adapting thrift-shop or "second-hand" clothing, custom color-styling garments by tie-dyeing or printing, creative sewing, adding appliques, and adopting styles of minority subcultures. Reverse status symbolism in fashion leadership can also

Youth leadership in fashion as exemplified by "Grunge," Seattle, 1992.

(*WWD*, Fairchild Publications)

prevail among the young when the norm of dress becomes cheap rather than expensive. These sorts of individuality can quickly spread within the youth culture and often outside to other social systems, as the "punk" look of the 1980s illustrates.

Society values youthful images, encouraging the diffusion of young styles to older segments of the population. The norms of young people favor innovation and change, making the youth culture a natural testing ground for new styles, and much of fashion merchandising is directed at youthful tastes. The active life-styles of youths also draw attention to their fashions. These conditions combine to propel young consumers to the center of fashion leadership.

The lower classes are also cited as sources of fashion trends. For instance, Field (1970) states that the first acceptance of men's mass-produced clothing came in the lower classes, and then diffused upward to other classes. He also points to men's work clothes, jeans, boots, and sleeveless undershirts as working-class styles that emerged as fashion trends. In women's wear, milkmaid and fishermen's styles are identified as historical examples of lower class influence, while miniskirts and blue jeans are more recent examples.

Several explanations for lower-class leadership are possible. Lower-class consumers have no traditionally honored social position to protect, and therefore can creatively choose any style (Troxell and Judelle 1971). They might engage in fashionable behavior to escape psychologically from poverty, or to appear upwardly mobile. Or, the lower class might have to originate its own styles because it is not catered to by the fashion industry, which emphasizes middle-income markets. Many lower-class styles are of necessity inexpensive, thereby accounting for their appeal to other consumers. Finally, the lower class may have its own standards of living that define a different norm of fashionability from those of the mass population. Such factors can account for the birth of new styles in the lower class, but it will still be necessary for some gapbridgers to endorse and legitimize the style if it is to diffuse.

Many of these explanations may apply also to leadership from other subcultural groups. This discussion has indicated that many forms of subcultural leadership exist and can influence fashion trends. When society is receptive to new trends in fashions, subcultures can be one of the sources to which consumers look for new ideals of aesthetic expression and fashionability.

THE INNOVATIVENESS AND COLLECTIVE SELECTION THEORY

Perhaps the most general theory of leadership argues that nearly any creative or innovative individuals can become leaders in fashion trends, provided that their innovative choices are reasonably in line with the social climate and life-styles of the times. The principal elements of such a theory have been outlined by sociologist Herbert Blumer (1968, 1969), a theorist in human collective behavior.

Like previous analysts, Blumer argues that fashion leadership is no longer confined strictly to the upper class. Instead he suggests that fashion is a process of "collective selection" and formation of collective tastes among a mass of people. In this process, many new styles of dress may be introduced at a given time, and these will compete for acceptance among consumers. Those that most closely represent the existing trends in consumers' tastes will be accepted and become fashionable. Initially tastes may be vague, but innovators' selections will give a more precise definition of these tastes, thereby establishing a clearer direction for the trend in new collective tastes. Blumer also notes that innovators' selections must be in line with the previous historical continuity of fashions to succeed (Blumer 1969). That is, new fashions usually evolve from and are not dramatically different from those they replace.

Blumer argues that prestigious people play an important role in leading the process of collective selection. By prestigious people he means persons "acknowledged as qualified to pass judgement on the value or suitability of the rival models" (Blumer 1969, 287) and this means many people in all classes, not just celebrities or the wealthy. He also argues that "not all prestigeful persons are innovators—and innovators are not necessarily persons with the highest prestige" (Blumer 1969, 281). This implies that prestigious leaders do not have to come solely from the upper class. However, he does clearly suggest that the prestigious leader could come from the upper class.

Blumer's thinking ties together previously established principles of fashion leadership and diffusion: the role of innovators, the need for leadership from centers of prestige, the requirement of historical continuity in fashion change, the existence of fashions as reflecting the spirit of the times, and fashions as manifestations of collective tastes. Identification of prestige as an attribute of successful leaders is particularly insightful. But Blumer's presentation of the processes of collective selection and formation of collective tastes is incomplete; therefore, they receive more detailed attention in the next chapter on the roles of social influence and interpersonal communications in fashion diffusion.

AN APPRAISAL OF LEADERSHIP THEORIES

It should now be apparent that many different types of fashion leadership can exist. In our heterogeneous society many types of people can engage in innovative behavior, and different people can emerge as leaders at any given time for any given trend. Therefore, the four theories of leadership contribute to an appreciation of fashion leadership as a diverse phenomenon.

The various theories offer several key points on the nature of the fashion process. All view the behavior of innovative consumers as the starting point of fashion diffusion, and the mass-market theory takes particular note of the leading role of innovators and opinion leaders operating within their own social systems. The theories also point to prestige or creativity as principal attributes of successful leaders. Finally, the theories point out that diffusion from centers of leadership to other consumers is a process of social emulation and formation of new social tastes. These are fundamental elements in the diffusion of all fashions.

The greatest limitation of several theories, but particularly the trickle-down theory, is their focus on social class processes of fashion leadership. Today's class structure is only hazily defined, as each broad class is composed of people with diverse life-styles, occupations, educational levels, and financial resources. Under these circumstances it is difficult to identify a trickle-down flow of fashion, or even a horizontal flow within classes. Instead, fashions may flow across social systems having similar life-styles and social tastes. This is different from saying that fashions diffuse down social classes over time or across all social classes simultaneously.

There are some controversial aspects of each theory, but by far the most controversy surrounds the applicability of the trickle-down theory to modern society. In the fashion industry there has been a long-standing belief that the upper class, the clientele of high fashion designers, and "the beautiful people" lead the acceptance of fashions. Therefore, these centers of leadership receive much publicity within the industry (e.g., in *Women's Wear Daily*), and exclusive styles of designers or high-fashion clientele are often copied by mass producers. But many executives and designers also are uneasy with the "beautiful people" approach and question the validity of the trickle-down notion in establishing mass fashion trends. They now speak of influence from youth, minority cultures, and average consumers in establishing dominant fashion trends. Although the trickle-down process may be prevalent in industry thinking, fashion leadership is now recognized by many as a far more complex process.[4]

Indeed, McCracken (1985) concluded in his appraisal of the current usefulness of the trickle-down theory that to be effective in explaining and predicting fashion change in contemporary society the theory's

> . . . rehabilitation requires several theoretic adjustments. First of all, the focus of the theory must be changed. Groups must be defined not only in terms of hierarchical social status but also in terms of status difference established by sex, age, and ethnicity . . . The theory must also attend to the cultural context of fashion innovation and diffusion. The provision of a cultural context enables the theory to account for the symbolic motives and ends of social groups engaged in fashion behavior. This in turn allows for a more penetrating analysis of the acts of imitation and differentiation in which the trickle-down effect consists. (PP. 50-51)

There are certain conditions under which each of the four theories discussed in this chapter might best explain the fashion process. For the upper class to lead, highly placed individuals—elites by virtue of occupational status, wealth, or public recognition—must be clearly the first to adopt the style. This can occur among the clientele of exclusive designers and stores. They must then receive almost immediate publicity as trendsetters in order to communicate the new style to innovators who will lead diffusion in other social systems. Furthermore, it is necessary that the fashion be made available to other segments of the population only after it has become well recognized as an elite fashion. The next step of mass emulation may then naturally occur, presuming that the aesthetics of the fashion as well as the status of its previous wearers are admired. However, later stages of diffusion are not likely to be a methodical class-to-class process; when mass production and communications take over, the mass-market process of simultaneous diffusion can be expected to direct the remaining phases of acceptance. The extreme example of this occurred in the 1986 royal wedding of the former Sarah Ferguson to Prince Andrew of England, in which it was widely reported that her wedding dress was copied and available for mass-market sales the same day as the wedding.

The mass-market process of fashion leadership requires a different set of conditions to operate. First, since this theory relies heavily on mass production of styles at all price ranges, the many producers in the fashion industry must have a like-mindedness on what fashions are wanted by consumers. The new style must be almost immediately mass-produced and retailed in a large number of stores and price ranges, assuring its availability to many social systems. But even this does not guarantee immediate acceptance across all social systems. For the mass-market theory to work, a high level of fashion interest and orientation to change must prevail throughout the population. Fashion leaders of most social systems must be in the market for new styles at essentially the same time, and must actually make similar purchasing and wearing decisions relatively independently of external influences other than the marketer's communications. Given these conditions, it would seem that the mass-market process of leadership would be difficult to activate, but nonetheless, the high level of fashion interest in the contemporary mass population makes this a process very likely to occur.

The collective selection theory requires similar circumstances. Leadership could initially come from prestigious figures of the upper class, but the theory implies that innovators from many if not all social systems will lend their prestige to the new style. Once the new taste is defined by innovators, it will spread simply because it will be recognized as socially appropriate to the life-styles of the times.

Subcultural leadership occurs when a subgroup of the population not traditionally in a position of leadership creates a new style. However, this

When the median age of the population is low, as it was in the 1960s, youth leadership in fashion becomes more prominent.
(The Bettman Archive)

will not force a fashion change until the style becomes admired by innovators from other social environments who then initiate the style within their own social systems. Idiosyncratic or faddish styles can also be created within the subculture, but only those consistent with existing norms and trends in aesthetic expression will be adopted and diffused by leaders from other social systems.

In an attempt to explain the complexities of fashion leadership between 1920 and 1985, one theorist has integrated components of several of these theories (Behling 1985). In this model (see fig. 5.1), two theories of

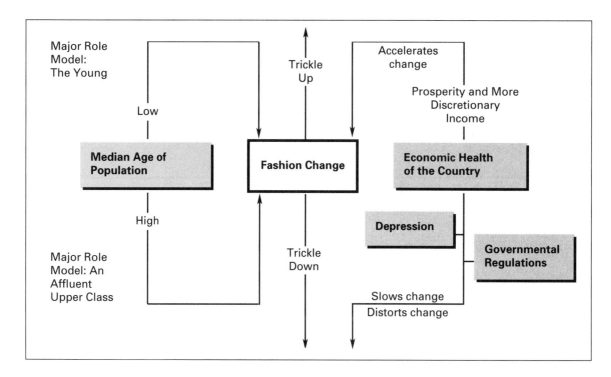

Major Role Model: The Young

Trickle Up

Accelerates change

Prosperity and More Discretionary Income

Low

Median Age of Population

Fashion Change

Economic Health of the Country

High

Depression

Governmental Regulations

Major Role Model: An Affluent Upper Class

Trickle Down

Slows change

Distorts change

Figure 5.1 Behling's Fashion Change Model
SOURCE: Behling (1985, 23)

fashion leadership are apparent: the trickle-down theory and the trickle-up theory. This flow of influence is affected by two variables: the median age of the population and the economic health of the country. According to Behling (1985)

> . . . the median age of the population determines who the role models will be for the majority of persons in our society and consequently determines whether fashion influences move in a downward direction from an older, more affluent class or upward from the street via the youth . . . .Change in the amount of disposable or discretionary income can speed up or slow down the fashion process (P. 20).

Thus, it appears fashion leadership and the fashion diffusion process is initiated and influenced by an interaction of social factors. It is unlikely that any dominant fashion trend may be initiated and propagated strictly by any idealized process. It is possible, for instance, for initial upper-class leadership to be supplanted by a mass-market process, or for subcultural leadership to diffuse quickly by upper-class or mass-market processes. However, for any emerging style to become widely diffused, it must effectively merge into a variety of consumers' value systems and life-styles. Thus some fads or brief fashions will ultimately diffuse to only certain segments of the population, and a few ideals will finally diffuse to a universal audience of adopters.

SUMMARY

Four major theories of fashion leadership in consumer behavior have been discussed. The theory of upper-class leadership suggests that fashion is an elitist phenomenon initiated by the highest socioeconomic classes and copied later by lower classes. The mass-market theory proposes that mass marketing makes new styles simultaneously available to all social classes, and that new fashions simultaneously spread across each social class. The subcultural innovation theory suggests that some new styles are creatively invented in subcultures or lower-status segments of the population, and then diffuse upward into the mass population. Finally, the theory of innovativeness and collective selection proposes that nearly any type of prestigious individual can be the innovator leading fashion trends, provided that the new style can pass the test of collective selection in the mass population.

These theories suggest that many different kinds of fashion leadership can exist. In our heterogeneous society, many types of consumers have the opportunity to lead trends. However, there is much debate as to how effective traditional upper-class leaders can be in originating trends in our modern social and marketing environments. Contemporary fashion leadership is often explained more completely by the mass market, subcultural and collective selection theories.

NOTES

1. The effects of mass production and communication of fashion trends are well documented in such varied sources as Foley (1894), Nystrom (1928), King (1963), Daves (1967), and Kidwell and Christman (1974).
2. See Blumberg (1974) for a more complete discussion of this perspective.
3. See Berk (1974) for a short introduction to collective behavior. Berk suggests that Blumer's theory of collective behavior is "outdated." Nevertheless, Blumer has much of interest to say about fashion-oriented collective behavior. Other theorists in collective behavior who offer interesting collective perspectives on fashion include Lang and Lang (1961) and Klapp (1969).

4. Based on numerous contacts with executives and designers at all levels of the fashion industry. Academicians also engage in debates on modern applicability of the trickle-down theory. Some believe the theory is obsolete, while others offer substantial support. See Hollander (1963) and Robinson (1963) for an interesting exchange of opinions on this subject, one that is relevant today.

DISCUSSION QUESTIONS AND PROJECTS

1. Outline the basic principles for each of the four theories of fashion leadership. Be specific as to what types of consumers are likely to be innovators, opinion leaders, followers and non-adopters under each theory.
2. Identify a new style of dress you believe will emerge in the coming six months to one year. Predict what types of consumers will be earlier and later buyers. How long will the trend last, and what level of acceptance do you expect? What market segments or groups of consumers are more likely and less likely to adopt? How confident are you of your forecast (fashion experts must make these prediction and then make choices of which styles to offer, thus risking the success or failure of their businesses daily!)?
3. Design a research project to identify the innovators and opinion leaders for new styles of men's and women's business wear. (This project may be done for any category of apparel that is of current market importance.) Hint: The classic studies of Katz and Lazarsfeld (1955), King (1963), and Grindereng (1967), among many others referenced in this chapter, offer ideas which you can modify and adapt for your particular study.
4. You are the marketing director for a large retail store in a major metropolitan area. Identify your major target markets, including the types of innovators and opinion leaders who will likely patronize your store. How does your understanding of fashion leadership contribute to understanding how these consumers may be motivated to visit and purchase items from your store?
5. Some fashion analysts strongly favor the proposition that the upper classes, the wealthy and similarly placed prestigious persons, are the key leaders of fashion today. In what ways do you agree with these analysts? Can you cite examples of leadership from such elite groups? What is the future role of such persons in the leadership of fashion?
6. Some fashion analysts argue forcefully that the elite groups are less influential on fashion adoption than they once were (see question 5).

Instead they suggest that fashion comes from the streets and from subcultures which are so visible in our multicultural world today. In what ways do you agree with these analysts? Can you cite examples of leadership from such multicultural groups? Is the "mass-market" process of fashion leadership still appropriate, or is it being replaced by some "multicultural market" process?

7. Overall, what theories of fashion leadership contribute to understanding today's fashion diffusion, and which have become less relevant to understanding contemporary trends?

SUGGESTED READINGS

The following are considered major historical readings establishing the basis for modern theories of fashion leadership.

Blumer, Herbert. "Fashion: From Class Differentiation to Collective Selection." *Sociological Quarterly* 10 (1969): 275-91.

Field, George A. "The Status Float Phenomenon: The Upward Diffusion of Innovation." *Business Horizons* 13 (August 1970): 45-52.

Katz, Elihu, and Paul F. Lazarsfeld. *Personal Influence.* Glencoe, Illinois: The Free Press, 1955.

King, Charles W. "Fashion Adoption: A Rebuttal to the 'Trickles Down' Theory." In *Toward Scientific Marketing,* edited by Stephen A. Greyser. Chicago: American Marketing Association, 1963.

Lang, Kurt, and Gladys Lang. "Fashion: Identification and Differentiation in the Mass Society." In *Dress, Adornment and the Social Order,* edited by Mary Ellen Roach and Joanne Bubolz Eicher. New York: John Wiley and Sons, Inc., 1965, 322-46. Reprinted from *Collective Dynamics.* New York: Thomas Y. Crowell Co., 1961, 465-87.

Robinson, Dwight E. "The Economics of Fashion Demand." *The Quarterly Journal of Economics* 75 (1961): 376-98.

Simmel, Georg. "Fashion." *American Journal of Sociology* 62 (1957): 541-58. Reprinted from *International Quarterly* 10 (1904): 130-55.

Sproles, George B. "Analyzing Fashion Life Cycles—Principles and Perspectives." *Journal of Marketing* 45 (1981): 116-24.

Recent works on fashion leadership:

Behling, Dorothy. "Fashion Change and Demographics: A Model." *Clothing and Textiles Research Journal* 4 (1985-1986, No. 1): 18-24.

Solomon, Michael R. (ed.). *The Psychology of Fashion.* Lexington, Mass: Lexington Books, 1985.

6

Social Process of Fashion Diffusion

OBJECTIVES

◆ To review the social processes involved in the diffusion of fashions in small groups.
◆ To describe how socially defined fashion norms develop and evolve within small groups.
◆ To examine the influence of reference groups on conformity in fashion adoption.

The diffusion of fashion centers on a process of social interactions and influence that spreads person-to-person. Behavioral scientists have used several sociological concepts—collective behavior, social contagion, social differentiation, social influence, and conformity to emergent social norms—to explain this process of socially-influenced consumer behavior. We will use these sociological concepts to explain the underlying process of fashion diffusion. Our analysis revolves around the central sociological principle that the processes of social interaction among people in group settings provide the mechanism through which the fashion process takes place.

Two basic social mechanisms of the fashion process will be discussed in this and the following chapter:

1. the diffusion of fashions through social interaction and definition of social norms in small groups (this chapter), and

2. the diffusion of fashions through the collective behavior of large masses of people and the social factors influencing the termination of fashion trends (chap. 7).

The analysis begins with a look at social origins of the fashion process that lead the way for fashion diffusion.

THE SOCIAL CONTEXT OF THE FASHION PROCESS

The initiation of the fashion process is influenced by a wide range of social forces in the consumer's environment. Modern mass society is oriented toward continuous change and progress, in that social change is equated with improvement of the human condition. Change is further stimulated by social mobility as people strive to better their position in life, and by our increasing and diversity of life-styles. Our extensive social contacts in urban mass society, in work life, and in abundant leisure activities set the social stage for the play of fashion. In concert with these forces, innovations in dress are constantly introduced to the consumer. In particular, fashion advertising and the fashion marketing system of designers, retailers, and the fashion media become powerful forces in creating new social and cultural meanings for fashions, thereby encouraging their acceptance by consumers (McCracken 1988). This environment constantly and powerfully seeds the beginnings of new fashions.

Within this environment, a great deal of consumer experimentation with new tastes occurs, and many differing centers of fashion leadership can emerge. Fashion theorists have identified upper-class elites, members of subcultures, or people at all levels of the population as potential leaders under different circumstances. This diversity of innovation-oriented consumers virtually guarantees the regular origination of new fashion trends. Research on large samples of adult consumers conclusively shows that fashion interest and keeping up with fashions are widespread in the consumer population (Sproles and King 1973; Sproles 1977; Horridge and Richards 1986). This virtually guarantees that new fashions will regularly gain popularity among many consumers.

At any given time, many new styles of dress compete for acceptance as fashions. In such an environment, many divergent and contrasting trends can occur simultaneously. This diversity happens because there are so many differing social classes, life-styles, subcultural and occupational groups in society. As discussed in chapter 3, the process of fashion diffusion involves the spread of fashion innovations within and across social groups, and the extent to which fashions diffuse is, in part, dependent upon communications among group members. Therefore, this chapter will center on the underlying and primary explanation for fashion diffusion: the processes of social interaction within each particular group that systematically define which specific tastes and emergent social norms of fashion will prevail. Let's first explore how fashion norms emerge and evolve within social groups.

EMERGENT SOCIAL NORMS AND GROUP BEHAVIOR

The fashion process, by definition, involves group acceptance of socially defined norms of what is considered "fashionable." It is especially important to understand the process of norm development to understand fashion diffusion within social groups. In group settings, individuals compare themselves with others and experience both internal and external pressures to conform to others in order to be socially "correct," to "fit into the group," or to avoid social sanctions. Subsequently, individuals within

Fashion norms evolve from comparing ourselves to others.

groups come to share a common sense of socially acceptable behavior, including the acceptance of socially approved fashion norms. Group norms, such as fashion norms, evolve from group processes and are constantly being revised through these processes. According to Ralph Turner, a leading sociologist in the area of group behavior, "when human beings act in any situation, they seek and create group norms to guide their behavior" (1990, 284).

Muzafer Sherif's work (1935, 1936) on the development of individual and group norms provides a basis for our understanding of the emergence of fashion norms within a group. In studying emergent group norms, Sherif experimented with the autokinetic phenomenon, one in which a stable pinpoint of light in a completely dark room will appear to move in an erratic manner. When separate groups of individuals were repeatedly exposed to this phenomenon, they developed unique ranges within which the light was seen to move. In these group situations, individual judgments came together to form a "group norm." Interestingly enough, when individuals were subsequently tested by themselves they conformed to the previously established group norms. This early work led researchers to study the development of group norms in various situations. It has been concluded that emergent group norms are dependent upon social comparison processes and the availability of pre-existing means for communication among group members (Turner and Killian 1987).

In applying this conceptual framework to the development of fashion norms, the parallels can easily be seen. Similar to the perceptions of light movement studied by Sherif, perceptions of "fashion" are often ambiguous and unclear. To provide a frame of reference and sense of structure to the stimuli, consumers turn to others for information and a frame of reference for fashion norms. The means for communicating fashion norms include social interaction and media coverage of fashion. Through personal and media communication processes, consumers discover a broad range of acceptable fashion alternatives. In their selection of specific fashion objects, they consequently contribute to the continuation of the group fashion norms. This emergent norm approach can be effectively applied to the explanation of fashion diffusion within small groups and organizations. These norms are especially powerful in small face-to-face groups. It is well known that social norms are more controlling when people are known to each other than when they are anonymous. This is one reason why we see greater conformity in clothing fashions in small groups and organizations than we do among the masses. It is because of this powerful and pervasive role of small groups in defining fashions that we now turn to an in-depth analysis of fashion diffusion as a group phenomenon taking place in small group settings. In the following chapters we will further explore these issues, but from the differing perspectives of fashion diffusion as a form of collective behavior among large groups and the individual's psychology and decision-making processes.

FASHION DIFFUSION IN SMALL GROUPS

The interactions of people in small social groups can be one of the most persuasive settings in which fashions are adopted and diffused. Indeed, the powerful forces of conformity take effect here: as fashion trends spread, consumers' latitude of choice narrows in favor of the normatively prescribed fashions. Clearly there are such prescribed standards of proper dress, and as Lauer and Lauer (1981) have persuasively argued, current fashion becomes a "coercive social fact" (p. 141). The consumer may indeed feel somewhat powerless to resist the trend approved by his or her reference groups.

Types of Small Groups

When we speak of small groups, we are referring to membership groups, peer groups, aspirational groups, and other types of reference groups. Reference groups exert some sort of influence on the individual. Such groups might influence the individual's attitudes, interests, opinions, values, or actual behavior. The individual may or may not be a member of the reference group. An individual might be influenced by many reference groups, or the influence might stem from a single reference individual. Thus the concept of reference groups describes a broad range of situations where individuals behave "in reference" to certain preferred groups. The influence of reference groups on conformity in fashion adoption will be discussed later in this chapter.

Membership groups are those in which two or more individuals come together for social interaction. Two basic types of membership groups are primary and secondary groups. Primary groups have regular, intimate, face-to-face interaction among members. The family is a primary group, as are many other informally established friendship and neighborhood groups. Secondary groups have a more formal organization, often focused on specialized needs or goals of members. Professional organizations, clubs, church groups, and other organized and long-lasting groups fall into this category.

In a **peer group,** the members are social equals. A peer group is a set of acquaintances or friends similar to one another in age, education, or social class, for example, who interact socially on a regular basis. Peer groups also include large groups of social equals, such as a doctor's professional organization, who occasionally interact face-to-face.

There are also groups of which a person is not a member, but which become important because they influence his or her behavior. **Aspirational groups** are those to which the individual would like to belong, and behavior can be modeled after that of the members of these esteemed groups. At the other extreme, out-groups are held in contempt or indifference. People avoid imitating the behavior of the members of these groups.

Behavior in Small Groups

The dynamics of social interaction and influence in small groups are complex: there are so many individual personalities and personal goals in situations of common interaction. Our present interests center on those basic features of social interaction that influence fashion diffusion in small groups. The following discussion describes some group processes that can exert this influence.[1]

Social behavior in groups starts with the formation of the group. The commonality of interests and goals among a number of individuals who know each other is one basis for group formation. People with similar attitudes, needs, and values may form small groups. People similar in age, social class, or profession can form groups as can those who live near one another or who work together. Social events drawing a lot of people together offer opportunities for chance meetings that can result in the formation of new groups or the addition of members to existing groups. Nearly any social contact between people with things in common can initiate group dynamics.

The size of the group is important. The smallest group is a dyad, or two-person group. This is an important group, for here much intimate interaction and social influence may occur. Of course we are also interested in larger small groups, those with five, fifteen, twenty-five, or even as many as fifty members. It's hard to define an exact upper limit on the small group's size, but the idea is to distinguish a small group from a crowd of hundreds, thousands, or even millions of people who might engage in collective behaviors other than personal face-to-face interaction.

Once formed, two primary characteristics of the small group are its levels of cooperative interaction and cohesiveness. To exist, the group must generate cooperation and control conflict among its members. As group activity becomes a cooperative venture, individual members become more cohesively related to one another. This cohesiveness is maintained through coopera-

Group uniforms are often worn by individuals in membership peer groups.
(Burt Ginn/Magnum Photos, Inc.)

tive behavior and from reinforcements or rewards group members receive from cooperating. A highly cooperative and cohesive group may also encourage members to conform to group norms in order to maintain their membership. On the other hand, conflict and disagreement make the group less desirable, and lead to lower cohesiveness or disintegration of the group.

Social communication is an important transaction in groups. It includes both verbal conversations between people and visual observations of the appearances presented in social interaction. These communications result in the dissemination of information and the formation and maintenance of group norms for behavior. Subjects of communications may range from informal small talk to topics crucial to the group's existence and objectives.

The group exercises social control over its members by setting standards of behavior to which the individual is expected to conform. Norms are established by the group and members are expected to behave in accordance with norms. In some groups norms may be rigidly defined and enforced, in others flexible or vaguely defined. The conforming member is rewarded with group approval and support, while deviants from norms are punished by being ignored or ostracized. Though the group's forces toward social control and conformity are substantial, there also is evidence that individuals seek personal uniqueness, or differences from as well as conformist similarities to others (Snyder and Fromkin 1980).

Many specialized social roles are performed by different group members. Of special interest are those related to leadership of the group. In general, group leaders are held in high regard, based on criteria such as their education, wealth, skills, and experience. Different leaders may emerge for different situations, and different leadership styles—authoritarian versus democratic, informal versus formally designated—can arise for each situation. Leaders also tend to be people whose actual behavior reflects the basic norms, values, and goals of the group. Thus the leader might be the perfect or model group member, and other members will often judge the adequacy of their own behavior by that of the leader.

Of special importance to leadership in small groups is the concept of **social power.** Certain people have a social power, or ability to stimulate and even control the behavior of others through communications (Miller and Butler 1969). This power sometimes operates through the **risky shift phenomenon,** which occurs when communication within a group, perhaps initiated by a leader, influences a change in group behavior to a more risky position than previously existed.[2] For example, the leader might initiate discussion of a controversial subject. The discussion could result in a change in group attitudes and behavior toward the subject, and a change of group norms. Obviously such a risky shift could be to a more conservative as well as a more liberal position.

The individual may belong to many social groups with different norms, and allegiances to these groups can vary from strong to weak. The driving force of the individual is acceptance by one or more important groups, and fashionable dress plays an obvious role in visually showing one's acceptability. The result is that many reference groups are influential in directing the individual's selected patterns of behavior. Human behavior does not occur in a vacuum, but rather it is directed by a wide range of social contacts and reference groups making up the social environment of the individual.

Consumer Socialization through Groups

One of the primary functions of small groups is socialization of its members. **Socialization** is a process through which an individual learns the knowledge and skills necessary to become a functioning member of his or her social and cultural environment through the teachings of others. Attitudes, values, and motives to conform to societal expectations are learned in the socialization process, which occurs in the context of interaction with other people (Mack and Young 1968; Moschis 1987).[3]

Small groups develop norms of fashionable behavior, 1955.
(UPI/Bettman Newsphotos)

Consumer socialization is a form of socialization through which an individual learns to function as a purchaser and user of products and services offered in the marketplace. This socialization begins in childhood and continues as a lifelong process of acquiring knowledge and skills needed as a consumer. Ward (1974) has stated some generalizations regarding this process.

1. Consumer socialization would be expected to begin within the child's family, since families are the major socializing agent in the child's early life. Studies suggest that this learning is subtle, rather than a result of purposeful parental training. For instance, the child may learn consumer behavior through observation and imitation rather than through specific teachings of parents.
2. As a child enters adolescence, the family becomes less important in consumer socialization, and peers become more important.
3. Early in life the child learns that products have "social meaning." That is, the individual uses products to help achieve social goals. The age at which products take on such a social function is not clearly defined, but it can occur very early in the child's development.

4. Early learning in childhood may influence consumer behavior later in life. For instance, studies suggest that such forms of consumer behavior as brand or store preferences may carry over from childhood to later life. Of course, as new social situations are encountered in later life, new learning rather than reliance on past experience might be required.

Consumer socialization in behavior related to clothing begins when the child learns how to put on and take off clothes. This complex process, a function of parental training, takes years. The child reaches substantial independence in dressing about age five; girls learn earlier than boys because physical coordination among girls develops faster. Complete independence in dress comes later, between six and nine.

Early in life a child is also being socialized about styles and functional purposes of dress, as the parents choose styles for different events in the child's life. What socializing influences do these style selections have on the child's preferences in later life? Does the well-dressed child become socialized in taste at an early age? Research has not answered these questions, but it is clear that parents can influence the child's development of aesthetic skills in dressing. The parents' attitudes, values, and behavior related to dress may also be observed and learned by the child, establishing a set of cognitive orientations toward dress that can carry forward to later stages of development. In this regard, it is notable that socialization into dress and fashion, once a phenomenon of teenage years, is happening now at earlier and earlier ages (culminating during the materialistic 1980s in many designer or brand-name lines and fashions, even designer diapers, aimed at young children).

The socializing influence of people from outside the family begins to take place at an early age. Around age three or four, the child begins to broaden social contacts with neighborhood children and school groups. As the child interacts with these new contacts, he or she probably learns that one way to gain attention is through clothes. Initially, this may occur through very direct methods such as the use of bright colors or new clothes. However, at this age the child may not recognize the role of clothing in establishing group membership and norms of social appropriateness.

However, appreciation and manipulation of these subtle aspects of dress may arise rather quickly. In the elementary school years, the child has increased social contact with playmates and peers at school, and socialization about styles and symbolic meanings of dress begins. The child may begin to conform to the dress of others because of fear of ridicule and teasing from other children. In these years the child also begins to be more independent in choosing clothing. The parents still do the buying, but around age nine to eleven the child often becomes a consultant on purchases, ultimately making the first independent purchase decision.

Knowledge the child acquires in the elementary school years carries over to the critical years of adolescence, when fashion-oriented behavior becomes central in peer interactions. Research has indicated that interest in clothing rises sharply from age twelve to about age eighteen, and declines thereafter (Ryan 1966). During these years young people experiment with many fads and fashions on what adults may consider a trial-and-error basis. As a result, the individual has extensive socializing experience with dress, which helps build social skills and self-confidence as the individual approaches adulthood.

As the person becomes an adult, social forces from the large society begin to expand the alternative ways of life the person can learn. In the adult years, social learning of norms for dress comes from combined influences of primary groups, secondary groups, and the collective behavior of mass society. Earlier experiences and learning can set the pattern for coping with adulthood. However, the adult is also confronted with new social experiences and groups that require learning of new forms of social behavior and complementary styles of dress.

The study of the effect of socialization agents on fashion adoption has received limited attention by consumer analysts. There is evidence, however, that parents play an important role in consumer socialization

Fashion conformity reinforces an individual's own fashion adoption.
(*NYT* Pictures)

with regards to dress. According to the consumer socialization perspective, children learn consumer skills from parents through observation and imitation (Atkin 1978; Ward and Wackman 1971). Researchers have shown greater parent-adolescent interaction in the purchasing of clothing than for other consumer goods. In their investigation of purchasing role structures for products consumed by adolescents, Moschis, Moore and Stephens (1977) found that adolescents tended to shop jointly with adult family members when purchasing clothing. In addition, May and Koester (1985) found that adolescents shopped more with their mothers than with anyone else when purchasing clothing. A study by Francis and Burns (1992) demonstrated that mothers may be long-term socialization agents for learning certain clothing purchase attitudes and behaviors. A sample of 70 mother/daughter pairs were surveyed about their attitudes toward clothing, clothing shopping and shopping behavior. Results indicated that daughters had attitudes and practices similar to their mothers' with regard to constructing their own clothing, acquiring their clothing at used clothing stores, garage/rummage sales, and department stores.

Fashion Adoption, Reference Groups, and Conformity

Now we turn to the influence of reference groups in conformity (similarity) in fashion adoption. First, a discussion of reference group and conformity theory will provide a foundation for the application of this work to fashion adoption. Next, research that has addressed factors underlying conformity in fashion adoption will be discussed.

Reference Group and Conformity Theory Conformity is change in an individual's behavior or attitude in the direction advocated by a group as a result of real or imagined group pressure (Kiesler and Kiesler 1970). Conformity research is primarily based on an empirical paradigm developed by Asch (1951). In the Asch procedure, subjects are asked to make simple unambiguous perceptual judgments in the presence of a group of confederates of the experimenter. Typically, the confederates unanimously give an obviously incorrect answer, and the researcher measures the change in the subject's judgment toward that advocated by the group. Using this procedure, Asch found that an average of 35 percent of the overall responses conformed to the incorrect judgments.

An important factor in the study of conformity is an understanding of the influence of the comparison group. These comparison groups are often referred to as reference groups. As suggested by Kelley (1952), reference groups can assume two functions:

1. **a normative** function by reinforcing an individual's conformity to group norms, and
2. **a comparison** function by serving as a standard of comparison by which the person can evaluate him/herself and others.

Appropriate reference groups provide information that allows individuals a means of developing and assessing their opinions, and also reinforces the individual for adherence to the modal opinion. Reference groups provide informational and normative social influences, two of the processes that are thought to underlie conformity. Informational social influence produces conformity when people evaluate and modify their opinions by making comparisons with the opinions of others (Deutsch and Gerard 1955; Festinger 1954). Normative social influence by a group produces conformity when the reference group is attractive to the individual and the individual desires acceptance by the group (Deutsch and Gerard 1955; Dittes and Kelley 1956; Festinger 1954). In a group situation, informational and normative social influence processes commonly operate together (Patel and Gordon 1960; Sistrunk 1973).

Reference Groups and Conformity in Fashion Adoption

Conformity in fashion adoption occurs within social groups when members adhere to distinct socially defined fashion norms. These fashion norms outline the range of styles that are socially acceptable to the particular group. Because an individual's conformity to the fashion norms of a group readily identifies the individual as a group member, fashions serve to visually distinguish group members from nonmembers. In other words, group unity may be achieved and displayed by means of members conforming in fashion patterns.

The processes involved in fashion conformity appear similar to the processes involved in the more basic study of conformity. Informational and normative social influence processes may play a role in conformity in fashion adoption and clothing behavior. **Informational social influence** is based on an individual's desire to gain socially correct information about social reality and to validate opinions by evaluation in terms of the opinion of others. Because fashion norms are also socially defined through group interaction, individuals often turn to others for correct information about fashion norms. For example, an individual who is unsure as to the appropriate clothing to wear for a social event may ask friends what they are wearing, or an individual may read a fashion magazine to acquire information as to the fashion industry's advice on current fashion trends.

In the study of fashion adoption, informational social influence results in awareness of the fashion norms for distinct social groups. Hendricks, Kelly, and Eicher (1968) and Kelly and Eicher (1970) found high agreement among adolescents in the identification of peers who were "best dressed" and peers who were "not dressed right," indicating high awareness of clothing fashion norms. Smucker and Creekmore (1972) further demonstrated that among high school sophomores, awareness of clothing norms was positively related to clothing conformity. To measure the subjects' awareness of clothing fashion modes, the subjects identified those fashion items "most everyone was wearing." The actual mode of the sample was determined by filming each subject and taking a fashion count of specific clothing items. A subject's awareness score consisted of a measure of the items of clothing correctly identified as what "most everyone was wearing." Conformity scores were calculated on the basis of clothing actually worn rather than that identified. Awareness of the clothing fashion mode was found to be significantly related to clothing conformity. These results suggest that fashion adoption is somewhat determined by information gained from others. Thus informational social influence appears to an effective process underlying conformity in fashion adoption.

Normative social influence is based on an individual's desire to be similar to and thus accepted into a group. Normative social influence may result in conformity to a group's norms as a means of seeking acceptance into the group. The operation of normative social influence is evidenced by the fact that the degree of conformity existing within a group has been found to be related to the unity or cohesion within the group (Hendricks, et al. 1968). Smucker and Creekmore (1972) found that conformity to a fashion was related to peer acceptance for adolescents. Subjects rated their classmates on a 3-point scale as to the degree to which they accepted that person as a friend. An individual's "peer acceptance" score was the sum total of his/her ratings. Conformity scores were determined by the degree to which an individual wore clothing in accord with the fashion for the group. Results indicated conformity to the fashion to be positively related to peer acceptance.

Four studies using similar methodologies (Hendricks, Kelly, and Eicher 1968; Kelly and Eicher 1970; Littrell and Eicher 1973; Williams and Eicher 1966) investigated the importance of clothing and appearance in the social acceptance of adolescents. In each of the studies, questionnaires and interviews were used to assign female subjects to one of the three categories of social acceptance: isolates, mutual pair memberships, and reciprocal friendship structures (RFS). The subjects were also asked their opinions concerning dress and appearance. Results indicated that social acceptance was, indeed, related to clothing conformity. Members of RFS held similar opinions regarding clothing, appearance, and group acceptance, which differed from the opinions held by non-group members. Hendricks, et al. (1968) further found that the extent to which members of RFS had similar opinions regarding clothing and appearance was positively related to the cohesion of the group. Littrell and Eicher (1973) extended the research by examining the relationship between opinions about clothing and movement from social isolation to social acceptance. Social acceptance and clothing opinions were measured when the subjects were grade nine, and again three years later. Results indicated that opinions about clothing appearance seemed important in the process of movement from social isolation. Social acceptance of isolates was found to be related to their conformity to the general opinion of the group in which they became a member. The results suggest that individuals conform to clothing norms as a means of seeking acceptance into a peer group. Therefore, in addition to informational social influence, normative social influence also appears to be an effective process in conformity in fashion adoption.

The relative influence of various reference groups on conformity in judgments of clothing fashionability was investigated by Davis and Miller (1983). Using established procedures for the study of conformity in opinion judgments, subjects made a reassessment of their original opinions of the fashionability of six women's suits after being exposed to opinions attributed to one of four reference groups: peers, career women, fashion experts, and housewives. Conformity was defined as the change between the subjects' initial judgments and the judgments they subsequently made after being exposed to the group influence manipulation. Results indicated that conformity in judgments of fashionability was affected by the perceived credibility of the reference group providing the social influence. Greater conformity to the opinion of others resulted when the opinion was attributed to fashion experts than when the opinion was attributed to housewives, college females, or career women. It seems that fashion experts, by virtue of their self-evident expertise, were perceived as the most credible reference group for judgments of the fashionability of garments.

These studies also imply that groups can apply social pressure to induce group members to conform in dress. Research by Venkatesan (1966) shows how effective this pressure can be. Using the traditional Asch procedure mentioned earlier, male college students were asked to evaluate and choose the "best suit" from three competing choices. The students were told that there were differences between the suits, but in fact the three suits were identical. Three experimental conditions were designed to apply different levels of social pressure on the student's choices. Under the first condition, students were asked to make independent choices of the best suit. In this situation of no social pressure to conform, it was found that each suit was equally likely to be selected as best. Under the second condition, students were formed into four-person groups, with three of the four students secretly instructed to indicate a strong preference for the same single suit. In this situation, strong social pressure to conform was placed on the fourth student, with the result that a majority of the fourth students conformed to the choice made by the other three. In the third experimental condition, students were also formed into four-person groups, but in this case three of the four members chose the same suit without indicating a strong preference for the choice. With this relaxed social pressure, the fourth group member was not nearly as likely to conform to the norm established by the other three members.

This study indicates the power social pressure can have in influencing, if not forcing, an individual to conform to a group norm. That pressure appears to be greatest when individuals are in face-to-face contact with peers and where the preferences of the majority are well-defined. However, Venkatesan's findings also suggest that when norms exist but are relaxed, social pressure may be modest. Also, peer group influence may be most effective in choices where it is difficult to evaluate and choose the best alternative objectively.

Fashion Adoption and Group Identification

One frequent observation is that conformity in dress becomes a symbol of group membership. That is, individuals identify with their reference groups by wearing the styles of dress socially accepted or prescribed by the group. Acceptance of the group's style of dress then becomes a mechanism of social control that identifies a conforming member and readily differentiates the deviant. Subsequently, social groups are often identified with fashion norms. For example, recently fashions have been associated with gang membership to the extent that some high schools have prohibited students from wearing the associated fashions.

An investigation by Clum and Eicher (1972) illustrates the use of dress in the identification of reference groups. Their investigation sought to determine whether adolescents conform to the dress of their school classes as a whole, or to their own specific friendship groups. When conformity in dress was related to friendship-group memberships, they found that

Conformity in fashion often becomes a symbol of group membership as with these skinheads, 1986.

(Reuters/Bettman)

individuals dressed more like members of their friendship groups than the class as a whole. Thus the reference group sets the basic standard for identification, and this standard acts to differentiate one group from another even though there is an overall norm for the social system. They also found boys to conform more to their reference groups than girls, perhaps because boys have a narrower range of styles to choose from than girls. It is also possible that the peer group exercises more influence on boys than on girls, or that boys have a greater orientation toward group conformity than do girls.

Eicher and Kelley (1974) reported the most extensive investigation to date supporting the relation between group membership and dress. The investigation involved a four-year study of relationships between friendship groups of high school girls and patterns of dress in different groups. The researchers identified groups by charting the network of social interaction among different individuals of the class. From these charts four main social groups and a number of subgroups were identified. Findings included:

1. the formation of the main groups was closely tied to social class and family background of the group members. Socially elite girls tended to cluster together, as did those of a more middle- or lower-class background, and little social interaction occurred across group lines.

2. the main groups differed not only in social class and family background, but also in their school club memberships, grades, popularity, and styles of dress. Dress was found to be one of several variables affecting the acceptance or rejection of a girl in social groups, while in others the standard focused more on neatness and cleanliness. Some individuals, particularly lower class girls, were excluded from group membership for being "not dressed right." The researchers also noted that overdressing can be as significant as underdressing in influencing social acceptance in groups.

3. A final conclusion was that each group may have norms prescribing a range of acceptable dress permitting some expression of individuality, but conformity to the overall group norms was evident.

Leadership in Small Groups

These studies show that fashions are substantially controlled by groups in which individuals are members. But what about leadership of fashion changes within small groups? Some approaches to fashion leadership suggest that leaders are widespread at all levels and social groups of the population (Katz and Lazarsfeld 1955; King 1963). However, not every group necessarily has members who are clearly leaders. In an investigation of fad rather than fashion leadership among college women, Janney (1941) found that individuals in a few prestigious cliques were the major initiators of faddish behavior. A few other cliques regularly experimented with fads that were not followed by others, but most individuals were conformists rather than initiators of fads. The investigations of Eicher and Kelley (1974) also imply that leadership may exist only in some social groups. In their investigations, individuals who were rated best dressed and most popular were members of different groups, but the most best-dressed members were found in higher status groups.

Those social groups that do not generate their own leaders imitate other reference groups. Such "leaderless" groups have their own internal standards of dress, which can differ to some degree from the standards prevailing in other groups. Also, a modest form of leadership in these groups can "bridge the gap" of fashion diffusion from one group to another. Indeed, all social groups probably need an "action leader" (Storm 1987, 299) to stimulate adoption, even if such action leaders do not qualify as true innovators or opinion leaders. And although some groups might not exercise a pure form of leadership or have true leaders, research has indicated the group's awareness of clothing norms in their social system can be high (Smucker and Creekmore 1972), and this awareness can stimulate the opportunity for style diffusion from other leadership groups to those groups where fashion leadership is limited.

Is the fashion leader also a leader in other social activities or functions of the group? A firm answer to this question has not been offered, but one can hypothesize that a general leader would also occupy the specific position of fashion leader. For example, a student body president or a corporate executive might be awarded a position of leadership in social tastes by virtue of a more formally recognized position. A few studies suggest this possibility. For example, Janney's (1941) study indicates that fad leaders were also leaders in other activities. Similarly, the Eicher and Kelley (1974) study indicates some important links between general leadership, popularity, and being well-dressed. These studies show that general leadership can often be associated with fashion leadership, but the exact nature of the association is not clear. One can say that fashion leadership is a specialized skill, and the role of the fashion leader may belong to the person who is most knowledgeable or who has the most demonstrated ability (taste) in this area. This skill does not necessarily coincide with the skills and abilities required for other forms of leadership.

There are also instances where individuals may become fashion leaders within their social environment even though they may not be members of any particular friendship group. For instance, Eicher and Kelley (1974) identified several twelfth-grade girls, one a social isolate and two who were close friends only with each other, who received an extremely large number of mentions as "best dressed" in the class. These girls were not clearly integrated into any small groups, and yet they could be reference points in establishing standards of dress. Thus individuals as well as reference groups may begin fashion diffusion in small groups.

The role of fashion leader contains substantial social rewards and risks. The leader's reward may be prestige but the risk is that selection of an innovative style may be perceived and reacted to as deviance from group norms. For instance, Cobliner (1950) points out that the person who wears a new style before the rest of the group is likely to be admired and envied. However, when the leader's role is informally perceived to belong to someone else, the innovative person might be viewed as "showing off." For the majority of group members, conformity is the expected and rewarded behavior. Only a few may safely exercise individualism and still win social approval of the group.

In summary, the formation of group norms for dress and the process of fashion leadership is very informal. Groups may engage in casual discussion and observation of each other's dress, and this can exert a subtle pressure toward conformity. The opinions, expertise, or good taste of certain group participants become dominant influences over the group's norms of dress. Certain prestigious leaders in the group may make innovative choices and encourage risk-taking toward the new fashion. Outside reference groups or individuals may also occasionally become models for the group's norms. Standards of dress in the group will change with time, but the group will continue to maintain social control over these overt symbols of its identity.

Fashion Diffusion in Organizational Groups

Our discussion of group identification through individuals' conformity to fashion norms brings us to a special case of fashion norms: the acceptance and diffusion of uniforms and occupational dress. Millions of Americans wear some type of occupational uniform, whether they be an airline pilot, nurse, bank teller, police officer, mechanic, or any other of the occupations that have uniform fashion norms associated with them. Millions of others may wear uniforms of membership groups. Team and club uniforms are examples. Although not all uniforms reflect fashion change, often we find fashion diffusion within various organization settings is reflected in the dress codes and standards set for the members or employees and the socialization processes that occur within the organization.

Uniform fashion norms within an organization vary to the degree of variation in dress that is allowed for the employees or members. Nathan Joseph (1986) developed a typology of uniforms and occupational dress in terms of the types of normative standards set. The **uniform** is the "legitimating emblem of membership within an organization" (Joseph 1986, 2). It serves as a visible group symbol worn by members. In doing so, it often emphasizes the role of the group membership and suppresses individuality within a group. Uniforms provide an efficient means for the identification of members and nonmembers, and are used for this purpose. Often, admission into the group or organization is symbolically indicated by allowing the individual to wear the uniform. Although group members control any change and variation in the uniform, tradition plays a strong role in maintaining the norms. Uniforms, especially those that are military-oriented, often shun the pressures of external fashion norms and remain consistent in styling over time.

Quasi-uniforms, on the other hand, often reflect current fashion norms. This type of uniform is typically found in bureaucratic organizations such as hospitals, airlines, service industries, and manufacturing industries. They are also found in membership groups that change membership on a regular basis, which creates greater opportunities for the membership to change or vary the uniform.

Standardized dress involves normative "pattern of dress arising among members of an occupation, or family of occupations, partly because they share similar social and physical conditions" (Joseph 1986, 144). The standardized dress norms evolved primarily because of the utility and function of the clothing. Fire fighters', mechanics', and cowboys' "uniforms" are examples of this type of normative behavior.

The use of **career apparel** and **dress codes** within an organization are means by which the group can set limits to the acceptable style norms, and continue to allow the expression of individuality in dress by group members or employees. Companies may provide employees with a range of acceptable "career apparel" that they can mix and match individually. Dress codes are common among many types of companies and organizations. They may be implicit or actually written limits of acceptable dress behavior.

Uniform fashion norms within a group or organization serve a number of functions for both the group member and the organization (Joseph and Alex 1972; Solomon 1987). First, because of their visibility, uniforms (including formal, quasi-standardized dress, career apparel, and dress codes) can be used to communicate a group or organizational image to others. This may enhance the perception of organizational characteristics that are deemed important by the organization. For example, organizations usually wish to appear contemporary and up-to-date, or at least not outdated. The uniform also implies a coherent group structure and may affect membership morale and feelings of belonging to a unified whole. For members of bureaucratic or hierarchal organizations, uniforms often minimize role (or rank) confusion and serve to equalize the membership in a particular role or rank.

Fashion diffusion within organizations has been investigated from a number of perspectives. The classic research of Form and Stone (1955) on the role of clothing in occupational life has pointed to several aspects of group identification through dress. They found that individuals relate their clothing selections to that of their face-to-face associates at work. However, there were substantial differences in these reference group orientations between office personnel (white collar workers) and manual laborers (blue collar workers). Dress among office personnel was oriented toward rather broadly defined reference groups, including the general public, the community, and their customers. Their dress was essentially aimed toward conforming to and securing the approval of these groups with which they dealt regularly. Manual workers emphasized obtaining approval from peers and coworkers with whom they had continuous, face-to-face contact.

Form and Stone also found that office workers were much more likely than manual workers to believe that their occupational dress was noticed by other people. White collar workers, the business class, feel the need to dress primarily to identify with and satisfy strangers with whom business must be transacted. In this environment of business dealings, relationships are relatively impersonal, but there still remains a set of social norms governing social interactions. On the other hand, members of the working class place less emphasis on clothing as a part of the total social interaction. Conformity in dress among peer laborers is maintained, but the strict use of clothing as a criterion of approval is less important in such direct and personal associations.

The contemporary saga of the "dress for success" movement in the 1970s and 1980s powerfully demonstrates these standardizing effects of occupational fashion as well. Perhaps one of the most widely researched phenomena of modern fashion (Forsythe, Drake and Cox 1984; Sherbaum and Shepherd 1987; Solomon and Douglas 1987), the wearing of appropriately defined business attire of quality and conservative fashion became a serious, sober uniform for upwardly mobile men and women. Initially this professional look conveyed status, rank and perhaps power to its wearer, but such symbolic values have life-cycles of their own that can decline as time passes. The style does persist in the 1990s within many professional settings, but has been moderated at least by women who are now achieving greater status in the workplace and perhaps concomitantly greater freedom to choose more variety in styling. But the power of proper and fashionably correct dress remains in this group setting, even as latitude of choice widens.

SUMMARY

This chapter has described the social context of the fashion process and the process of fashion acceptance among small social groups. The discussion of the subjects has revolved around the basic sociological principle that social interactions among people provide the primary mechanism through which the fashion process takes place.

The fashion process in our society takes place in a fluid social environment, one filled with continual social changes, social mobility, and abundance of resources and life-styles. In such a social environment, there is continually an open invitation to a lot of consumer experimentation with new tastes, and many competitive centers of fashion leadership may emerge. Although informational and normative social influences creates conformity in fashion adoption within small groups, a look at fashion acceptance in small groups reveals a great deal of diversity. Small groups of people who interact with one another on a regular face-to-face basis directly influence the individual's adoption of fashions. The norms and social pressures developed in groups can become more important to the individual in defining standards of dress than are the more broadly defined and collective forces of mass society.

NOTES

1. For introduction to the processes of social interaction and group dynamics, see Lambert and Lambert (1964), Sherif and Sherif (1964), Phillips and Erickson (1970), Ostlund (1973), Snyder and Fromkin (1980), Lauer and Lauer (1981), Storm (1987), or a basic social psychology text. Much of the following general discussion is derived from these references.
2. See Woodside (1974) and Reingen (1974) for perspectives of risk-taking and the risky shift phenomenon in consumer behavior.
3. See Janney (1941), Stone (1962), Ryan (1966), Smucker and Creekmore (1972), and Moschis (1987) for further perspectives on consumer socialization related to dress. Much of the following is influenced by these sources.

DISCUSSION QUESTIONS

1. Name several social groups evident on campus whose members can be identified by their patterns of dress. Who are the groups and what fashion norms are unique to these groups? Do all group members conform to the fashion norms of the group? Are fashion leaders within the group readily evident?
2. Are there individuals or media sources you turn to for information about fashion? If so, who/what are they? Why are they useful sources of information? To what extent do you conform to the information received from these sources?

3. Think of a situation in which you wore a type of group uniform. What do you think the purpose of the uniform was? How similar in appearance were the uniforms? Was any deviation from the uniform allowed? Were others able to identify you as a group member by the uniform? What were the advantages and disadvantages of wearing the uniform?

4. Think of a time when you felt out of place in a situation because you were not dressed similar to others in the group. What was the situation? Why do you think you felt awkward? Did you receive comments or feedback from others in the group?

SUGGESTED READINGS

Davis, Leslie L. and Franklin G. Miller. "Conformity and Judgments of Fashionability." *Home Economics Research Journal* 11 (1983): 337-42.

Francis, Sally, and Leslie Davis Burns. "Effect of Consumer Socialization on Clothing Shopping Attitudes, Clothing Acquisition, and Clothing Satisfaction." *Clothing and Textiles Research Journal* 10 (Summer 1992): 35-39.

Joseph, Nathan. *Uniforms and Nonuniforms: Communication Through Clothing.* New York: Greenwood Press, 1986.

Littrell, Mary Bishop, and Joanne B. Eicher. "Clothing Opinions and the Social Acceptance Process Among Adolescents." *Adolescence* 8 (1973): 197-212.

Smucker, Betty, and Anna M. Creekmore. "Adolescents' Clothing Conformity, Awareness, and Peer Acceptance." *Home Economics Research Journal* 1 (1972): 92-97.

7

The Mass Diffusion and Termination of Fashion Trends

OBJECTIVES

◆ To discuss fashion diffusion among large groups of people.
◆ To describe collective behavior in fashion adoption.
◆ To examine social processes that contribute to the termination of fashion trends.

In the last chapter, we focused on conformity and fashion diffusion within small groups of people. In addition to conformity in fashion adoption within these small groups, certain fashion trends become widely visible and dominant in society. Thus, in this chapter we will focus on fashion diffusion among large groups of people. Some theorists explain this mass fashion diffusion as a process of collective behavior among large numbers of people. From this perspective, fashion diffusion is likened to the behavior of people in crowds, mass meetings, or even mobs or riots. Such large groups engage in collective behavior when they cooperatively pursue a single activity or interest for a short period of time. Although collective behavior can occur spontaneously—sometimes even irrationally—recent theorists contend that collective behavior is based upon emergent norms (Turner and Killian 1987). In their book *Collective Behavior*, Ralph Turner and Lewis Killian (1987) note several such norm-associated features of collective behavior.

1. Initially there is a temperament among individuals within a group to "transcend, bypass or subvert established institutional patterns and structures." (p. 7)
2. They subsequently translate these perceptions, feelings and ideas into action that is feasible and timely.
3. Then through internal and external pressures to conform to the other members of the group, the action takes place collectively rather than singly, and is justified and coordinated through emergent group norms.

Similar to the norm development in small groups as discussed in chapter 6, we will find that emergent group norms also form the basis for mass fashion diffusion.

COLLECTIVE BEHAVIOR IN FASHION ADOPTION

Sociologists Lang and Lang have described the fashion process as "an elementary form of collective behavior, whose compelling power lies in the implicit judgment of an anonymous multitude" (Lang and Lang 1961, 323). Central to this proposition is the notion of anonymity in our society. In a complex and heterogeneous mass society, social contacts between individuals are typically limited and impersonal. Most people have direct associations with small groups, but the vast majority of the society is to the individual an anonymous multitude. Nevertheless, individuals frequently react to and adjust their behavior to this anonymous society surrounding them. This reaction is evident in mass fashion adoption when people perceive and judge the appropriateness of their behavior by what they see in the larger society. Individuals may perceive societal fashion norms on television, in magazines, in movies, and on the streets of cities, and subsequently evaluate their own fashion adoption in light of these perceptions. Under such circumstances, the style of fashion selected becomes a reflection of a collectively endorsed standard that the individual perceives. This theory implies that the fashion process involves a continuous mechanism of collective conformity to a newly emerging societal norm.

Herbert Blumer, one of the early theorists on collective behavior, has offered a similar but expanded view of the fashion process. He proposes that fashion should be analyzed as a process of collective selection of a few fashions from numerous competing alternatives. Innovative consumers may experiment with many possible alternatives, but the ultimate test in the fashion process is the competition between alternative styles for positions of fashionability. Exactly how this collective selection happens is not well defined, but Blumer points to three factors shaping this process:

Fashion adoption is a form of collective behavior.
(© Robert Fox/Impact Visuals)

1. the **historical continuity of fashion change,** in which new fashions evolve from those previously established by the society;
2. the **influence of modernity,** through which fashions constantly respond to and keep pace with change in the larger mass society; and
3. the **gradual formation and refinement of collective tastes,** which occur through social interaction among people with similar interests and social experience, with the result that many people develop tastes in common (Blumer 1969).[1]

The appropriateness of these perspectives is reinforced by the continued popularity of fashion magazines, the coverage of fashion trends by major newspapers, and research that shows a substantial portion of consumers, well over 50 percent, watch what others are wearing and keep informed on trends (Horridge and Richards 1986; Sproles 1977). This widespread social monitoring of fashion may be the most pervasive of the massed, collective forces of the fashion process.

A principle derived from these theoretical ideas is that increasing social visibility of a new style is the key to collective behavior in fashion. At any given time many styles compete for attention and gain some limited visibility when adopted and worn by a few members of society. However, some styles become more socially noticeable than others due to the styles being seen worn by early adopters, being promoted in the media, or hanging on the racks in fashion-forward stores. The increased visibility for a particular style further stimulates consumers' awareness of the style and motivation to accept it, propagating the style to even higher levels of mass acceptance.

But all styles receiving this high social visibility do not become collective fashions. Indeed, theorists argue that only those styles most consistent with the current sociocultural environment win in the test of collective selection. For example, despite widespread social visibility, the midi-skirt failed to obtain mass adoption by women in the early 1970s primarily due to the style's inconsistency with the social values of the times. Similarly, although socially visible male rock stars wore colorful eye makeup in the early 1980s, this trend was not adopted by the masses of men.

Research on Collective Fashions

Although research is limited on the processes of mass fashion diffusion, several studies have offered inferential evidence of collective behavior in the fashion process. One study involved investigation of norms for dress among high-school boys and girls in nine states (Western Regional Research Cooperative Project W-98, 1972). The states were Colorado, Hawaii, Michigan, Minnesota, North Dakota, Nevada, Utah, Washington, and Wisconsin. Norms of dress were identified among students in a selected high school in each state. An observational technique was devised to identify modal (normative) styles worn by students. When the modal styles were compared across states, considerable similarities in norms of dress across the geographic areas were found. For boys, similarities existed in such areas as trouser length, shoe styles, and trouser types. Among girls, similarities were found in such areas as hosiery styles, dress silhouettes, and skirt length. The greatest differences were connected with climate (lots of bare leg styles in Hawaii), or cultural differences (as in a small, conservative Utah community used in the research).

A study by Smucker and Creekmore (1972), conducted in a single high school and using methods like those of the preceding study, offers similar evidence. They identified modal patterns or dress among tenth-grade boys and girls, and they found that individual awareness of and conformity to norms were significantly linked with social acceptance by peers. These findings suggest how a collective norm of dress can facilitate social interaction within large groups.

Research by Clum and Eicher (1972) also supports the existence of a collective norm of dress, but their investigation stresses the importance of

specific norms among small groups. The researchers identified modal patterns of dress among a class of high school sophomores in the 1960s, using films of the dress worn by each class member. Among boys the modal dress was a conservative haircut, blue button-down sport shirt, and tight black ankle-length trousers. For the girls the mode was a brown A-line skirt, one or two inches above the knee, worn with plain nylon hosiery and loafers. After identifying these basic norms, the researchers compared the degree to which individuals conformed to this broadly defined norm or to a more specific social norm of their particular friendship groups. Findings indicated that individuals tend to conform more to the standards of their personal social group rather than to the more broadly defined norm.

None of these investigations was designed to test the theory of collective behavior in fashion, and one cannot infer how the collective norms within each school were formed. Of course high schools are relatively self-contained social environments where widespread social contacts take place on a daily basis among a very fashion-oriented segment of the population. There could be no more fertile ground for collective fashion diffusion among members of the large groups as well as among members of small groups within the larger entity. Similarly our business and professional environments, country clubs, local communities, or other formal and informal social organizations offer arenas for collective fashion norm development. Thus we must conclude that these studies have contributed a base of inferential evidence suggesting that broad norms, resulting from collective behavior, do exist among large groups of people.

Social Forces Favoring Collective Behavior

What are the conditions that cause society to behave collectively, to react in mass to fashion change? Mass fashion marketing and mass communication of information on new styles tend to homogenize consumer tastes, because the styles manufactured and promoted often resemble one another, even when many different manufacturers and retailers are involved in the fashion business. The fashion industry is notorious for "knock-off" copying—manufacturers frequently copy each other's styles—thereby inducing "sameness" in many styles offered. The media and fashion advertising or editorials in particular also confer social status and prestige on new fashions, building their social desirability and encouraging consumers to accept them. Other social forces, such as the forces of urbanism, the social-class system, physical mobility, and increasingly active life-styles, can also create social visibility for a style and thus propagate collective behavior.

Urbanism and the concentration of populations in general also favor collective fashions. During the past century, cities with large populations have grown substantially, and in the past half century this growth has extended to suburbs. Social interactions in this concentrated environment are regular and diffuse, ranging from those daily contacts with friends and coworkers to casual contacts with strangers. Consumers receive repeated exposure to styles of dress, and the social visibility of certain styles is particularly high. These styles can spread through the urban environment and

Classics are adapted to fit in with current fashion detailing.
(*WWD*, Fairchild Publications)

become collective norms of dress. Of course urban environments are socially diverse in values and life-styles, favoring formation of different norms of dress within subsegments of the population. Rarely if ever would one find a single collective norm in an urban area.

The current class structure in the United States also favors collective behavior toward fashions. Though our social structure is not rigid, a majority of the population falls into the broad middle of the status hierarchy. This majority might therefore be expected to have similar orientations toward fashions, and to behave collectively in accepting new fashions.

Physical mobility also stimulates collective behavior toward fashions. Physical mobility takes many forms, such as occupational moves from one location to another, business travel, vacations, and local mobility—local travel by car or mass transit. Mobile people are exposed to accepted styles in areas they visit, encouraging their recognition of new ideals for dress. The collective diffusion of fashions will be influenced as mobile people communicate these ideals from one community to another.

Mass fashion trends are typically associated with dominant life-styles within any society. For example, one key characteristic of the American lifestyle—our informality in living—influences fashion trends within the

United States. Our life-styles differ in personal interests, roles, activities, and levels of social participation. But the underlying theme of casual and informal living is pervasive. Many people have adopted this norm of behavior, and the norm is reflected in our collective tastes for casual fashions.

Concluding Comments

Theories of collective behavior suggest that there must be a great deal of cooperative interaction among participants if a collective movement is to occur. In the behavior of mobs or crowds, this can be the case since large numbers of people will be brought together face-to-face and with common interests or goals in mind. Collective behavior can then occur spontaneously, assuming the group receives some form of leadership or other inspiration to act.

However, collective behavior toward fashions may be far more complex than collective behavior in a crowd or mob. For one thing, a collective fashion trend has to occur over a much longer time. The trend also has to occur over many different geographic regions, each having its own leaders or inspirational figures to initiate diffusion. Furthermore, a considerable degree of competition and social differentiation, rather than cooperative behavior, is possible as new styles are selectively adopted by fashion leaders or status-seekers. For these reasons, mass fashion trends are not uniform throughout the population. Rather, there can be a number of subtrends within different social systems and geographic regions as the collective behavior progresses. The outcome may reflect a democratic, collective choice of the cooperating majority, but the opportunities for competition in collective behavior toward fashions must be taken into account.

Theories of collective behavior have traditionally suggested that collective movements are irrational, a judgment implicit in expressions like "the herd instinct," "mob psychology," "joining the bandwagon," or "social contagion." Mass movements in fashion in particular have been cited as examples of irrational behavior. However, Berk (1974) has made a case for collective behavior as rational and goal-directed. The individual might be swayed to some extent by social contagion and enthusiasm as more participants join the collective movement, but at the same time the individual may carefully assess the potential costs and benefits of participating. Thus, one should assess the element of rationality in collective movements and question the credibility of social contagion as the sole explanation of collective behavior. This is particularly true in mass fashion changes, for the individual frequently has the time and private opportunity to decide before participating in the movement.

To conclude, the collective theory of fashion diffusion differs from the basic theory of diffusion discussed in chapter 3. The theory of collective behavior suggests that fashions occur as sweeping mass movements stimulated by the immense social visibility a style can receive. Certain leaders can establish direction to this movement when they present alternative styles for selection, but the trend is formed only as collective tastes become adopted among an increasing number of people. In contrast, the theory of diffusion of innovations (chap. 3) suggests that innovations are spread systematically from one social group to another through a communications process. Innovators and opinion leaders in each social group initiate and propagate acceptance of the fashion within their immediate social environments. The mass system of fashion marketing also stimulates and accelerates this diffusion, perhaps causing simultaneous diffusion into many social groups. Therefore, the theory of diffusion differs from that of collective behavior, though there are basic similarities between the theories in the roles of leadership and social visibility. Both of the theories offer plausible explanations of how mass fashion movements can occur.

THE SOCIAL TERMINATION OF FASHION TRENDS

Ultimately, fashion trends end. Terminations can occur for three reasons:

1. further physical modifications or changes to a trend are no longer possible (the rule of excess);
2. the marketing system can induce terminations through the strategy of synthetic obsolescence; or
3. certain social forces may induce consumers to reduce and finally terminate wearing the fashion.

The following discussion briefly reviews the first two of these and discusses the third in detail, since social forces predominate in these influences.

One well known sort of termination is expressed as the "rule of excess," attributed to one of the first internationally known French designers, Paul Poiret (Robinson 1958). The rule states that fashion trends end when they reach an extreme point where further change of styling cannot physically occur. For example, trousers can only get so tight before it is physically impossible for them to get tighter, skirts can get only so short or so wide before a physical boundary of change is reached, or fabrics may become only so colorful or patterned before they will be evaluated as gaudy or overdone. Thus, physical boundaries set limits on fashion changes, and

Mass fashion breeds social saturation of styles.

(*WWD*, Fairchild Publications)

extremes of sensory stimulation (bright colors, for example, or excessive design details) result in over-stimulation. Thus termination of a fashion trend may occur when the extreme is reached.

Excess is not the only reason that fashion trends may come to an end, however. Some analysts also say that the marketing system can induce planned or synthetic obsolescence of fashions, because marketers seasonally introduce new styles of dress to the retail market, presumably making older fashions obsolete. If an older, established fashion is no longer available in the market, this will eventually result in termination of the trend, as consumers wear out or discard the style from their wardrobes. Flooding the market with new styles reinforces this termination. In these cases, the termination is forced or imposed on consumers, whether or not their demand for the fashion has actually been exhausted. However, remember that marketers may not be nearly so successful at controlling the direction and duration of fashion trends as this theoretical situation might suggest.

But perhaps the most common fashion terminations are those in which consumers *willingly* take part. Specifically, fashions often become obsolete for socially induced reasons. When these social forces arise, consumers discard older fashions in favor of newer and more socially desirable or appropriate styles. Now for a look at these forces.

Social Saturation of a Style

One of the most important explanations for the social termination of fashion trends lies in the concept of **social saturation.** A fashion becomes socially saturated when most or all potential adopters actually wear the fashion. Consumer demand for the fashion has been economically exhausted, and the fashion may be marketed only through low or sale prices. More importantly, however, the style has reached its highest point of consumer use, and a recognizable uniformity in use of the style for many social occasions is evident. This uniformity or social saturation, inherent in mass fashion trends, breeds the boredom and sameness that leads to a termination of the fashion. From a psychological point of view, the individual is likely experiencing habituation, or is becoming insensitive or unstimulated by the aesthetics of the style (Sproles 1981; Woods and Padgett 1987). He or she has become used to it, and it has lost its sensory appeal or excitement. Termination then occurs when the fashion begins to be transferred from wearing status to a relic in the closet by an increasing number of people.

Theoretically, the widespread adoption of a fashion across social situations creates an overuse leading to termination. As a practical matter, however, some fashions do not get a massive level of adoption; such fashions might ultimately end for a lack of social saturation. For example, a fashion receiving a modest level of acceptance can begin to decline when its adopters recognize that the trend has reached a social limit, and will receive no further social endorsement. Though such fashions can keep a certain exclusiveness, and thus receive continued use for some time, they may also reach a point of social resistance and end much earlier than more widely adopted styles.

If social saturation leads to termination of fashion trends, then why do classic fashions such as blazers, trenchcoats, or five-pocket jeans enjoy popularity over an extended period of time despite market saturation? There are several reasons why social saturation may not be an influence on

Widely diffused status symbols, such as Calvin Klein jeans, typically fade in popularity as they ease their status symbolism.
(*NYT* Pictures)

fashion termination in the case of such classic styles. Remember, few fashions ever reach that status of "classic." Those that do possess a basic simplicity and a versatility. Classics can often be adapted to fit in with current fashionable detailing. For example, the color, fabric or detailing of a classic blazer may change, adhering to fashionable norms. Classics may also involve informal traditions which are immune to fashion change. Buttons on the sleeves of blazers, satin stripes on tuxedo pants and epaulets on trenchcoats are traditional styling details that are seldom affected by fashion change. The classic may decline in the number of users and frequency of use as new fashions emerge as its competitors, but as long as the classic retains its consistency with the social environments where it has been accepted, it may continue hand-in-hand with newer fashion trends.

Social Differentiation

The classical explanation of fashion change focuses on the motivation of social differentiation as the underlying force for change. Theoretically, a widely diffused fashion loses much of its symbolic prestige and exclusivity, and is no longer a valued social object. Such a fashion has lost its ability to distinguish those people who desire differentiation, their leading motivation for adopting the style in the first place. Therefore, those who seek social differentiation will end their use of the established fashion and search for a new style.

The classic trickle-down theory of fashion is built on this concept of the upper classes continually seeking social differentiation. But the motive of social differentiation might occur within any social network, and does not necessarily show a differentiation between social classes (subculture leadership). For instance, a subculture might wish to display its uniqueness through dress, but this becomes increasingly difficult as a particular subcultural style diffuses to a larger population (Polhemus and Proctor 1978). If any particular group of the population wants to assert its uniqueness, it can do so simply by terminating use of old symbols and developing new ones. For example, the youth subculture favors social differentiation through unique fashions. However, the innovative fashions of the youth subculture continue to percolate upward and are often adopted by all ages.

Social Change

Termination can occur when a fashion trend is made obsolete by a change in the social environment. That is, fashion trends may be terminated when they become irrelevant to the social orientations, values, or functional uses

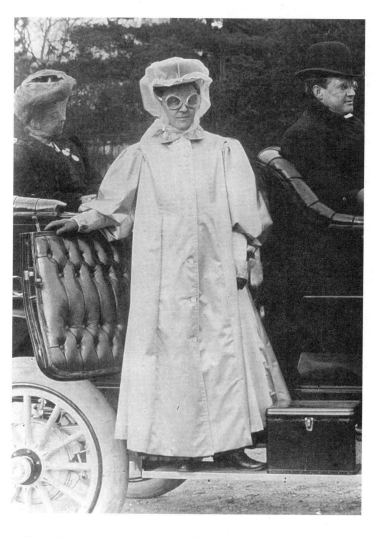

Riding in a motor car in the early 1900s required a duster and goggles.
(The Bettman Archive)

with which they were initially linked. Fashionable hats, helmets, scarves, and goggles worn by motor car drivers and passengers in the early 1900s soon went out of style as automobiles became enclosed. The invention of panty hose for women in the early 1960s made corsets and garter belts almost obsolete, until they were revived in the 1980s. Over the past twenty-five years, the rise of casual life-styles and extensive participation in social activity has made many formal styles of dress irrelevant, while increasing the fashionability of sportswear.

In general, we might expect that the termination of any social activity or tradition would be accompanied by termination of its related symbolic behavior. Thus the principle that fashion change will accompany social

TEXTURED TIGHTS
AND PANTY-HOSE
for Misses and Girls

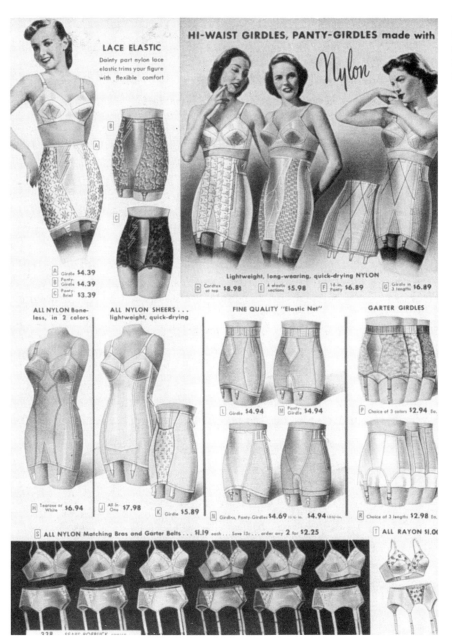

change appears relevant not only to explaining the emergence of new fashions, but also for the termination of behaviors that have no functional purpose in a changing social environment.

Normative Boundaries of Social Appropriateness

Fashions are controlled by social norms prescribing standards of social appropriateness for dress in different situations. These norms are often flexible, and a variety of similar styles will be approved with little notice. But it's difficult to be sure how flexible a particular norm is until a fashion trend reaches or exceeds it, and social resistance mixed with indignation is expressed by an increasing proportion of nonadopters. Here the termination of a fashion trend comes under social influence.

The most familiar of these normative boundaries pertain to bodily exposure, sexual attention, and moral decency. A trend in bodily exposure can go only so far before people's standards of morality will no longer tolerate it. Normative boundaries are also expressed by dress codes, which limit styles worn in such social environments as businesses or schools. These codes are primarily for social control, but they also serve to place a terminal point on the continuation of school fashion trends. Nearly every social interaction has some boundaries of what is socially acceptable. Unless the norms prescribing these boundaries become more flexible as the boundary is reached in a fashion trend, the norms will ultimately specify when the trend must end.

Two bathers being escorted off the beach by a policewoman for violating a law banning abbreviated bathing suits, 1922.

(UPI/Bettman)

Concluding Comments

There are powerful social processes through which fashions are terminated: social saturation of a style, the need for social differentiation, social change, and normative boundaries of social appropriateness. It is important to consider that fashion termination can involve unique processes, for it is deceptively simple to dismiss terminated fashions with the casual statement that they are "out-of-fashion" and "old-fashioned." There is much more to a complete understanding of the fashion process than simply studying the emergence of a new style into fashion acceptance.

Complex questions surround the social processes of fashion termination, questions not fully answered by the studies done to date. Therefore, the concepts of fashion termination are unstructured compared to other aspects of fashion theory. This indefiniteness is particularly true of the concepts of social saturation and social appropriateness, abstractions requiring a specific definition for each social situation. Nonetheless, these concepts offer a basis for studying the last phase of the fashion process, which prepares the ground for the emergence of new fashions.

SUMMARY

This chapter has described the phonomenom of collective behavior in mass fashion diffusion and the social termination of fashion trends. The phenomenon of collective behavior in mass fashion diffusion is one of the ways new fashions are selected from the competing alternatives. Fashions are collectively selected in mass society as a result of widespread interactions between fashion innovators, followers, a changing social environment, and the direction of a collective taste established in the society. A major force in collective behavior is the social visibility created for a fashion in the course of extensive but anonymous interaction among the members of mass society.

Though the process of collective behavior tends to homogenize mass fashion, a look at fashion acceptance in small groups reveals a great deal of diversity. Small groups of people who interact with one another on a regular face-to-face basis directly influence the individual's adoption of fashions. The norms and social pressures developed in groups can become more important to the individual in defining standards of dress than the more broadly defined and collective forces of mass society.

The termination of fashion trends is subject to unique social forces: social saturation of fashions when they are in extensive use; the motive of social differentiation; the effects of social change; and normative boundaries, which act to define what styles are socially unacceptable. Therefore, fashions do not die simply because they are "out-of-fashion," but because of powerful social influences that encourage consumers to willingly stop using them.

NOTES

1. Blumer's theory of collective behavior has been criticized by Berk (1974), largely on the grounds that it views collective behavior as "irrational." However, Blumer's presentation of fashion as collective behavior suggests a great deal of rationality among consumers in the acceptance of mass fashion change. See chapter 5 for more discussion of this theory.

DISCUSSION QUESTIONS

1. Consider the fashions you are wearing today. Which fashions or fashion components do you think are a reflection of mass fashion norms; which do you think are a reflection of fashion norms developed within smaller groups?
2. Based upon your answer in question 1, what conclusions can you draw about the types of fashions or fashion components that are more prone to influence from mass fashion norms and those that are more prone to influence from fashion norms developed within small groups?
3. Look in a fashion magazine from ten, twenty or thirty years ago. In the magazine, find a picture of a fashion that is no longer in style. Describe the fashion. Explain why you think the fashion went out of style. Have any components of the fashion been revived in a later period? If so, which components have been revived?
4. In the same magazine that was used in question 3, find a fashion that could be worn today. Describe the fashion. Why has this style had such lasting power?

SUGGESTED READINGS

Blumer, Herbert. "Fashion: From Class Differentiation to Collective Selection." *Sociological Quarterly* 10 (1969): 275-91.

8

Fashion Adoption and the Individual

OBJECTIVES

- To review classic works on the psychology of dress that serve as a foundation for our current understanding of fashion and the individual.
- To discuss current theories on the social psychology of fashion adoption.
- To examine social psychological functions of fashions within contemporary society.
- To explore the psychological motives underlying an individual's fashion adoption.
- To discuss the social comparison processes that affect an individual's fashion adoption.

Today there are no laws which make us accept a fashion. No fashion is imposed upon an individual by force. Generally, the acceptance or rejection of a fashion is up to the individual, and he is free to make his decision as to what his actions will be. (Hurlock 1929, 8)

Fashion adoption is a personal choice. How can we explain this individual-centered phenomenon—that some individuals are quick to adopt a new fashion and others are slower to adopt or may not adopt the fashion object at all? Considering the number of fashionable styles available to a consumer, what determines the consumer's selection of one fashion object over another? Many of the answers lie in understanding the psychological and social-psychological motives underlying a consumer's adoption of fashion.

Fashion adoption is the process by which a new style is adopted—bought and worn—by the consumer after its commercial introduction. Individual consumers adopt fashions for a wide range of personal, social, economic, and cultural reasons. This chapter will focus on the psychological and social-psychological motives underlying a consumer's fashion adoption. First, a review of the classic works in the social psychology of fashion will provide a foundation for the current approaches to understanding fashion adoption. Next, three theoretical approaches toward examining psychological and social-psychological motives for fashion adoption will be discussed: satisfaction-of-needs approach, psychological approach, and social-comparison approach.

FOUNDATIONS OF THE SOCIAL PSYCHOLOGY OF FASHION ADOPTION

To better understand current theories on the social psychology of fashion adoption, it is useful to review some early classic works on the social psychology of dress. Early in this century several exploratory psychological studies on dress and fashion gave legitimacy to fashion as a topic of interest to behavioral scientists. From these works several enduring principles for the study of fashion-oriented consumer behavior emerged. These principles form the foundation for later theoretical approaches on the social psychology of fashion adoption.

Historical Perspectives

The social psychology of dress had its beginnings as a scientific area of investigation in the early 1900s. At that time early analysts conducted exploratory research on the psychology of dress. Similar to later investigations, the goal of these early studies was to examine the reasons underlying individuals' adoption of certain clothing and the effect of clothing on individuals' attitudes and behavior. In one of the earliest investigations, Flaccus (1906) studied attitudes toward dress among female students and found that clothing affected their feelings of physical well-being, sociability, social acceptance, and personal worth. A later survey by Hurlock (1929), using a sample of 1452 men and women of all ages, found that most subjects favored conformity, inconspicuousness, modesty, and "expressing their personality" in their dress. Barr (1934) conducted a similar study and her findings further supported the social psychological importance of conformity and modesty in dress. Significantly, both

Hurlock and Barr also found that a large proportion of their subjects believed it was important to be in fashion.

Early researchers also investigated social-psychological motives for fashion change and fashion adoption. In his classic work *Economics of Fashion* (1928), economist and marketing professor Paul Nystrom hypothesized that a wide range of social-psychological factors prompted the emergence of new fashion. The foremost were boredom with the old and seeking the excitement inherent in something new. He also suggested that fashionable behavior is stimulated by such diverse desires as personal recognition, self-assertion, rebellion against convention, attraction of the opposite sex, the hunger for ownership, improvement of appearances, and social conformity. In another classic study Hurlock (1929) discussed similar motivation, including the desire for approval, "self-advertisement," display of wealth, imitation, conformity, the fear of ridicule or social disapproval, and the battle for recognition within the sexes. Other analysts expanded on these viewpoints. For example, Harms (1938) suggested that clothing is a form of intellectual and artistic expression as well as an expression of the individual's mental traits. Dooley (1930) discussed such fashion motives as the imitative desire and the contrasting drive for novelty and distinction. Jacobson (1936) pointed to three basic motives of fashionable behavior: the desires for self-assertion, social approval, and conformity. She further suggested that fashion leadership may stem from a person's superior knowledge of fashions, whereas followers may assume their position because they don't want to learn enough about fashions to become leaders. Finally, Jacobson noted that fear of ridicule, feelings of inferiority, and the risk of being socially ignored motivate conformity to fashions.

These early investigations yielded several fundamental principles on the social psychology of fashion adoption, which are today's foundations for psychological studies:

Adoption of fashions may be used for personal stimulation

This is manifest when adoption of fashion objects is used to seek novelty, uniqueness, individualism, excitement in life, or escape from boredom. Of these, the pursuit of individualism in fashion has become the watchword of contemporary life.

Fashion adoption provides a vehicle for self-expression

Fashion provides one of the most visual and easily manipulated means for presentation of the individual's personality, self-concept, and social roles. It is also a means for self-assertion, differentiation of oneself from others, and expression of one's aesthetic sensitivity or knowledgeability. Today we term this impression management.

Fashion adoption provides a vehicle for self-expression.

(© 1993 Linda Eber/Impact Visuals)

Fashion adoption may satisfy the individual's need to seek social identity   Most importantly, conformity in dress is a method for seeking group membership, or for attaining the friendship and companionship of others. That fashions are accepted as a means to conform seems a timeless principle.

Adoption of fashion objects may establish a means for maintaining or increasing the feeling of personal security   Selecting the appropriate type of dress may have the direct effect of reinforcing self-satisfaction and self-assurance. Conforming to the dress of others also has the effect of increasing one's personal perception of security, in that conformity is a means for achieving social approval and reducing the fear of ridicule or social disapproval. Contemporary analysts may even suggest the role of appropriate fashion in promoting mental health.

Each of these principles has become a well-established guide to the analysis of the social psychology of fashion-oriented behavior. Each is elaborated in three current social-psychological approaches discussed in this chapter: satisfaction-of-needs approach, psychological approach, and social-comparison approach.

SATISFACTION-OF-NEEDS APPROACH TO FASHION ADOPTION

The most general approach, and the approach that stems most directly from the earlier works on the social-psychological factors affecting fashion adoption, is the **satisfaction-of-needs** approach. Fashionable clothing is a functional product with a number of useful purposes that satisfy certain needs of an individual. According to this approach, each act of consumer behavior in the selection and use of fashion occurs with some purposeful function—satisfaction of needs—in mind.

It is useful to consider the kinds of needs an individual can have. The classic "hierarchy of needs" proposed by Maslow (1954) can be used as a model for this purpose. Maslow suggests that humans are motivated to satisfy five basic needs, and that those needs fall into a hierarchy extending from "lower" (satisfied first) to "higher" (satisfied later) needs:

1. **Physiological needs,** or needs related to proper functioning of the human body (food, drink, rest, activity).
2. **Safety needs,** including the related needs of physical security, protection from the environment, and reduction of fear or anxiety.
3. **Love needs,** including the needs to receive affection from others and to secure a feeling of "belonging" among other people.
4. **Esteem needs,** or needs for feelings of self-esteem, self-worth, recognition, and social approval.
5. **Self-actualization needs,** or needs related to success in personal achievements, expression of personal creativity, and "self-fulfillment."

The selection and wearing of particular clothing serve partially to satisfy these needs. For instance, one function of clothing is to satisfy some of a person's physiological and safety needs (comfort and protection). Although functional clothing such as a firefighter's uniform, mountain-climber's gear, or football uniform are the most obvious in terms of satisfying safety needs, fashions may also satisfy this need (albeit safety is possibly of secondary importance). In more subtle ways, clothing may also be used to satisfy higher needs; this is manifested when clothing is purposefully used to enhance the individual's social identity and interaction with others (love and esteem needs) as when an adolescent dresses in a manner similar to his/her friends or when an employee adheres to a company's dress codes. Individualistic and creative dress may be selected perhaps for purposes of self-actualization, such as wearing fashions that reflect personal tastes, attitudes, and values (e.g., wearing fashions made of fabrics

Clothing as a form of intellectual and artistic expression is illustrated here with "Celebration Cape IX" designed by Robert Hillestad. This hand-knitted cape with fringe is made of rayon tape and yarn and raffia.

(Robert Hillestad; Photographer: Roger Bruhn)

**Functional clothing
often takes on a
fashion aspect.**
(Reuters/Bettman)

that do less harm to the environment as a expression of one's environmental concerns). In short, clothing can satisfy significant physiological, psychological, and social needs. With this background in mind, we can make a more detailed analysis of the functions of clothing. The analysis will focus on intrinsic functions of clothing and social-psychological functions of clothing.

Intrinsic Functions of Clothing

Many of the needs satisfied by fashion adoption are related to the intrinsic functions of clothing. Early writers in the area of the psychology of clothing concentrated on explaining social-psychological motives for humans wearing clothing (Dunlap 1928; Flugel 1930; Hurlock 1929). These psychologists noted four intrinsic functions of clothing: protection, modesty, immodesty, and adornment.

The **protective function** of clothing is based upon clothing's intrinsic characteristic of covering the body in some manner. This body covering may be as extensive as a full-length fur coat or as bare as body painting. The covering of the body, however, is what provides humans with a sense of protection. Examples of clothing that serve this protective function can be classified into two broad categories: (1) protection from the elements, and (2) protection from evil. Clothing that protects individuals from the elements includes any clothing that provides comfort and guards the body from climatic conditions, vegetation, animals, or other humans. This occurs when clothing effectively screens out direct contact between the body and the natural environment. Protective clothing includes everyday wear such as umbrellas, visors, parka and gloves, as well as specialized functional clothing such as bullet-resistant vests worn by police officers and hockey uniforms, just to name a few examples. Comfort is enhanced when clothing maintains the individual's preferred body temperature (e.g., putting on a jacket in cool weather or wearing shorts in warm weather), and perhaps when the individual receives pleasant sensations from contact between body and fabric (e.g., wearing silk fabric next to the skin; Branson and Sweeney 1991; "Comfort," 1985).

Clothing that protects individuals from evil includes any clothing that has mystical, magical, or religious qualities that are believed to guard the individual or the individual's soul from harm by evil forces. Amulets, ornamental charms or other symbols designed to protect the wearer from evil or aid the wearer in some way, may include tattoos, jewelry, or other meaningful clothing (e.g., lucky fishing hat).

Although the main goal of clothing fashions is not necessarily protection, fashions may incorporate protective elements. For example, protective bicycling helmets may be made in bright fashionable colors. In addition, fashion designers may get inspiration from strictly functional or protective clothing. Sports clothing and western "cowboy" wear are two types of functional clothing that have recently served as inspiration for fashions. When this happens, the protective function of the clothing often becomes secondary to the fashion function of the clothing.

The second intrinsic function of clothing fashions is **modesty/immodesty.** These two functions will be discussed together because the concepts are interrelated. The term modesty in clothing is often associated with related terms such as decency, appropriateness, sexiness, and properness. For the most part, modesty and immodesty in clothing are associated with the amount of body exposed by the clothing or the degree to which the clothing draws attention to the body. Color, fit, or design details of fashion can be used to emphasize or draw attention to one's body or parts of one's body. In our society, covering one's body with clothing is associated with preservation of personal modesty. Underlying this function of dress is the

Perceptions of modesty and immodesty in dress are related to social norms and to individuals' attittudes and values.
(UPI Bettman)

social judgment, derived from the Judaic-Christian belief, that a covered body is good while an exposed body is shameful. Though humans are not born with this outlook, it is quickly learned that social encounters require some form of appropriately modest dress.

One unique characteristic of clothing is that it can both conceal the body and draw attention to the body at the same time. For example, a pair of tight jeans may cover the lower torso, but may also draw attention to the wearer's buttocks. The reason that clothing can at the same time be both erotic and moral is because clothing is used to differentiate between the sexes (Steele 1985). Thus it is impossible to discuss modesty in clothing without taking into consideration immodesty in clothing. Feelings of immodesty arise when we believe we are exposing our bodies or drawing attention to our bodies more than what is considered decent. Although it was once believed that modesty was the main reason humans initially started to wear clothing, it is now the accepted belief that the wearing of clothing was not the result of modesty but the cause of modesty.

Because modesty in clothing is socially and personally defined, it varies with culture, era, situation, and individual attitudes. Within each culture, mores (socially defined norms of morality) regulate the degree of bodily exposure considered decent. Within a single society, definitions of modesty can change over time (e.g., swimwear considered immodest in the 1920s would be considered tame today). What is considered modest or immodest can also vary among situations and among individuals (e.g., a male appearing bare-chested may be considered immodest in a business situation but not on the beach). Thus it is difficult to label specific clothing items as modest or immodest without taking into consideration cultural, social, and personal factors.

Fashion change may facilitate change in perceptions of modesty of clothing. A clothing item once considered immodest may achieve greater perceived modesty by becoming socially defined as fashionable. This is accomplished by increased social visibility and acceptance of a fashion object. Consequently, fashion symbolizes changing perceptions of modesty. For example, when rock star Madonna originally appeared wearing lingerie as an outer garment, it was considered immodest. Now that the fashion industry has legitimized the look, it does not have that same connotation. However, a fashion object will not be accepted by individuals if it does not fit within the society's definition of modesty. For the most part, European definitions of modesty are much less restrictive than those in the United States. Fashions perceived as daring or immodest by many Americans, such as bare-breasted women on the beach or the thong bikini, have been readily accepted by European society.

Although modesty and immodesty are not regarded as the primary explanations for fashion change or fashion adoption, they reinforce the association between fashion and modesty in clothing. It is interesting to note that most of the discussion of modesty in clothing concentrates on women's clothing. This is due to the fact that fashions symbolizing "sexiness" in women's clothing are associated with the perceived immodesty of the clothing. This is not necessarily the case for men's clothing. As noted by Steele (1985),

> The female role as "sexual object" undoubtedly contributes to the relatively greater sexual display of women's clothing. These historical facts seem to explain adequately why women's dress was (and is) both more modest and more erotic than men's clothing. (P. 28)

Perhaps the most significant and universal function of clothing that is evident in fashion is personal decoration and **adornment.** Adornment in clothing is used

- ◆ to enhance physical attractiveness of the clothing or the person,
- ◆ to symbolize social status and identity, or
- ◆ to raise a person's self-esteem (Ebin 1979).

Tattoos are one of the oldest known forms of corporal adornment.

(Bettman Newsphotos)

There are two basic forms of adornment involved with clothing and fashion: (1) corporal (bodily) adornment and (2) external adornment (Flugel 1930). Corporal adornment involves decorating the physical body itself. Corporal adornment can be a permanent change in the body texture, shape, or color. Examples of permanent corporal adornment include scarification, tattooing, permanent binding or contortion of the body, piercing of the body, and plastic surgery. Corporal adornment may also involve a temporary change as is the case with makeup, body paint, styling or shaving of body hair, or lotions that are applied to the skin to change its texture.

External adornment involves decorations that are:

- wrapped around the body (shawls, togas, sashes),
- suspended from the body (ponchos, necklaces, bracelets),
- pre-shaped to fit the body (jackets, shoes, trousers),
- clipped to the body or to other clothing (earrings, pins, tie clasps),
- applied to the body with adhesives (false mustaches, eyelashes, fingernails), or
- hand-held (handbags, briefcases, umbrellas) (Roach and Musa 1979).

Early punk style included body piercing, such as safety pins through the cheek or ear, 1978.
(UPI/Bettman)

External adornment can be used to:

- increase the apparent height of an individual,
- increase the apparent width or size of an individual,
- emphasize the movement of the body,
- draw attention to or emphasize the body shape or particular parts of the body,
- embellish fabrics and garments themselves (Flugel 1930).

Fashion objects may incorporate characteristics of both corporal and external adornment, and acceptance of a fashion object may be due to the object's qualities of adornment. Often the acceptance and wearing of fashion objects are to increase one's attractiveness, status, and feelings of self-worth. These goals are frequently achieved through corporal or external adornment. Although we usually think of fashion objects in terms of external adornment, fashion objects may also incorporate elements of corporal adornment (e.g., trimming or shaving of facial hair, earrings that pierce the ear lobe, cosmetics that color the skin).

In the book, *The Agony of Fashion,* Cremers-van der Does (1980) examined one type of corporal adornment, contortion, and traced the history of the fashionable body shape. As she writes, "Mankind (woman in particular) has through the ages reshaped the body in order to be beautiful and to obtain the figure, the silhouette or 'line' which the current fashion decrees" (p. 9). Her analysis of fashionable silhouettes over the centuries indicates that contortion has been achieved in two main ways. First, "paring down" has been achieved through the use of tight corsets and other types of bindings and constrictors (e.g., breast binders). Second, "adding on" has been achieved through the use of padding and other devices that add height and width to the silhouette (e.g., epaulets, petticoats).

Social-Psychological Functions of Fashion

In addition to these intrinsic reasons for adopting fashions (protection, modesty/immodesty, and adornment), fashion adoption satisfies other social-psychological needs including one's:

- need to be up-to-date,
- need to adjust to a changing society,
- desire to escape boredom,
- need for symbolic differentiation,
- need for social affiliation.

In fact, adoption of the fashion object may be due to one or more of these social-psychological needs that are satisfied by adopting the fashion object. Although all individuals have some degree of these social psychological needs, individuals vary as to the level to which they need to be satisfied.

Adoption of fashion objects may satisfy an individual's social-psychological **need to be modern and up-to-date.** Because the emergence of fashion objects is influenced by current events and happenings in the larger social context, fashion is always "modern" (Blumer 1968). From the consumer's viewpoint, modernism in dress may be thought of as a function wherein certain new forms of dress symbolize that their wearers are up-to-date with, and perhaps ahead of, a changing social and cultural environment. Consumers' acceptance of the newest fashions, or selection of innovations in the design and manufacturing of fashions (e.g., new fabrics and finishes), may be analyzed with this function in mind. Moreover, consumers' acceptances of fashions may mean more than just a preference for novelties or conformity to current tastes; acceptance of modern objects may show the person's awareness of current events in his/her environment, willingness to accept change, and desire to be an active participant in those changes. Thus through fashion adoption individuals communicate to themselves and others that they are aware of and accepting of current modes of thought.

Fashion adoption also satisfies an individual's **need to adjust** to a changing society. Because fashion legitimizes and perpetuates social change, fashion adoption provides individuals with a means of coping and adjusting to these changes. Blumer (1969) outlined what he calls "the societal role of fashion," a role that involves fashion's ability to move from the present into the future.

1. First, **fashion adoption introduces order to social change.** In the area of clothing, fashion provides a logical and predictable progression to changing styles. Manufacturers and retailers of fashion systematically select the styles they believe will have the greatest acceptance by consumers. Thus the fashion industry limits the number of alternative styles available for purchase by consumers. By doing so, the fashion industry helps individuals accept and cope with the change.
2. Second, fashion adoption allows individuals the **freedom to move in new directions** and to try new ideas. In our society a premium is placed on being up-to-date; it is socially desirable to be considered modern and new. Because of this, adoption of changing fashions is considered appropriate and good. Consequently this allows individuals the freedom to be innovative and to try new ideas because they know they will not be socially chastised for such behavior.
3. Third, fashion adoption allows individuals to **get accustomed to and prepare for the future.** New fashions are constantly being introduced and made socially visible through the media. These are essentially previews of the future that give individuals the chance to know what will be considered fashionable in the immediate future and to become accustomed to the new styles.

Fashion adoption also satisfies an individual's **desire to escape boredom.** According to Sapir (1931),

> *the fundamental drives leading to the creation and acceptance of fashion can be isolated. In the more sophisticated societies, boredom, created by leisure and too highly specialized forms of activity, leads to restlessness and curiosity. (P. 140)*

It is this restlessness and boredom with existing styles that may cause individuals to strive for newness and excitement in fashion innovations.

Similarly, fashion adoption may be due to an individual's "spirit of adventure which impels individuals to rebel against the confinement of prevailing social forms" (Blumer 1969). Such rebellion against social norms may lead to the overt disposal of current modes and acceptance of innovative fashions.

Fashion adoption also satisfies an individual's need for **symbolic differentiation.** Consumers may use unique forms of dress to differentiate themselves from other consumers. This symbolic function of dress can satisfy needs related to personal recognition, prestige, status, esteem, and self-actualization. Nearly everyone's dress is in some way unique and individual. Although social norms prescribe the general form for dress, rarely do we encounter two people identically dressed, with identical apparel, accessories, hair styling, and cosmetics. In our society, the con-

Fashions perceived as status symbols often satisfy an individual's need for symbolic differentiation, 1989.

(© 1989 David Maung/ Impact Visuals)

sumer wants to say "I am different" and to enhance his/her self-esteem through this uniqueness. Thus consumers often use clothing to communicate their unique self-concept and social identity. This human need for uniqueness will be discussed more thoroughly later in the chapter in the section that deals with the social-comparison approach to fashion adoption.

In one of its most important and frequently analyzed functions, fashion adoption helps **satisfy affiliation needs,** including social acceptance, social approval, and a feeling of belonging. This social function occurs when members of a social group adopt similar styles of dress, as a result of some relatively well-defined norms governing dress that have emerged within the group (e.g., written or unwritten dress codes). In one way, such similarities merely serve to identify the group and its members. But an individual's conformity to these norms for dress also becomes a major step in achieving and maintaining social affiliations with other group members. When used in this manner, dress can be a powerful method of maintaining social control within the group. Specifically, the conformist who adopts the prevailing styles of the group is likely to be rewarded with social acceptance and approval. This acts to control behavior by encouraging conformity. The deviant, on the other hand, invites disapproval, even rejection from the group. In these situations, satisfaction of the person's needs for social affiliation may depend on the consistency of his or her dress with what the group perceives to be appropriate.

PSYCHOLOGICAL APPROACHES TO FASHION ADOPTION

Fashion adoption is considered a personal choice and clothing fashions are a visible reflection of this personal choice. Because of this, the adoption of specific fashion objects has long been a focus of psychologists interested in understanding individual differences in fashion adoption. In an early essay on fashion Sapir (1931) noted that "fashion concerns itself closely and intimately with the ego" (p. 143) and that fashion acceptance is in part based upon a "ceaseless desire to add to the attractiveness of the self" (p. 140). As put by William James, a turn-of-the-century psychologist:

The old saying that the human person is composed of three parts—soul, body, and clothes—is more than a joke. We so appropriate our clothes and identify ourselves with them that there are few of us who, if asked to choose between having a beautiful body clad in raiment perpetually shabby and unclean, and having an ugly and blemished form always

spotlessly attired, would not hesitate a moment before making a decisive reply. (1890, 292)

Therefore, this section will discuss fashion adoption from a purely psychological approach. This perspective will include two specific areas of psychology as they relate to fashion change and fashion adoption. First, the psychoanalytic perspective of psychology will be discussed as it relates to fashion adoption and fashion change. Second, the relationship between fashion adoption and individuals' personality characteristics, attitudes, and values will be discussed to better understand individual differences in fashion adoption.

Psychoanalytic Approach to Fashion Adoption

The psychoanalytic approach to fashion adoption and fashion change is based upon the writings of Sigmund Freud. Freud's theories of personality, psychosexual stages of personality, and unconscious mental activity influenced fashion theorists as they attempted to explain fashion adoption and fashion change. Perspectives of fashion based upon psychoanalytic theory focus on the sexual symbolism of fashion (Flugel 1930; Steele 1985), and the theory of shifting erogenous zones (Bergler 1953; Laver 1969).

Sexual Symbolism of Fashion   Since dress is a presentation of the human body, it inevitably generates some sexual implications (Squire 1974). And frequently dress is intentionally used to stimulate sexual consciousness and attraction between people. One of the first fashion theorists to use psychoanalytic theory to explain the sexual symbolism of clothing was Flugel (1930). He noted that "clothes not only serve to arouse sexual interest but may themselves actually symbolize the sexual organs" (p. 26). As he stated,

> *a great many articles of dress, such as the shoe, the tie, the hat, the collar, and even larger and voluminous garments, such as the coat, the trousers, and the mantle may be phallic symbols, while the shoe, the girdle, and the garter (as well as most jewels) may be corresponding female symbols. (P. 27)*

Flugel went on to hypothesize that interest in clothing by individuals was based upon their sexual admiration of their own bodies and appearances.

While psychoanalytic theory as it relates to sexual symbolism in clothing has not been used extensively in research on fashion adoption, authors have noted how fashion has developed sexual connotations throughout history. For example, using psychoanalytic theory as a foundation, Steele (1985) examined the relationship between sexual symbolism and feminine beauty in Victorian fashion. She noted the erotic basis of the ideal of beauty and the typical female silhouette of the time which "was essentially formed by two cones—the long, full-structured skirt and the tailored, boned bodice—intersecting at a narrow constricted waist" (p. 51, 52). Fashion adoption during this era appeared to be based upon women's striving to achieve this ideal sexual beauty. Other researchers have also noted the sexual symbolism in Victorian fashion (Lauer and Lauer 1980; Roberts 1977).

In *The Language of Clothes,* Alison Lurie (1981) highlighted several current sexual signals in clothing from a psychoanalytic perspective. For example, according to Lurie, hats, umbrellas, walking sticks, excess jewelry, neckties, and breast pocket kerchiefs have served as phallic symbols throughout history. Lurie also notes that the most recognized sexual indicator in women is the purse or handbag. The purse supposedly not only serves as a "portable identity kit and a repair kit" but also "conveys erotic information." For example,

> *a tightly snapped, zipped and buckled purse suggests a woman who guards her physical and emotional privacy closely, one whom it will be difficult to get to know in either the common or the Biblical sense. An open-topped tote bag suggests an open, trusting nature: someone who is emotionally and sexually more accessible. A handbag may also be small or large, stiff or soft, and brightly colored or dark. It may have many compartments, suggesting an organized mind or a woman who plays many roles in life; or it may consist of only one compartment in which everything is jumbled together. The handbag may also be extremely "feminine"—soft, flowered and fragile-looking—or it may resemble a man's briefcase. The executive woman who carries both a handbag and a briefcase appears to have two contradictory sexual identities; perhaps for this reason, wardrobe consultants strongly advise against the practice. (P. 243)*

According to psychoanalytic theory, individuals subconsciously adopt and wear these sexual symbols in clothing to fulfill hidden sexual drives and communicate sexual desires. In a test of this assumption, Edmonds and Cahoon (1984) examined the sexual symbolism of various styles of women's clothing (styles ranged from "demure frocks to revealing swimwear," p. 171) and the extent to which women who perceived themselves as sexually attractive preferred such styles. The results of the study showed that the women in the sample could accurately assess the sexual impact of their clothing on men and that women who perceived themselves as sexually attractive preferred sexually arousing styles of clothes. However, actual purchase behavior of clothing was not measured and perceived sexual attraction of clothing may not be the primary motive for clothing purchase behavior and usage (McCullough, Miller, and Ford 1977).

Theory of Shifting Erogenous Zones   Just as the perceived sexual attraction of a fashion may affect individual adoption of the fashion, sexual connotations associated with fashion have been used to explain changes in fashion. According to the "Theory of Shifting Erogenous Zones," changes in fashion occur because of changes in perceived erogenous zones of the human body. This theory is based upon the assumption that clothing is worn to attract attention to the body as a sexual object. Because complete nudity is anti-erotic, clothing is a primary source for creating sex appeal. Bergler (1953), drawing from this basic assumption, explained how our characteristic permanent eroticism is kept alive through altering the erotic emphasis in clothing. He hypothesized that one and then another part of the body is emphasized by succeeding styles, thus instigating fashion change:

> *Fashion is no more than a series of permutations of seven given themes, each theme being a part of the female body: the breasts (neckline), waist (abdomen), hips, buttocks, legs, arms, and length (or circumference) of the body itself. Organs "appear" and "disappear" as the theme of fashion changes, and one and then another part of the body is emphasized by succeeding styles. (P. 117)*

In the past legs have been emphasized by tight trousers or short skirts, waists have been emphasized by the use of belts, and breasts have been emphasized by low necklines. According to this hypothesis, changing fashions stimulate sexual interest by constantly shifting sexual attention to different parts of the body, the erogenous zones. As one part of the body may lose its sexual appeal from overexposure, new styles emerge to conceal the old appeal and draw attention to a new appeal. And, with so many erogenous zones to expose, there is no lack of opportunity for continual renewal of sexual attractiveness through changes in fashion.

Laver (1969) expanded on this theory explaining female fashion changes by what he called the "seduction principle." He concluded that fashion serves to maintain interest in the body by concealing parts of it long enough to build up its "erotic capital." According to Laver, the female body consists of erogenous zones (i.e., legs, back, breasts, derriere) that are the point of interest for the innovative fashion item. The erogenous zone is always shifting and fashion pursues it without ever actually catching up with it. The innovative fashion is considered by society as daring, and the obsolete fashion is considered by society as dowdy; that is, it has exhausted its accumulation of erotic capital. Thus, according to Laver, fashion change is in part a function of this seduction principle.

Individual Differences in Fashion Adoption

Because fashion adoption is a personal choice, individuals differ as to when they will adopt a fashion, what fashion they will adopt, and why they adopt a specific fashion. In an attempt to understand these individual differences in fashion adoption, researchers have investigated the relationship between individuals' adoption of certain clothing styles and their personalities, values, and attitudes.

Fashion Adoption and Personality   Individuals tend to be consistent in their responses toward the world around them. These "persistent qualities in human behavior" (Kassarjian 1971, 409) are known in psychology as "personality." In relating personality to fashion adoption, researchers have assumed that if they could understand individuals' personalities, they would be able to understand why individuals buy and wear the clothing fashions they do.

The most common approach to personality theory used to predict and explain relationships between personality and clothing fashion adoption is the trait-factor approach. Trait-factor theorists believe that personality is composed of a set of traits or factors that are enduring and distinctive and relatively stable across situations (Cattell 1950). Researchers following this theoretical approach select one of many personality inventories and attempt to find a relationship between personality traits and, in this case, factors related to clothing/fashion selection and use.

Using the trait-factor approach to the study of personality and clothing factors, early investigations suggested that different orientations toward dress may reflect individual differences in personality. For example, Aiken (1963) correlated five general orientations toward dress with various personality characteristics, and found the following relationships:

1. **Decoration in Dress** Individuals who scored high in using clothing for decoration tend to be conscientious, conventional, stereotyped, conforming, nonintellectual, sympathetic, sociable, and submissive. Aiken concluded that people emphasizing dress for decoration tended to be "uncomplicated" and "socially conscientious."
2. **Comfort in Dress** High scorers on the comfort dimension tended to be self-controlled, socially cooperative, sociable, thorough, and deferent to authority. Aiken concluded that these people were "controlled extroverts."
3. **Interest in Dress** High scorers on clothing interest tended to be conventional, conscientious, compliant before authority, stereotyped in thinking, persistent, suspicious, insecure, and tense. Aiken concluded that these people were "uncomplicated" and "socially conscientious," but also might have certain "adjustment difficulties." It should be noted that the findings for this group tend to be similar to the "decoration" group.
4. **Conformity in Dress** Individuals having higher orientations toward

conformity in dress tended to be socially conforming, restrained, conscientious, moral, sociable, traditional, and submissive. In short, conformists in dress tended to have a variety of personality characteristics surrounding conventionality and general conformity.

5. **Economy in Dress** People with higher scores on economy tended to be responsible, conscientious, alert, efficient, precise, and controlled. In other words, people who emphasize economy in dress tended to have personality characteristics that favored "resourcefulness," intelligence, and efficiency.

In a conceptually related study, Gurel, Wilbur, and Gurel (1972) analyzed how orientations toward specific styles of dress were associated with two specific personality characteristics: authoritarianism and dogmatism. Those favoring a highly uniform style of dressing had the highest scores on authoritarianism and dogmatism, thereby indicating their high tendency toward conformity. Those favoring simple classic styles were next highest in conformity, those wearing the most current fashion were next, and finally, those who were lowest in conformity were wearers of unconventional, "hippie" dress. The researchers concluded that individual preferences for individualistic or conformist styles were associated with their underlying general orientations toward conformity as measured by the authoritarianism and dogmatism scales.

More recently, the trait-factor concept of personality has led to many studies that have examined differences in the personality characteristics of fashion leaders and fashion followers. Because of their early adoption of fashion and their impact on others' adoption of fashion, fashion leaders and their characteristics have been investigated by both market researchers and social psychologists. Market researchers have investigated the psychographic, demographic, and personality characteristics of fashion leaders. The goal of this research has been to establish criteria that differentiates fashion leaders from fashion followers in an effort to better market new products to them. Psychologists and social psychologists have studied innovativeness and opinion leadership as personality traits that are possessed, to some degree, by all individuals. The goal of this research has been to better understand the psychological motives underlying early adoption and opinion leadership of fashion.

It should be noted that several studies suggest fashion leaders are not identified by basic personality variables. For example, Robertson and Myers (1969) related basic personality traits assessed by the California Psychological Inventory to opinion leadership and innovativeness. Although innovativeness in clothing was correlated with sociability, over-

Fashion innovators, such as Cher, may perceive less risk in wearing innovative fashions than other consumers, 1986.
(UPI/Bettman)

all there was little relationship between personality characteristics and fashion leadership. Darden and Reynolds (1972) found that, other than fashion interest and fashion venturesomeness, predispositional characteristics were not predictive of opinion leadership for men's apparel fashions. Baumgarten (1975) conducted research on the personalities of male innovative communicators and found that fashion-oriented variables rather than personality characteristics were the most significant discriminators between innovative communicators and noninnovative communicators. However, innovative communicators were found to be higher in impulsiveness, exhibitionism, and narcissism, and lower in intellectual interest than noninnovative communicators. Summers (1970) also found that attitudes and values were more powerful predictors of opinion leadership for women's fashion than were personality factors, although more opinion leaders in this sample perceived themselves to be assertive, likeable, less depressive, and less shy.

Other researchers have found specific personality characteristics to be associated with fashion leadership. For example, fashion-oriented women have been found to possess and show greater emotional stability, ascendancy (Greeno, Sommers, and Kernan 1973), competitive exhibitionism, venturesomeness, self-confidence, gregariousness, assertiveness, attention seeking, and leadership than non-fashion-oriented women (Sproles and King 1973). Individuals identified as fashion opinion leaders have been found to have lower levels of debilitating anxiety (Brett and Kernaleguen 1975), lower levels of cognitive complexity (Lennon and Davis 1987), and in general, personalities favoring conformity (Schrank and Gilmore 1973) as compared to those identified as fashion followers. Individuals identified as innovators have been found to be higher in tolerance of ambiguity, self-acceptance, security (Pasnak and Ayres 1969), and cognitive complexity (Lennon and Davis 1987), and have lower levels of dogmatism and anxiety (Jacoby 1971) than those identified as "noninnovators."

In addition, researchers have discovered several cognitive orientations that are related to innovativeness and opinion leadership in fashion adoption: perceived risk, fashion involvement, fashion awareness, fashion knowledgeability, and fashion interest. Cognitions are personal perceptions and mental understandings of, in this case, clothing and fashion. Individual differences in cognitive orientations toward fashion influence the timing and content of fashion adoption.

The first cognitive orientation that may affect the timing and content of fashion adoption is the **level of risk perceived** with adopting (buying and wearing) an innovative fashion object. Researchers have categorized perceived risk into five types: social-psychological, economic, physical, performance, and temporal (Cox and Rich 1964; Jacoby and Kaplan 1972). Social-psychological risk involves the chance of social disapproval or humiliation, economic risk involves the fear of loss of money or other resources, physical risk involves fear that the product will cause harm, performance risk is the chance that the product will not perform satisfactorily, and temporal risk involves the loss of time spent in buying, caring for, or fixing the product. Although fashion adoption can include any of these risk classifications, "a good that is subject to fashion may be perceived as having greater economic, social, psychological, and performance risks than goods that are not subject to fashion" (Winakor, Canton, and Wolins 1980, 48). To reduce these uncertainties, the consumer seeks information to identify the best choice, reduces the amount of money at stake by buying a cheaper brand, or postpones the choice until greater certainty is assured. It appears that individuals who perceive less economic, social-psychological and performance risk involved with adopting a new fashion will adopt the fashion earlier than someone who perceives a greater risk involved with the adoption of the fashion (Sproles and King 1973; Schrank and Gilmore 1973). For example, an innovative fashion adopted by consumers immediately after its introduction may be relatively expensive compared to other styles or very different from what others are currently wearing. In other words, the innovative fashion may be perceived as economically and socially risky to the consumer. On the other hand, a fashion adopted later in time, after the price has come down or after the fashion has been adopted (and therefore legitimized) by other consumers may be perceived as less risky to the consumer.

In addition to the perceived risk associated with adopting a new fashion, fashion adoption is also related to the consumer's **fashion involvement.** Fashion involvement incorporates five fashion-related dimensions: (1) fashion awareness, (2) fashion knowledgeability, (3) fashion interest, (4) fashion interpersonal communication, and (5) fashion innovativeness (Tigert, Ring, and King 1976). It has been found that individuals who are highly involved with fashion adopt a new fashion earlier than individuals who are less involved with fashion (Baumgarten 1975; Darden and Reynolds 1974; Polegato and Wall 1980). Thus fashion involvement may serve as an underlying reason for fashion adoption.

Fashion awareness refers to an individual's recognition of fashion objects and their meanings. Positive relationships have been found between fashion awareness and fashion innovativeness (Polegato and Wall 1980). Fashion awareness has also been found to be positively related to views that quality in clothing is more important than price, that shopping for clothes is a pleasurable activity, and with the amount of time devoted to shopping for clothing (Horridge and Richards 1984). In addition, it is assumed that because fashion leaders use fashion media more than others (Polegato and Wall 1980), they would also be more aware of fashion.

There are three levels of awareness:

1. awareness of body-related elements such as skin color and shape of the body,
2. awareness of clothing-related elements including the silhouette, the style details, the color, and the texture of the material, and

3. awareness of the clothing on the body.

Researchers have developed methods to assess consumers' clothing awareness. For example, Rosencranz (1972) used projective data collection techniques including word association tests and a clothing Thematic Apperception Test to measure awareness. Awareness was inferred from the amount of clothing-related themes in individuals' answers to each text. In general, the findings indicated:

1. Students who have studied home economics, arts, humanities, and social sciences are more aware of clothing than are those in engineering or sciences.
2. Women are far more aware of clothing than are men.
3. Younger women are far more aware of clothing and fashion than are older women.
4. Younger men are slightly more aware of clothing than are older men.
5. Among women, clothing awareness increases with higher levels of social class, income, educational level, verbal intelligence, number of organizational memberships, number of magazine subscriptions, and husband's occupation (white collar).
6. Upper class men tend to have higher clothing awareness than do men from other classes.

Using semantic differential scales and stated likelihoods of individuals with certain personalities wearing certain clothing (and vice versa), Miller, Feinberg, Davis, and Rowold (1982) measured and found individual differences in sensitivity to appearances. While this has been related to impression formation (Miller, et al. 1982; Rowold 1984), individual differences in the sensitivity to appearance cues may also be related to fashion awareness.

Fashion knowledgeability is the amount of information obtained and used by consumers in fashion decisions. Fashion selection requires a considerable degree of aesthetic skill in coordinating colors, fabrics, and styling of items for each outfit. Judging quality in fabrics and construction also requires knowledge. Knowledge of fashion is accumulated from personal experience and from reception of informational communications. A large amount of fashion information is transmitted to consumers through fashion magazines, fashion editorials, advertisements in newspapers, and exposure to styles through television and movies. Information on fashions is also received from the consumer's interactions (e.g., observation, conversation) with others.

Interest in fashion may be expressed in terms of the amount of time, energy, money, and personal commitment a consumer applies to the selection and use of clothing fashions. Interest may also be measured by how well consumers keep informed on current fashion trends and keep their wardrobes up-to-date with changing fashions. A series of studies using a measure of this sort showed a relatively consistent pattern of fashion interest across populations (Sproles and King 1973). The studies indicated that approximately 10 percent of the adult female population has the highest level of fashion interest and keeps up with most changes in fashion. Approximately one-third or more of the respondents in the studies indicated a substantial interest in keeping informed about new fashion, though these consumers might not adopt each new trend. For the remainder of women, fashion interest appeared to be at a lower, fashion-follower level, although less than 15 percent of those studied indicated no fashion interest at all. Whereas similar data on males have not been published, it is known that levels of fashion interest here are substantially lower overall.

Thus fashion adoption may be related to an individual's cognitive orientations such as level of perceived risk associated with the fashion and involvement (e.g., awareness, interest, knowledge, interpersonal communication, and innovativeness) with fashion. These orientations will affect the timing (e.g., early or late) and level of fashion adoption by the individual.

Values, Attitudes, and Fashion Adoption

Studies have also found important relationships between an individual's values and attitudes and the wearing of clothing that the individual feels reflects those values and attitudes (Buckley and Roach 1974; Christiansen and Kernaleguen 1971; Kness and Densmore 1976; Levin and Black 1970; Unger and Raymond 1974). To better understand these relationships, we first must distinguish between "values" and "attitudes." The concept of value is broader and more fundamental than the concept of attitude. Values are general standards that are applied across situations of what we believe is important; whereas attitudes are predispositions both positive and negative toward objects in a given situation (Milsap 1986; Rokeach 1973). An individual's attitudes are usually thought to be based upon their set of basic values (Allport 1961).

Theoretically everyone has a basic set of **values** prescribing what he or she believes is a personally or socially important way of behaving. Research indicates that people's general values are reflected in their specific orientations toward clothing fashions (Ryan 1966). For example, those whose values favor aesthetics may be interested in the color and style of fashions; those whose values favor personal prestige and status may prefer fashions that are also viewed as status symbols; those whose values favor economy of resources may prefer purchasing classic fashions; and those whose values favor social acceptance and participation may favor fashions that conform with their peer group.

Attitudes are predispositions to behave in certain ways with respect to a specific object, such as style of fashion, or to a situation, such as use of clothing. One can have many attitudes toward a particular style or brand of clothing, some positive, some negative, some strongly held, and some of slight consequence. The consumer can form attitudes toward colors, fabrics, brand names, stores, quality, fit, and social appropriateness of varied styles of fashion. A combination of these attitudes influences the consumer's preferences for styles or brands, intentions to buy, and the actual purchases made. During the 1970s, several researchers investigated the relationship between social attitudes and the adoption of clothing fashions

Dress often reflects personal values and attitudes.
(Reuters/Bettmann)

that stereotypically communicated those attitudes (Buckley and Roach 1974; Christiansen and Kernaleguen 1971; Kness and Densmore 1976; Levin and Black 1970; Mathes and Kempher 1976). In general these researchers found that individuals with more conservative social attitudes dressed more conservatively (e.g., classic, subdued styles) than those with more liberal social attitudes, and vice versa. However, few relationships were found between liberal sexual attitudes and the wearing of clothing associated with liberal sexual attitudes (Mathes and Kempher 1976).

SOCIAL-COMPARISON APPROACH TO FASHION ADOPTION

In the previous discussion of theoretical approaches to fashion adoption (satisfaction-of-needs approach and psychological approach) it was noted that fashion adoption is a personal choice that is related to individual needs, psychosexual desires, personality traits, attitudes, and values. In addition to these personal orientations, fashion adoption is also affected by social comparison processes. That is, we compare our appearance to others and evaluate these comparisons which, in turn, influence the timing and content of our fashion adoption. This section will discuss social comparison processes as they relate to fashion adoption. First, an overview of social-comparison theory will provide a foundation for the specific approaches discussed. Next, applications of social-comparison theory to the explanation of individuals' fashion adoption are proposed as they relate to self-concept theory and uniqueness theory. A third application, reference group and conformity theory, was discussed in chapter 6.

Social Comparison Theory

In 1954, Leon Festinger published "A Theory of Social Comparison Processes" which outlined why and how humans compare their thoughts and behaviors to other people, and the effect of these comparisons on the individual's own thoughts and behaviors. For almost forty years, this theory has formed the foundation for research in self-concept development, human pursuit of uniqueness, and the influence of reference groups on conformity. Goethals (1986) summarized the basis tenets of social comparison theory as follows:

1. People strive to evaluate their opinions and abilities.
2. When there is no physical reality against which they can assess them,

they compare themselves with other people.

3. It is necessary to compare themselves with others who are similar in order to precisely evaluate opinions and abilities.

4. As a result of the importance of comparative evaluation with similar others, there are pressures toward uniformity in groups.

5. Uniformity can be achieved by changing opinions or performance levels or by ceasing comparison with others and rejecting them from the group. (P. 262)

Social comparison theory can effectively be used to explain fashion adoption. As a form of human behavior, fashion adoption is subject to social-comparison processes as is any other type of human behavior. Individuals strive to evaluate their appearance and behavior towards clothing through comparing this behavior to others. This results in either positive or negative evaluations of their behavior towards clothing. Consequently, as a result of these comparisons, behavior may be maintained or changed, or the comparative group may be changed. The social-comparison processes as they relate to fashion adoption can be highlighted through the examination of conceptual extensions of social comparison theory: self-concept theory and uniqueness theory. Reference group and conformity theory, discussed previously, is also an extension of the social comparison foundation.

Fashion Adoption and Self-Concept

A natural extension of social comparison theory is the development of the self-concept. **Self-concept** is a person's perceptions and perceptual organization of his/her own characteristics, roles, abilities, and appearance (Ryan 1966). One's self-concept is based in part on how one compares to other individuals with regard to traits, opinions, and abilities (Pettigrew 1967). Humans learn and form impressions about themselves by comparing themselves to others (Mead 1934). Cooley (1902) called this the "looking-glass self" or reflected appraisal. In other words, the self-concept grows out of the reactions one receives from parents, friends, teachers, and others.

Self-concept can have a number of dimensions which evolve from social comparisons and evaluations (Walters 1974). The self-concept consists of

- the actual self (how a person perceives him/herself),
- the ideal self (how a person would like to perceive him/herself), and
- the social self (how a person presents him/herself to others).

These selves might be similar, but note the potential differences or conflicts that could exist.

Appearance is an extremely important part of the self-concept. Through personal appearance—dress, cosmetics, fashion expressions, body movements—an individual presents personal identity, attitudes, moods, and value or self-worth (Stone 1962). In addition, individuals receive positive and negative evaluations from others with regard to appearance. Hence, appearance is one of the most prominent ways to display and reinforce a self-concept. A chosen appearance can also represent a particular self-concept.

Consequently, fashion adoption can be related to the individual's self-concept. In consumer research it is argued that the social self is achieved through the purchase and use of products that portray an image that is consistent with (or a compromise between) the consumer's actual and/or ideal self-concept. As Tucker (1957) states

There has long been an implicit concept that consumers can be defined in terms of either the products they acquire or use, or in terms of the meanings products have for them, or their attitudes toward the products. (P. 139)

According to researchers in the area, individuals perceive clothing they own, would like to own, or do not own in terms of the symbolic meaning to themselves and others. Congruence between the symbolic image of a garment and an individual's self-concept will then lead to a positive evaluation of the garment (Jacobi and Walters 1958). Thus the social self is often demonstrated through an individual's purchase and use of clothing fashions that are symbolic of an individual's actual and/or ideal self-concept. Steele (1985) argues that

our appearance is a form of self-presentation, a look that has meaning, involving a compromise between who we are and who we would like to be, our personal self-image and a "self-for-others." (P. 46)

In relating self-concept to fashion adoption Gibbins (1969) and later Gibbins and Gwynn (1975) found that certain clothing items (in this case, women's clothing shown in current fashion magazines was examined) communicate a meaning of fashionability and individuals select clothing which represents an image that is a compromise between their actual and ideal self-concepts. They supported the derivative propositions that fashionable clothing conveys a generalized self-concept, and that the actual self-concept of fashionable people is closer to their ideal self-concepts than the actual self-concepts of unfashionable people.

Fashionable clothing communicates not only "fashionability," but other desirable social traits (Gibbins and Gwynn 1975). Thus people accept fashion objects that they believe express a desired image. If "fashionability" was their desired image, then the fashions adopted would be viewed as communicating "fashionability;" if "professional" was their desired image, then the fashion objects adopted would be viewed as communicating "professionalism." Eventually this meaning will be diluted and will fade, to be replaced by newer, more meaningful, yet temporary, symbols.

Fashion Adoption and Uniqueness

A second extension of social comparison theory used in better understanding fashion adoption is Snyder and Fromkin's (1980) theory of uniqueness. According to this theory, humans strive towards individuality and unique-

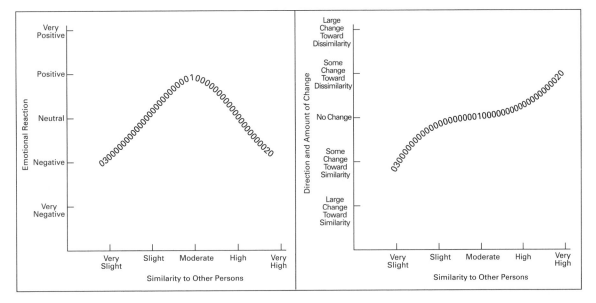

Figure 8.1 Hypothesized Emotional Reactions to Another Person as a Function of Similarity Relative to That Person
SOURCE: Snyder and Fromkin (1980, 35)

Figure 8.2 Hypothesized Direction and Amount of Change as a Function of Similarity Relative to Another Person
SOURCE: Snyder and Fromkin (1980, 37)

ness. In addition, humans also strive toward a certain level of similarity with others. Through social-comparison processes, individuals evaluate their level of uniqueness in relation to others, resulting in both emotional and behavioral reactions (see fig. 8.1 and 8.2). It appears that individuals have the most positive reactions when they perceive themselves as moderately similar to others. The most negative reactions occur when individuals perceive themselves as either dissimilar or very similar to the comparison individual or group. Consequently, change toward similarity occurs when perceived similarity is very low. Change toward dissimilarity (uniqueness) occurs when perceived similarity is very high. Individual differences in the need for uniqueness also contribute to the emotional and behavioral reactions to perceived similarity (Fromkin and Lepshitz 1976; Snyder and Fromkin 1977).

According to Snyder and Fromkin (1980) clothing is a "commodity" that has special value in terms of uniqueness. Because of its visible nature and its link with the self-concept, clothing is one means of presenting uniqueness and conformity to others. Although the existence and maintenance of conformity in fashion behavior is an important underlying factor affecting fashion adoption (as was discussed in detail in chapter 6), we also know the

Opportunity to buy scarce nylon stockings brought this crowd to a department store in 1946. The store had advertised the sales of 26,000 pairs, one pair to a customer.

embarrassment and negative emotions that arise when two people appear at a social event wearing the same clothing. Thus the theory of uniqueness can be used effectively in explaining the dichotomy of individuality and conformity in fashion adoption. In light of this theory, fashion adoption may be a function of the perceived similarity with a comparison individual or group. Perceived high similarity (i.e., wearing the same garment as someone else) would lead to negative emotions and behavioral change toward dissimilarity. Perceived low similarity (i.e., the only person wearing jeans when everyone else is in suits) would also lead to negative emotions, but would lead to behavioral change toward similarity. Perceived moderate similarity (i.e., wearing a similar style, but different clothing than others) would lead to positive emotions and little behavioral change.

Researchers have demonstrated that individuals assign positive traits to clothing perceived as unique or scarce. It appears that the value of clothing is enhanced when people believe that it is unavailable to others. For example, Fromkin, Olson, Dipboye and Barnaby (1971) found that individuals assigned higher prices to fashions (in this case, nylon hosiery was examined) that were perceived as scarce (and therefore unique). Several studies have demonstrated a similar occurrence with perceptions of designer label clothing (Baugh and Davis 1989; Davis 1985). In these studies clothing with designer labels was viewed as higher quality and higher status. Apparently, because a designer label projects an image of uniqueness, it enhances the value of the clothing that carries the label. However, individuals do differ in their need to be unique. Research has shown that compared to others, people who have a higher need to be unique see scarce objects as more desirable (Fromkin, Williams, and Dipboye 1974).

Studies of individuation (Maslach, Stapp, and Santee 1985) and freedom in dress (Lowe and Anspach 1978; Lowe and Buckley 1982) are relevant here as well. In essence, these approaches suggest that there are people who are individualists who wish to publicly differentiate themselves, to express "freedom" in dress, so to speak. The closely related ideas of individuality, uniqueness and freedom in dress offer a simple yet persuasive explanation for such diverse fashion-oriented behavior as innovativeness in choosing new fashion as well as the similarities (but not identicalities) between people when major fashion trends are propagated.

Just as individuals strive toward uniqueness and individuality in appearance, individuals also strive toward similarity with others. In chapter 6, the social processes underlying conformity (similarity) in fashion adoption were discussed. Comparison groups, also known as reference groups, play a major role in influencing conformity in dress. Thus reference group influence and conformity is an extension of social comparison theory. Because we compare ourselves to others, we are aware of how different and of how similar we are to the comparison group. Fashion provides a vehicle to satisfy these conflicting needs.

SUMMARY

This chapter has examined the individual psychology and social psychology of fashion from a variety of fundamental psychological perspectives. We began by stating four basic principles of dress which help us understand, in part, the psychology of fashion adoption: (1) adoption of fashion may be used for personal stimulation, perhaps most important to pursue individualism; (2) fashion adoption provides a vehicle for self-expression, to engage in impression management; (3) Fashion adoption may satisfy the individual's need to seek a social identity; (4) and fashion may establish a means for maintaining or increasing the feeeling of personal security.

Based upon these principles, we identified three contemporary psychological and sociological approaches which help us understand fashion-oriented behavior: the satisfaction of needs approach, the psychological approaches, and the social-comparison approach. The satisfaction-of-needs approach suggests that dress is a functional product that has useful purposes. These begin with basic needs such as protection, modesty, immodesty, and adornment, as suggested in the historical literature. Contemporary literature also suggests the importance of social-psychological functions such as modernism (being contemporary, up-to-date), escape from boredom, symbolic differentiation (prestige, recognition, status), and social affiliation.

The psychological approaches to fashion are many and varied. The psychoanalytic approach focuses on sexual symbolism and sexual attraction, suggesting the important role of changing fashions as a means for communicating sexual desires and seeking sexual attention. Another psychological approach focuses on measuring individual differences and correlating these with acceptance of fashions. It has been found that individuals having different personalities, attitudes, values and other cognitive states vary significantly in acceptance of fashion. In particular, fashion leaders (e.g., innovators, opinion leaders) have unique individual psychologies compared to followers of fashions, as demonstrated in a variety of studies.

The social-comparison approach to fashion is based upon the proposition that individuals strive to evaluate their own behavior and thoughts through comparisons with others. Subsequent behavior is affected by these evaluations. Social-comparison processes result in self-concept development and awareness of our similarities and differences from others. In applying this approach to fashion adoption, we assume that individuals compare their appearance to others and that evaluations of one's own appearance are made based on these comparisons. An individual's self-concept arises from interactions with others. As a form of self-presentation, consumers often adopt fashions that are consistent with their self-concept. Through social-comparison processes, individuals are aware of their similarity to others. Fashion adoption also has the unique quality of satisfying a consumer's need to express individuality as well as the need to conform to others. It may be that the ideas of individuality, uniqueness and conformity are among the most simple yet persuasive psychological explanations of fashion innovativeness and the mass conformity (similarities of dress) we see as fashion trends develop.

DISCUSSION QUESTIONS

1. Write down ten characteristics relating to your (1) personality, attitudes, and values, (2) social roles, and (3) physical appearance that define who

you are. How are each expressed in the fashions you select and wear?

2. What aspects of the clothing you are wearing satisfies the following functions: protection, modesty/immodesty, adornment, modernism, desire to escape boredom, need for social affiliation, need for symbolic differentiation, need to adjust to a changing society. Think of two other examples of fashions that meet each of these needs.

3. Bring in a fashion advertisement that uses sexual symbolism to advertise the fashion. Is a specific "erogenous zone" emphasized in the advertisement? What image is the advertisement communicating? In what way does the fashion conceal and draw attention to the body at the same time?

4. Explain the statement "because complete nudity is anti-erotic, clothing is a primary source for creating sex appeal."

5. Think of a time in which you felt psychologically uncomfortable because of the clothing you were wearing. What was the situation? Why did you feel uncomfortable? Did you receive overt responses from others?

SUGGESTED READINGS

For a historical perspective:

Flugel, John Carl. *The Psychology of Clothes.* London: Hogarth Press, International Psychoanalytic Library, 1930.

Laver, James. *Modesty in Dress.* Boston: Houghton Mifflin Co., 1969.

Stone, Gregory P. "Appearance and the Self." In *Human Behavior and Social Processes,* edited by Arnold M. Rose. Boston: Houghton Mifflin Co., 1962.

More recent work:

Robertson, Thomas S., and James H. Myers. "Personality Correlates of Opinion Leadership and Innovative Buying Behavior." *Journal of Marketing Research* 6 (1969): 164-68.

Steele, Valerie. *Fashion and Eroticism.* New York: Oxford University Press, 1985.

Tigert, Douglas J., Lawrence J. Ring, and Charles W. King. "Fashion Involvement and Buying Behavior." *Advances in Consumer Research* 3 (1976): 46-52.

9

The Symbolic Dimension of Fashion

OBJECTIVES

- To consider fashion symbolism as a form of nonverbal communication.
- To discuss social perception and interpretation of fashion symbols from a social cognition perspective.
- To discuss fashion symbolism as it relates to symbolic interaction theory.
- To review applications of fashion symbolism in impression management and costume design.

FASHION AS A SYMBOL

In its basic form, a **symbol** is an item that serves to represent something else. Humans use symbols, whether they be verbal or nonverbal, as a means of communicating with one another. Our verbal language is based upon our use and shared understanding of symbols—the letters of the alphabet and the words and sentences made up of these letters. Nonverbal symbols can also be used to communicate with one another. For example, we understand that a nod of the head means agreement and a shake of the head means disagreement. In order for symbols to be effective means of communication, they must possess shared meanings for a group of people. The meaning of the symbol may be shared by a large group of individuals, such as the national or international use of a particular language in communication. The meaning of the symbol may be shared by a smaller group of individuals as a means of communication within that group. For example, friends may use their own "sign language" as a means of communicating among themselves.

Fashion objects can be viewed as symbols possessing meaning beyond their tangible characteristics. This meaning of fashion symbols is considered to be the "images, thoughts, sentiments and sensibilities communicated by a new or old fashion and the symbolic means by which this is done" (Davis 1985a, 16). The wearing of fashion symbols conveys to a perceiver the notion of modernity, of being "in style," and of being a "fashionable" individual. In addition, because they are a form of nonverbal communication, fashion objects often symbolize much more than just the "fashion-ability" of the person. Fashion objects may symbolize a person's life-style, personality, or social values. To further our understanding of fashion symbolism, this chapter will examine the extent to which fashion symbols can be considered a language, the characteristics and categories of the symbols, how symbols are connected with and acquire social meaning, the process by which fashion symbols are communicated and interpreted, and applications of fashion symbolism in impression management and costume design.

THE LANGUAGE OF FASHION SYMBOLS

Virtually every fashion object can be considered a fashion "symbol." The study of symbols, known as semiotics, has been used to explain a possible systematic organization of fashion symbolism. Many semioticians contend that fashion symbols can be viewed and studied as a language of artificial symbols that approximate the semiotic concept of a "code" (Barthes 1983; Davis 1985a; Eco 1979; Simon-Miller 1985). Similar to letters of the alphabet, the "code" of fashion is sometimes thought to include the type of fabric, the texture of the material, the color and pattern of the material, the volume and silhouette of the structure, and the occasion for which it is worn. The specific combinations of these components of the fashion code can be used to convey specific social meanings to others. For example, a suit made of dark blue pin-stripe wool fabric would convey a different meaning than a similarly styled suit made of light yellow silk fabric because of the varying color and fabrics of the two suits.

In the study of semiotics, theorists and researchers have attempted to demonstrate that appearance is a visual language with its own distinctive grammar, syntax, and vocabulary (Lurie 1981). For example, Fowles (1974) noted that in a system of fashion language, fabrics and colors were the phonemes, dress items the words, wardrobes the vocabulary, outfits the sentences, and the pattern of putting an outfit together the grammar. Lurie (1981) outlined the "vocabulary of fashion," which included archaic words (e.g., out-of-date fashions), foreign words (e.g., fashions from other cultures), slang (e.g., fads adopted by a small number of people), adjectives and adverbs (e.g., trimmings or accessories that serve as "modifiers" of the fashion object), and lies and disguises (e.g., costumes).

In *The Fashion System*, Roland Barthes (1983) used a semiotic approach to analyze the language used to describe fashion. According to Barthes, "for any particular object (a dress, a tailored suit, a belt) three different structures exist: one technical; another, iconic; the third, verbal" (p. 5). The technical structure is the actual fashion object, the garment itself. The iconic structure is any photograph, picture, or image of the object, and the verbal structure is the written or spoken description of the object. Thus the "language of fashion" is essentially the translation from the technical structure to the verbal structure, the words used to describe actual fashion objects. Fashion acquires its meaning through its "language"; that is, the descriptions of fashion objects in media sources such as fashion magazines, advertisements, or newspaper articles (e.g., "a sweater with a boatneck collar," "a pullover with a closed collar," "a hat with a high crown," p. 63). And the meaning of the technical structure of fashion can best be studied by analyzing these descriptions. Thus, according to Barthes, to understand the meaning of fashion one must understand how the fashion is described.

Although the semiotic approach to the study of fashion symbols can provide us with a useful analogy of equating fashion with language, fashion symbols are unique in several respects that prohibit a direct parallel between "language" and "fashion symbolism" (Davis 1985a; Hoffmann 1984).

1. First, unlike verbal communication, messages transmitted through **fashion symbols are often emotional impressions** or, what Hoffmann (1984) called "illusions." Fashion symbols can communicate impressions or illusions such as physical attractiveness, femininity and masculinity, power and dominance, and self-confidence and assurance. Fashion designers, aware of clothing's ability to represent feelings and ideas, often use fashion symbolism to convey emotional and expressive content in their designs (DeLong 1987). For example, a black leather jacket elicits different emotions than a light pink cashmere sweater. Through aesthetic expression in fashion symbolism, fashion designs can communicate feelings such as excitement, calmness, strength, or delicacy.

2. Second, **messages transmitted through fashion symbols are nonlinguistic.** Receivers of verbal communication usually respond to this communication with additional verbal communication; you may answer a verbal question with a verbal response. On the other hand,

receivers of communication conveyed by fashion symbolism often do respond to this communication through the use of fashion symbols. One may get verbal reactions to fashion symbols in the form of comments such as "How nice you look" or "Is that a new suit?" However, the remainder of the response is nonlinguistic in terms of judgments of and attitudes toward the cultural meaning associated with the symbol.

3. Third, the **code used to transmit fashion symbol messages** does not have the same characteristics as the code used for verbal messages. The code of any language consists of specific units that can be combined based upon rules of syntax. The speaker is both "constrained and empowered by the code" (McCracken 1988, 63). Although the speaker is constrained by the use of the established language code (such as letters of the alphabet) in order to convey meaning, the speaker also has the power to create new meanings by combining the codes in new ways. One has the ability to create new words, sentences, and paragraphs by combining letters and words in ways that had not been done before. Fashion symbols, however, do not allow the speaker this power.

In fact, according to Grant McCracken (1988, 64), when fashion symbolism "as a code is most like language, it is least successful as a means of communication." In other words, the newest and most innovative fashions may often elicit the most varied meanings. To better understand fashion symbols as language codes, McCracken examined the various categories of interpretation individuals use when they draw meaning from fashion symbols. He examined individuals' responses to a series of slides which pictured a variety of contemporary fashions. He discovered that:

1. The first level of interpretation was a social salience category in which individuals interpreted the symbols in a general stereotypic manner. Single-word descriptions such as "housewife," "hippie," "wealthy" were common.
2. In the next level, when cues were not easily associated with a stereotypic image, individuals had difficulty interpreting the cues and often relied on the most salient feature from which they drew meaning (e.g., most evident color or style detail).
3. In the third level of interpretation, cues were presented in new and unique ways. Because of this, the cues were perceived as ambiguous in meaning and difficult to interpret.

Thus, it appears to be impossible to use fashion symbols as a code in creating new meanings. The perceiver examines a fashion statement "not for

a new message, but for an old one fixed by convention" (McCracken 1988, 66). Because of this, McCracken inferred that fashion symbols would be most effective in communicating culturally defined categories, principles and processes (e.g., age, sex, social norms) that have emerged through human interaction. These levels of interpretation will be discussed in greater detail later in the chapter. We will see in the next section that fashion symbols are best studied not as a parallel to language but as a form of nonverbal communication whose meanings emerge and change over time and among individuals.

FASHION SYMBOLS AS NONVERBAL COMMUNICATION

The study of our fashion-related appearances can best be accomplished by analyzing them as a form of nonverbal communication. Nonverbal communication generally refers to human communication that transcends the spoken or written word (Knapp 1978). According to scholars in the area

Fashion symbolism often elicits stereotypical responses, e.g., wealthy.
(WWD, Fairchild Publications)*

(Ruesch and Kees 1956), nonverbal communication includes sign language (e.g., gestures and facial expressions), action language (e.g., touching behavior), as well as object language (e.g., the human body and the clothes that cover it). In addition to symbolizing the idea of fashion, modernity, and innovativeness, fashion as object language can communicate a number of other aspects of the individual, society, and environment. Clothing, as the primary component of our fashion-related appearance, is used universally as a form of nonverbal communication. In virtually every society clothing is and has been used to communicate personal traits as well as social norms. As Alison Lurie (1981) explains in her book, *The Language of Clothes*:

> *Long before I am near enough to talk to you on the street, in a meeting, or at a party, you announce your sex, age and class to me through what you are wearing—and very possibly give me important information (or misinformation) as to your occupation, origin, personality, opinions, tastes, sexual desires and current mood. I may not be able to put what I*

observe into words, but I register the information unconsciously; and you simultaneously do the same for me. By the time we meet and converse we have already spoken to each other in an older and more universal tongue. (P. 3)

Drawing from research in the areas of social cognition and symbolic interaction (Davis 1985a; Kaiser 1990; Lennon and Davis 1989a, 1989b), there appear to be general characteristics of fashion symbols as a form of nonverbal communication. First, **fashion symbols are context dependent.** In other words, fashion symbols often gain meaning from the social context of which they are a part. For example, one would interpret a male dressed in a tuxedo seen in the context of a wedding differently than if the male in a tuxedo was seen in the context of an informal backyard barbecue.

We tend to have expectations of people's appearance for social contexts based upon social norms. These expectations consequently affect the meaning we attribute to appearance symbols. Damhorst (1984-1985) found that perceptions of males and females dressed in formal and informal attire were affected by the office context in which they were perceived. Rees, Williams, and Giles (1974) found that how appropriate students were perceived when wearing ties varied between two situations: job interview and college campus. Students on campus were rated more intelligent when not wearing ties and students on a job interview were rated as more intelligent when wearing ties. Apparently, "dress worn by a person takes on meaning within the context in which the interaction takes place" (Damhorst 1984-1985, 40).

Second, **fashion symbols are a visual medium.** Fashion symbols project themselves by their very presence. This visibility permits group statements through uniform display of fashion symbols by members of a group. We perceive individuals dressed in uniforms as a unified group. Indeed, uniforms are often used by organizations to portray a professional or unified image to the public. The visibility of fashion symbols also prevents private communication. It is often impossible to control to whom we are communicating through our appearance. Also, because of the visibility of the symbols, to change the meaning of the message we must either alter, remove, or conceal the fashion object, or change the social context in which the symbol is being perceived. For example, it is common for men or women in business suits to loosen their ties or remove their jackets after work to communicate a less formal situation.

Third, there is a **high degree of variability of interpretation** of fashion symbols. The meaning attributed to many fashion symbols is often ambiguous since not all fashion objects have an obvious communication function,

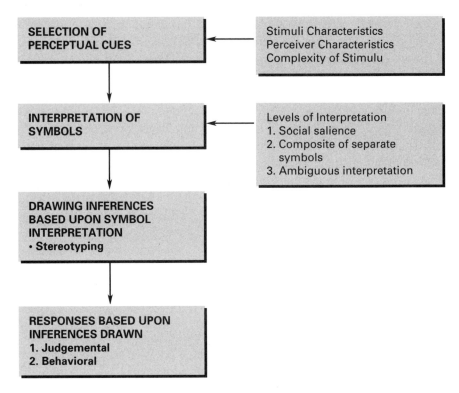

Figure 9.1 Process of Perceiving and Interpreting Fashion Symbols

SELECTION OF PERCEPTUAL CUES ← Stimuli Characteristics / Perceiver Characteristics / Complexity of Stimulu

INTERPRETATION OF SYMBOLS ← Levels of Interpretation / 1. Social salience / 2. Composite of separate symbols / 3. Ambiguous interpretation

DRAWING INFERENCES BASED UPON SYMBOL INTERPRETATION
• Stereotyping

RESPONSES BASED UPON INFERENCES DRAWN
1. Judgemental
2. Behavioral

or the meaning of the symbol may be unclear. In addition, the same fashion symbols may connote different meanings to different people. Although there may be some general consensus regarding the meaning attributed to certain fashion symbols (e.g., wedding gown, business suit), even for these stereotypic symbols, individuals may interpret the meanings slightly differently. For example, Davis (1990) found that when interpreting the meaning of a man dressed in western attire and riding a horse, virtually all respondents focused on some aspect of cowboys or the rural west. However, the range of responses varied from personal characteristics (e.g., rugged, macho) to personal connotations (e.g., my trip to Montana last summer) to extended inferences (e.g., "Marlboro Man"). The important idea is that the connotations still exist and even the varying interpretations are meaningful.

THE PROCESS OF PERCEIVING AND INTERPRETING APPEARANCE SYMBOLS

Social psychologists have investigated how one perceives and interprets appearance symbols from a social-cognition perspective. With its basis in

cognitive psychology, social cognition deals with the perceptual processes used in our perceptions and interpretations of any social object or event (Fiske and Taylor 1984). According to this perspective, fashion symbols, due to their visible nature, impact this social perception process and the meanings given to the appearance of others.

By virtue of their uniform clothing, we tend to group these individuals together in our perception of them.
(Costa Manos/Magnum Photos, Inc.)

To better understand fashion symbols as a form of nonverbal communication, it is important to consider these underlying processes by which an individual perceives and forms impressions of others. Lively and Bromley (1973) outlined a four-stage process that people go through as they perceive others and make judgments about them: (1) selection of perceptual cues/symbols, (2) interpretation of the symbols, (3) drawing inferences about the person based upon the symbol interpretation, and (4) responding to the person based upon the inferences drawn (see fig. 9.1). Often as we are perceiving and interpreting fashion symbols and forming impressions of others based upon these interpretations, we do not even realize that we are going through this process. We may go through it unconsciously or go through several of the stages almost simultaneously. Let's consider each stage separately.

Perceiving Fashion Symbols

The first stage of the process is the **selection of cues or symbols.** This selection process (how and what fashion symbols are selected) varies among individuals, which in turn affects the resulting impression formed. For example, people differ in their awareness of fashion symbols and their ability to accurately interpret fashion symbols. Research shows that people do indeed vary in their sensitivity to appearance cues in impression formation (Miller, Feinberg, Davis, and Rowold 1982; Rowold 1984). Littrell and Berger (1985-1986) investigated school counselors' and law enforcement officers' perceptions of male adolescents who were either well-groomed or poorly groomed. They found that law enforcement officers noted more appearance cues and based their perceptions on more specific appearance cues than did school counselors. In this case, occupational background affected individuals' ability in assessing appearance symbols.

The selection of cues is also dependent upon the complexity of what's being perceived. Our understanding of cue selection in our perceptions has its roots in Gestalt psychology (Koffka 1935; Kohler 1929). According to Gestalt doctrines, we tend to organize our perceptions of others by means of grouping similar and dissimilar cues; and that the perception of the total has greater meaning to us than perceptions of individual cues. We tend to group similar and dissimilar clothing items together in our perceptions. Buckley (1984-1985) found that for women's clothing in general, individuals tended to group varying styles into three basic categories: special occasion, bifurcated (i.e., divided into two branches, such as pants, trousers, shorts), and skirt or dress based upon grouped similarities and differences.

When perceiving a person wearing a fashion ensemble, we would tend to notice (and give meaning to) the outfit as a whole rather than focusing on separate pieces. However, if cues were seen as dissimilar, such as unfashionable shoes being worn with a fashion suit, we would also notice the dissimilarity. In the study conducted by McCracken (1988), perceivers had difficulty interpreting separate components of the outfit when the components did not appear to "go together" or had inconsistent symbolic meaning. In an effort to make sense of the discrepancies and give meaning to the appearance, respondents tended to "explain away" the inconsistencies or interpret the most salient component. Indeed, Lennon and Miller (1984-1985) studied the influence of cues when they were systematically added to the fashion ensemble worn by a target person. In this study, fashion symbols conveying social (e.g., designer jeans, boots) and intellectual (e.g., glasses, blazer) traits were examined. They found that the systematic

We strive to reconcile inconsistent appearance cues by explaining them away. Sneakers worn with a business suit are perceived as functional shoes for walking.
(*WWD*, Fairchild Publications)

addition of similar cues (conveying either social or intellectual traits) made little impact on the overall impression. The addition of dissimilar cues, however, influenced the overall impression. Again, it is apparent that when individuals are faced with fashion symbols to which they attribute inconsistent meanings they strive to reconcile the inconsistencies by revising their interpretations of the cues.

This same process holds true for our perceptions of groups of individuals. When we see a group of people dressed similarly, we tend to notice the similarity among them rather than other less obvious characteristics. On the other hand, when we notice one person dressed differently among the group, that difference stands out and we notice it.

Giving Meaning to Fashion Symbols

The second stage of the process is that we **interpret the symbols and give meaning to them.** Where do the meanings associated with fashion symbols come from? Why does one specific fashion object convey the meaning of "fashionable" and another may convey the meaning of "unfashionable"? As we noted previously, fashion symbols convey much more than "image" and "fashionability." Where do the other meanings that fashion symbols communicate come from? There are several perspectives that help us to explain how fashion symbols acquire social meaning. "Symbol production" is often attributed to designers, manufacturers, retailers, trade media and mass media who describe and promote the fashion object (Hirschman 1980; McCracken 1988). However, socially visible consumers also take an active role in the production of the symbolic meaning of fashion goods.

The Law of Association   Much of the symbolic meaning associated with fashion can be attributed to the law of association; which posits that if people see two things paired together repeatedly, then they will come to believe that this pairing is always true. McCracken (1988) noted that fashion advertising and dimensions of the fashion process serve as means by which social/cultural meaning is infused in the object through the law of association. In fashion advertising we see specific fashions paired with some image (that has cultural meaning): young, attractive, active males modeling denim jeans; athletes modeling underwear or sweats; or wealthy businessmen and -women modeling designer jewelry are just a few examples. Because of this association, the fashion acquires the cultural meaning with which it has been associated. In fact, "there are, in our society, layers of fashion, some of which have associations with the past; some have associations with the present (or with the future)" (Polhemus 1973, 74).

Dimensions of the fashion process work in much the same way. Because fashion opinion leaders are associated with "fashionable" clothing and life-styles, their social visibility allows them to transfer these same meanings to the objects they own and wear. Similarly we associate "fashionable" merchandise with stores that are considered high fashion. When we perceive new merchandise in these stores, we automatically categorize it as "fashionable" simply because of the store in which its seen. Advertisements, articles, and editorials in fashion magazines also serve as a vehicle for the transfer of meaning from culture to the fashion object. If we see or read about individuals with a certain life-style wearing specific fashions, then we tend to associate the life-style with the fashion. For example, in the 1960s, and again in the 1980s, fashions worn by surfers became associated with their unique active lifestyle, and subsequently were adopted by those outside the surfing community. For years fashion has been promoted in the media with young, thin models and, therefore, has been associated with youth and thinness. It is no surprise then that Lennon (1988) found younger models were seen as more attractive than older models, and thinner models were seen as more attractive than heavier models. Similarly, because fashion can be used as a group statement, if we see a certain group wearing specific fashions we tend to associate the fashion with the group, and will assign group membership to someone dressed similarly.

Levels of Interpretation   As mentioned earlier in the chapter, results of the study conducted by McCracken (1988) suggests that there are levels of interpretation of fashion symbols. The first level of interpretation is social salience of the symbol, or the first aspects noticed and interpreted about a person. Davis (1990) conducted a study that investigated what people notice first about others. In this study, individuals were asked to write down the first word or image that came to their minds when perceiving individuals shown in five slides. Each slide depicted a person within a social context (e.g., woman wearing a robe and curlers standing in a kitchen, man in western clothing riding a horse). Content analysis of the words and statements indicated that initial impressions fall into one of five categories:

1. personal and social roles (e.g., housewife, cowboy),
2. personal characteristics (e.g., rugged, happy),
3. extended inferences (e.g., showing "Marlboro Man" as the cowboy slide),
4. context (e.g., the west, kitchen), and
5. appearance characteristics (e.g., ugly robe, leather chaps).

It appears that in this initial level of interpretation, impressions of others are often based upon salient stereotypic images.

In the second level of interpretation, the combination of symbols did not convey to the perceiver a general stereotypic image and so perceivers attempted to **draw meaning from the separate symbols.** There was particular difficulty in interpreting the separate symbols if these symbols did not appear to "go together" in the perceiver's mind (for example, if a man wearing a conservative business suit was also wearing sandals). In these situations, the perceiver either tried to reconcile what they perceived as contradictory messages or reverted back to the most salient stereotypic descriptor. In their investigation of this second level of interpretation, Gibbons and Coney (1981) examined whether the interpretation of a total ensemble varied directly with the dimensions of the ensemble components. Subjects interpreted pictures of females dressed in clothing that varied according to three factors: skirt width, skirt length, and type of top worn. When interpreting the combination of the appearance symbols, dimensions of the skirt did not interact with each other or with top variations. Impressions of combinations of the dimensions were determined by one or more of the individual components. Thus it appears that at this second level of interpretations, the perceiver strives toward simple and understandable meanings by focusing on certain salient symbols.

The third level of interpretation occurs when the **fashion symbols are combined in new and unique ways.** Innovative, avant-garde street fashions may be interpreted at this level. Under these conditions McCracken (1988) found the perceiver to have the greatest amount of difficulty interpreting the meaning of the symbols. At this level the perceiver was often unable to interpret the novel combination of symbols. Thus, it appears that fashion symbols are best at communicating personal and social aspects that have shared stereotypic cultural meanings associated with them. Gibbins and Coney (1981) noted that complex meanings of fashion symbols may "only occur when and if particular outfits become so familiar as to acquire idiosyncratic meanings" (p. 720).

Variation in the Interpretation of Fashion Symbols   As noted earlier, although some fashion symbols elicit stereotypic impressions, there is still a great deal of variation in the meanings attributed to fashion symbols. In fact, according to Hoffmann (1984, 7), "it is very rare that wearing apparel carries messages that permit unequivocal interpretation (the exceptions are national costume and uniforms)." Davis (1990) found that despite general consensus regarding the "theme" of initial impressions of others, individuals varied as to the specific interpretation. For example, the picture of the woman dressed in a robe and curlers standing in a kitchen elicited responses focusing on her role (e.g., housewife, maid), personality (e.g., tired), physical appearance (e.g., ugly robe), context (e.g., kitchen) and extended inferences (e.g., my aunt Mildred). Individuals apparently have their own unique "framework of interpretation" (Noesjirwan and Crawford 1982) that is used in interpreting fashion symbols. An individual's framework of interpretation consists of the cultural and social norms and values that he/she has personally adopted.

The development of this framework of interpretation is based upon the fact that we acquire our norms and values through human interaction. This premise forms the basis of the area of sociology known as **symbolic interaction.** The symbolic interactionist approach contends that individuals respond toward objects on the basis of the meanings that these objects hold for them and the meanings are derived through social interaction (Blumer 1969; Mead 1934). According to sociologist Nathan Joseph (1986)

Dustin Hoffman, as Tootsie, exemplifies the use of appearance to change perceptions of gender.
(The KOBAL Collection)

Clothing is very much a social artifact—a form of communication— which can best be understood by sociological concepts. My premise is that all signs derive meaning from their social contexts and may serve some function for individuals, groups or institutions. (P. 1)

Thus through our social interaction, we give meaning to fashion symbols based upon how we respond to them within the social context (Kaiser 1983-1984; 1990, chap. 2). Because people come into a situation with unique experiences, interpretation of objects varies among them. For example, based upon individuals' differing exposure to high fashion, they may interpret the meaning of a fashion differently. Some individuals, who may have seen the fashion advertised or exhibited in fashion magazines or displayed in high fashion stores and have therefore associated the object with high fashion, will perceive it as such. Others, who may never have seen the object before, may view it as "weird" or even "old-fashioned."

The Meaning of Fashion Symbols   What meanings do we associate with fashion symbols? Research has demonstrated that both personal and social variables are communicated by appearance cues (Kaiser 1990, chap. 13). People use fashion symbols (and perceivers interpret fashion symbols) to convey personal variables such as

◆ **Gender** fashion symbols associated with or typically worn by males (e.g., facial hair) or females (e.g., dresses, high heels)
◆ **Age** fashion symbols associated with youth versus adult roles
◆ **Occupation** fashion symbols associated with the type and status of occupations including uniforms and dress codes
◆ **Marital Status** fashion symbols such as wedding bands, which are associated with being married or single
◆ **Religion** symbolic items associated with a particular organized religion (e.g., cross, Star of David)
◆ **Economic Status** status symbols associated with social value or class standing (e.g., gemstones, expensive fabrics)
◆ **Self-esteem** fashions that may symbolize how one feels about him/herself
◆ **Attitudes and Values** fashions that symbolize social, political, or economic attitudes and values.

For each of these it is easy to think of examples of fashion-related appearance symbols that communicate these traits. In his study of what clothing communicates, Hoffman (1984) identified ten messages communicated by appearance-related symbols (see table 9.1).

Fashion symbols are also used to define social characteristics (Kaiser 1985, chap. 7) such as

◆ how formal the situation is: fashions that symbolize casualness (e.g., jeans, sweats) versus formality (e.g., tuxedo);
◆ the roles and identities of interacting individuals: fashion symbols associated with specific social or occupational roles;
◆ how important the situation is to that person: fashions that convey the idea the wearer took time and effort because the situation was important to him/her; and
◆ if it is possible for the individual to engage in physical activity: fashions that provide for inactivity or restrict movement (e.g., high heels) versus

TABLE 9.1 MESSAGES COMMUNICATED BY APPEARANCE-RELATED SYMBOLS

Messages	Communicated By
Manliness	Trousers, heavy materials
Femininity	Skirts, delicate materials
Sexual Provocation	Emphasis of secondary sexual characteristics
Naïveté	Drawing attention away from or covering sexual characteristics, small patterns, playful shapes and styles
Dominance	Stiff fabric, fur, leather, high hats or collars, dark colors, metal, freedom of movement
Submission	Soft materials, pale colors, lace, frills, impairment of movement, swinging clothes
Social Power	Expensive materials, classical lines, designer clothing, demonstrative use of clothing, dress privileges
Social Weakness	Cheap materials, ill-fitting clothes, second-hand clothes, out-of-date clothing
Autonomy	Casual fit, unironed clothing, rolled-up sleeves
Fitting In	Impeccable fit, creases, starched fabric, stiff collars

SOURCE: Hoffman (1984)

fashions that provide for activity or enhance movement (e.g., athletic shoes).

Of these social aspects communicated by fashion symbols, the most common aspect conveyed is social role. For example, in her investigation of the social salience of fashion symbols Davis (1990) discovered that the slide that elicited the most consistent responses was of a woman dressed in a suit standing in an office. For this slide, 34% of the responses were about her social role (e.g., business woman, executive), and an additional 22% of the responses were about appearance aspects related to her role (e.g., professional dress).

Because new fashions are associated with varying cultural meanings, the specific fashion items that are used to symbolize these personal and social aspects change over time and among different groups of people. What is considered fashionable by individuals at any time and place apparently communicates characteristics desired by the individuals within that social context (Gibbins and Gwynn 1975). Gibbins and Gwynn (1975) related the meanings attributed to fashions to the self-images of individuals who selected the fashions. They found that fashionable clothes conveyed different meanings than did unfashionable clothes, in that "fashionable clothes reflect the consensus of ideal self-images in the images they cast of the wearers" (p. 2). The consensus of ideal self-images are the social characteristics desired by the wearers. For example,

> if "rebellious" is seen as a desirable characteristic and short skirts are seen at the time to express this, this style will be adopted, but as it becomes widely accepted it will become "ordinary" and cease to convey the original "rebellious" meaning (Gibbins and Gwynn 1975, 2).

It appears that as fashions move through their life cycles, the meanings attributed to them change. At its introduction stage, a fashion conveys the characteristics desired by fashion innovators. However, as the fashion becomes generally adopted, its message changes and it no longer conveys characteristics desired by fashion innovators. In fact, it may now convey characteristics desired by fashion followers. Thus when a fashion no longer reflects the consensus of ideal self-images of a group of individuals, then the fashion is no longer considered fashionable at that time by that particular group. In this manner, fashions can be said to have a **symbolic life cycle,** representing the changing symbolic meanings associated with the fashion.

Drawing Inferences from Symbols

The third stage in the person-perception process is drawing inferences about the person based upon the meanings attributed to the fashion symbols. We often categorize people and draw inferences about them in terms of stereotypic characteristics in order to simplify the perceptual stimuli. In **stereotyping,** individuals are grouped according to some visual trait (often the trait that is most salient) and thereby presumed also to possess similar personality or behavioral characteristics. Appearance-related stereotypes are common and include stereotypes associated with perceived age, hair color, perceived social status, race or ethnic identity, and sex. We extend the inferences made about a person beyond the direct meaning associated with the symbol itself. For example, we may assume that all individuals wearing status symbols are wealthy and drive expensive cars; or that individuals wearing unfashionable clothing are "nerds." Thus we extend our inferences about the person beyond the immediate interpretation of the fashion symbols perceived.

Damhorst (1990) conducted a qualitative meta-analysis of person-perception literature to discover common themes that are inferred about individuals based upon their clothing. She developed a content-category system to organize the person-perception literature and to use as a taxonomy of inferences made about others.

1. The first category was **evaluation** which included descriptors related to the positive/negative components of the person's character (e.g., trustworthy-untrustworthy, sloppy-neat), sociability (e.g., cool-warm, pleasant-unpleasant), or mood (e.g., happy-sad, lighthearted-somber).
2. The second category was **potency.** These were assessments of power (e.g., aggressive-passive, delicate-rugged), competence (e.g., reliable-unreliable, successful-unsuccessful), and intelligence (e.g., shallow-deep, theoretical-untheoretical) of the person.
3. The third category was **dynamism** which related to perceptions of the person's physical and mental activity (e.g., fast-slow, dynamic-static), control (e.g., relaxed-tense, natural-unnatural), and stimulation (e.g., usual-unusual, thrilling-soothing).
4. The fourth category was **quality of thought** which included inferences about the flexibility (e.g., open-minded—closed-minded, conservative-liberal), objectivity (e.g., idealistic-realistic, pessimistic-optimistic), and tangibility (e.g., clear-vague, direct-indirect) of the person.

Judgments and Behavioral Response

Based upon the meanings and extended inferences we give to the cues, we **respond or behave** toward the person in a certain manner. This behavioral response is the fourth stage of the person-perception process. It is the response to the person that is often the outcome of our perception and interpretation of the fashion symbols. Research has demonstrated that if we interpret the clothing of an individual as meaning they have similar values and attitudes as ourselves, we are more likely to respond to them in a favorable manner. This is based upon the notion that we are attracted to those whom we perceive as similar to ourselves because the perceived similarity reinforces or confirms our own attitudes or behavior (Byrne 1971). Experimental investigations in this area have manipulated "perceived similarity" by having stimulus persons vary their clothing/fashion cues and then measuring the effect of these clothing variations on other's compliance or helping behavior toward the stimulus persons. In general, this research, conducted primarily in the 1970s, found that conventionally dressed middle-class adults were less likely to comply with a request, such as donating to a charity, giving change for a dime, signing a petition, or giving directions to someone whose appearance was perceived as "sloppy" or resembled a "hippie" stereotype than to someone with conventional or "straight" appearance (Bryant 1975; Chaiken, Derlega, Yoder, and Phillips 1974; Darley and Cooper 1972; Emswiller, Deaux, and Willits 1971; Hensley 1981; Kleinke 1977; Lambert 1972; Samuel 1972; Schiavo, Sherlock, and Wickland 1974).

The interpretation of an individual's clothing symbols as meaning weakness and dependency has been found to affect their ability to obtain assistance or help. Harris and Bays (1973) found that women wearing "feminine" attire (i.e., ruffled blouse, high heels, and curly hair) as compared to "masculine" attire (i.e., man's shirt, jeans, tennis shoes, and straight hair) were more likely to be helped, particularly by men and particularly if the woman made what was considered a feminine request for help ("My shopping cart is stuck. Can you help me?"). However, feminine attire was not more effective than masculine attire when the request was of a more neutral nature ("Do you have change for a dime?"). Similarly, Miller and Rowold (1980) found that sexual meanings attributed to a female's clothing affected the type of help she received. When asking directions to a large store, the female received more detailed directions from men when wearing clothing interpreted by males to mean sensuousness and sexuality (i.e., tube top) than when wearing either a "feminine" blouse or a tailored blouse. Thus it appears that men's perceptions of a woman's femininity affects their responses to her.

The perceived fashionability of appearance symbols has been found to affect interpersonal distance in social interaction. Workman (1987) investigated how close someone was willing to stand next to a stranger dressed in either fashionable or out-of-date clothing. She discovered that individuals were willing to stand closer to strangers dressed in fashionable clothing than to strangers dressed in out-of-date clothing. Apparently, people interpret out-of-date clothing in a negative manner, which affects interpersonal distance.

The person-perception process constitutes the basis for the impressions one forms of others. Individuals select, interpret, and draw inferences from fashion symbols worn by the target person which subsequently affect their judgement and behavioral responses toward the person. Appearance symbols are most important in first-impression situations when other information is not available about the person. Once other information is available (e.g., we talk with the person, the person is perceived over time) then appearance cues are less important to the impression-formation process.

APPLICATIONS OF FASHION SYMBOLISM

We have discussed the theoretical ideas and concepts surrounding the analysis of fashion symbolism. However, fashion symbolism can be studied from an applied perspective as well. Two direct applications of fashion symbolism will be discussed: 1) the use of fashion symbols in symbolic consumption and impression management and 2) the use of fashion symbolism in costume design.

Symbolic Consumption and Impression Management

The symbolic meaning associated with fashion symbols may affect its adoption and use. The study of symbolic consumer behavior is based upon the idea that "products may serve as symbols, and hence may be evaluated, purchased and consumed based upon their symbolic content" (Hirschman 1980, 4). In fact, with fashion-oriented goods, the symbolic meaning may be the most important evaluative criterion used in a consumer's decision-making process. Consumers are often motivated to purchase products because the products are perceived to communicate a certain image, social role or status. It may be that certain fashion objects are selected because the person views the products as being symbolic of "who they are" or "who they would like to be." Gibbins and Gwynn (1975) noted that "any individual is hypothesized to choose clothing which is a compromise between the message that says how she would like to be and how she feels she really is" (p. 2).

Social roles are also associated with specific products. Because of this, the behavioral patterns associated with the role may be facilitated by the wearing of the specific fashion symbols associated with the role. Thus individuals in a new social role may adopt the symbols associated with the role as a way of demonstrating to others (and possibly themselves) the accuracy of their role behavior. In other words, people often adopt and wear the costumes that help them play the various roles in their lives. Solomon and Douglas (1987) investigated whether confidence and experience in a social role, attitudes toward symbolic consumption, and the type of information sources consulted would affect the symbolic interpretation of fashion symbols associated with the role of female executive. They found that attitudes toward symbolic product consumption, more than role-related factors, affected the diversity of product symbolism associated with the executive role for women. In their study of female bicyclists' interest and use of bicycling apparel, Casselman and Damhorst (1990) found that compared to less involved bicyclists, highly involved bicyclists were more concerned with expressing their competence in cycling through the bicycling apparel. Thus their adoption of specific role symbols was related to their involvement with the social role.

The notion of symbolic consumption forms the basis for an application of fashion symbolism: **impression management.** As previously discussed, the impressions formed through person perception processes affect subsequent interpersonal behavior. Because of this well-known fact, individuals can manage their appearance and verbal cues in order to convey an image that will elicit a certain impression in perceivers' minds and consequently affect the perceivers' behavioral responses. All people control, to some extent, their self-presentation or how they appear to themselves and to others. A person may intentionally select and wear certain fashion symbols for a first date or for a job interview or may practice a speech so that it sounds relaxed and professional. This is done so that others form a certainimpression and react in the desired way. The study of impression management focuses on the premise that people take an active role in managing the impressions that others form of them (Schlenker 1980; Tedeschi 1981). The use of fashion-related appearance symbols is only one means by which impression management is carried out (the others include verbal self-presentations, nonverbal expressive behavior, and intentional behaviors). However, in most social situations, the use of appearance symbols is an imperative component of impression management.

We often think that the only reason a person manages impressions is to "make a good impression." However, there are several reasons why people may use appearance symbols in their image management strategies. One of the most common reasons to use fashion symbolism in impression management strategies is to establish power and influence others. Through the use of power-related status symbols a person can communicate power-oriented qualities such as expertise, credibility, attractiveness, prestige, and status. Another reason for using fashion symbolism in impression management may be to define the social situation and identify respective norms associated with social roles. For example, specific fashion symbols in the form of uniforms and dress codes are often required for employees in service industries (i.e., restaurants, hotels, retail stores) so that customers can easily identify who the employee is. By controlling the visual presentation

Wearing a business suit is one way by which impression management is carried out.

(*WWD*, Fairchild Publications)

of the employee, the desired impression of the company can be elicited. Ceremonial dress (e.g., graduation gown, wedding dress) is often used to help define the situation and individuals' roles within the situation. A third reason for employing fashion symbolism in impression management strategies may be to influence others' behavioral responses in order to enhance or maintain one's self-esteem. Often we will direct fashion-related appearance cues toward increasing perceived social attractiveness. By doing so, we often receive positive feedback (compliments, social approval) from others which, in turn, enhances self-esteem. We may also utilize impression management strategies in order to appear similar to others and influence these people's liking for us and subsequently influence their behavior toward us.

Costumes are used to communicate traits of the character (James Dean, 1955)

(The KOBAL Collection)

Costume Design and Fashion Symbolism

Costume designers have realized the importance of fashion symbolism in characterization and have constructed identities visually through the use of costumes. Manner of dress and physical appearance have been used effectively to characterize people in plays, films, and television. Costume design must take fashion symbols and make them meaningful to an audience. According to costume designers Barbara and Cletus Anderson (1984), the "primary function of the costume is to enhance the characterization of a role" (p. 3). Fashion symbols most often used in costume design include those that communicate sex of the character, age of the character, occupation of the character, social status of the character, the geographic area where the story is taking place, the season of the year, the time of day, a particular activity in which the character may be engaging, the historic period of the story, and personal or psychological traits of the character. It is the philosophy of costume designers that the "costume should give as much meaning to the character as possible" (Anderson and Anderson 1984, 40) without symbolizing the role. In such a manner, the fashions on stage parallels and provide similar meanings as do the fashions worn in real life.

SUMMARY

Fashions can be considered symbols that convey meaning beyond their tangible characteristics. To some extent fashion symbols can be viewed as a "language of fashion" with nouns, verbs, modifiers, slang, foreign words, and archaic words. Unlike verbal language, however, the messages transmitted through fashion are often emotional impressions and typically are not responded to with similar (in this case fashion) symbols. It is also difficult, if not impossible, to create new meanings by combining fashion symbols in new and unique ways. In fact, fashion symbols become more ambiguous the farther they get from stereotypic images.

In virtually every society, clothing, as the main component of fashion-related appearance, has been used as a means of communicating personal and social characteristics. Fashion symbols, as a form of nonverbal communication, are context-dependent in that their meanings are dependent on the social situation in which they are perceived. Fashion symbols are also a visual medium that often are interpreted in many ways. Individuals go through four stages in using fashion symbols as a form of nonverbal communication. The first stage involves how and what fashion symbols are selected for interpretation. From a Gestalt perspective, perceivers apparently group similar and dissimilar fashion cues in the selection process.

The second stage involves how we interpret and give meaning to the fashion symbols. Fashions often acquire their meaning from that with which they are associated, whether it be a time period, an individual or group of individuals, a store, advertisement appeals, or any other aspect of the society. Interpretation of fashion symbols occurs at three levels, based upon the perceived ambiguity of the symbols. The first level is the social salience of the symbols, or what we notice first about the fashion. At this level, interpretations are consistent with stereotypic images. Beyond this, perceivers strive to form an overall impression, drawing meaning from separate symbols. At the third level, when the symbols are new to the perceiver, it may be impossible for the perceiver to interpret the symbols. It appears that individuals interpret fashion symbols based upon their own frame of reference, which consists of the cultural and social norms and values they have adopted. The fact that individuals' frameworks of interpretation vary contributes to the wide variety of interpretations given to fashion symbols.

Fashions communicate both personal characteristics (e.g., age, sex, occupation, marital status, religion, economic status, self-esteem, attitudes, and values) and social characteristics (e.g., formality of a situation, social roles, importance of the situation, and evidence of physical activity). The specific fashions that communicate these various cultural meanings change over time and among different groups of people. It can be said that fashions have a symbolic life cycle that represents the changing meanings attributed to them.

The last two stages of using fashion symbols as a form of nonverbal communication involve our judgments of and responses toward the wearer of the fashion. Based upon our interpretations of the symbols, we often infer characteristics about the wearer of the fashion and may possibly respond to the wearer in a certain manner based upon these inferences.

Because of the symbolic nature of fashion, individuals may purchase fashions because of their communicative qualities. Symbolic consumption, as this practice is known, forms the basis for impression management, the active management of self-presentation cues. The symbolic nature of fashion also forms the foundation for costume design when the designer wants to portray aspects of the character by means of the costume worn.

DISCUSSION QUESTIONS

1. Think of a first impression situation in which fashion-related appearance symbols served as a primary source of information about another individual. What was the situation? What was the person wearing and what impression did you have of the person? In this situation, why do you think appearance cues were important in the your first impression of the person? Did you interact with the person? If so, did your first impression change because of this interaction?
2. What personal and social characteristics are being communicated by the clothing you are wearing? Are these messages "accurate" indicators of who you are? Why or why not? Identify two examples of fashion-related appearance cues that communicate each of the personal and social characteristics listed in this chapter.

3. Bring in a fashion advertisement. What images/characteristics are being associated with the fashion? Does the fashion being advertised convey this meaning in society?

4. Think about two social roles you play in your life (e.g., student and basketball player). Do you wear different clothing for these two different roles? Why or why not? Does the clothing you wear communicate any aspects regarding these roles? If so, what aspects are communicated?

5. Impression management involves the purposeful manipulation of appearance cues to convey a particular image. For example, an interviewee may purposefully wear an expensive suit to a job interview to convey a professional image. However, the images conveyed may or may not be an accurate reflection of the individual. Therefore, what are the ethical implications of impression management? Are there ways in which perceivers can identify and "see through" false appearance cues?

SUGGESTED READINGS

Damhorst, Mary L. "Meanings of Clothing Cues in Social Context." *Clothing and Textiles Research Journal* 3 (1984-85): 39-48.

Damhorst, Mary L. "In Search of a Common Thread: Classification of Information Communicated Through Clothing." *Clothing and Textiles Research Journal* 8 (1990): 1-12.

Davis, Fred. "Clothing and Fashion as Communication." In *The Psychology of Fashion,* edited by Michael R. Solomon. Lexington: Heath/Lexington Books, 1985, 15-27.

Joseph, Nathan. *Uniforms and Nonuniforms: Communication Through Clothing.* New York: Greenwood Press, 1986.

Kaiser, Susan B. "Toward a Contextual Social Psychology of Clothing: A Synthesis of Symbolic Interactionist and Cognitive Theoretical Perspectives." *Clothing and Textiles Research Journal* 2 (1983-84): 1-9.

Lennon, Sharron J., and Leslie L. Davis. "Clothing and Human Behavior From a Social Cognitive Framework. Part 1: Theoretical Perspectives." *Clothing and Textiles Research Journal* 7 (1989): 41-48.

Lennon, Sharron J., and Leslie L. Davis. "Clothing and Human Behavior From a Social Cognitive Framework. Part 2: The Stages of Social Cognition." *Clothing and Textiles Research Journal* 8 (1989): 1-9.

Solomon, Michael R., and Susan P. Douglas. "Diversity in Product Symbolism: The Case of Female Executive Clothing." *Psychology and Marketing* 4 (1987): 189-212.

10

Fashion Communication Channels

OBJECTIVES

◆ To describe how different sources of information on fashion, such as mass media and personal friends, transmit information about new fashions to consumers.
◆ To focus attention on the unique and complementary roles performed by impersonal communications and personal communications on fashion adoption.
◆ To suggest how specific sources of information may be received by specific audiences, such as fashion magazines, by fashion innovators.

Communication of information is a direct force shaping consumers' decision processes in adopting new styles. Consumers receive information on fashions through many channels, ranging from formal advertising campaigns by fashion businesses to informal and casual conversations among peers. This chapter describes how various elements of communications—**sources,** or sponsors of communications, **messages,** or information contents of the communication, and **channels** of communication such as TV or newspapers—influence the adoption and diffusion of fashions. We focus on the two broad categories of fashion information received by consumers, **impersonal** and **personal** communications.[1]

SOURCES OF INFORMATION

The consumer receives a great amount of fashion information through various communications. Here are several kinds of communications, each offering differing types of messages and informational contents:

Advertising and Promotion in the Mass Media   A major channel of fashion communication is fashion advertising and promotion through the mass media. Newspaper advertising has become one of the most important channels for promoting selected styles available to consumers in the local markets. The specialized men's and women's fashion magazines offer exhibitions of the newest and sometimes most avant-garde offerings of the fashion industry. General-interest and men's- and women's-interest magazines also include occasional fashion promotions as features in their diversified contents. Catalogs featuring fashions targeted toward an assortment of market segments have become mass disseminators of information and influence. Fashions are advertised on television and radio, and though the advertising often emphasizes brand names or store names rather than specific fashions, the endorsement of specific fashions is powerful. The central feature of all these mass media communications is that the messages and channels selected are **marketer-controlled,** and the specific styles promoted are determined almost exclusively by the marketing system.

Nonpromotional Communications through Mass Media   Fashions are indirectly exposed to consumers through the nonpromotional content of media. Television programs, movies, magazines, and newspapers are carriers of fashion information by virtue of their emphasis on visual communications. For instance, a TV program or movie shows clothing worn by actors and stars, and the consumer sees a great deal of fashionable behavior through these media. Thus the consumer is exposed to a variety of styles and related life-styles, which can have an effect on fashion choices. For the most part, this exposure is nonpromotional, although occasionally a star's wardrobe may be furnished by a designer or fashion manufacturer.

Retailer Promotions at the Point of Sale   The retailer uses a number of promotional techniques within the store, of which fashion displays are the most prominent. Fashion shows, labels on clothing, and styles worn by store personnel are other communications at the point of sale.

Consumer Education and Information   Fashion information is transmitted through education-oriented communications such as fashion

Television programs, such as *Murphy Brown,* communicate fashion information through the clothing worn by characters (*Murphy Brown,* 1992).

(CBS Files; Photographer, Richard Cartwright)

editorials, consumer education columns in newspapers or magazines, home sewing features, "how-to-wear-it" information, home economics extension programs, and news releases. The sources of these communications are professionals in the clothing field, and messages tend to emphasize semi-technical information on characteristics and uses of a fashion. Some of these educational communications are under the control of marketers, while others are controlled by neutral or consumer-oriented sources.

Visual Observation   One of the most powerful fashion communications is the visual observation of styles being worn by other people. An individual has considerable opportunity to receive this nonverbal communication every day.

Verbal Discussions   Fashion is sometimes a topic for face-to-face discussion among people. This is an important category of fashion communications in that a wide variety of fashion topics might be chosen for verbal discussion and evaluation at the discretion of those engaged in the conversation.

These kinds of communications differ in their sources, messages, channels of transmission, audiences receiving the messages, and effects on consumer decision-making. Some communications transmit factual or objective information about price, sizes, functional characteristics, and store availability, for example, while others might present normative or subjective appeals ("the latest thing," "something for every well-dressed man or woman"). Consumers seek information from some sources and channels, while other communications may come unbidden. Many are picked up incidentally in the course of daily life. Since so many communications simultaneously compete for consumers' attention, some are never received while others are received but ignored. Some communications are perceived by consumers as more honest or credible than others, and these sources have the greatest potential impact on decision-making. Friends or peers may be perceived as particularly trustworthy, whereas advertising or salespeople have less credibility in some cases, yet both convey information and influence shaping decisions. Ultimately the myriad of informational messages received and learned by the consumer are combined for application in the consumer's decision-making process.

All of this leads to the proposition that information seeking and processing (use) is widespread. In fact this has been documented in many types of consumer behavior (Bettman 1979; Wilkie 1990), even leading to possible *information overload,* the use of too much information for some purchases which leads to mental stress and confusion. Of course it goes without saying that many purchases are routine and habitual, requiring little information, while still others may come from purely impulsive or unplanned behavior (D'Antoni and Shenson 1973). We have seen extensive private data of retailers and business firms indicating substantial impulsive purchasing, especially in less expensive and trendy sportswear and casual fashions. But in categories where newness and social visibility are important, or when considerable expense or other perceived risks are involved, we should expect more concerted information seeking and decision-making by the consumer. Such is the case with multitudes of fashions, and as we shall see there is much monitoring and processing of information in the specific category of fashion.

Fashion communications can be divided into two broad categories of *impersonal* and *personal* communications. Impersonal communications are transmitted "one-way" from a source to receiver, such as the transmission of information through the mass media. Such communications are impersonal in that the source is not necessarily known to the receiver, the receiver cannot question the source, and the channel used in the communication encourages passive reception of information. Personal communications, on the other hand, are those in which two or more people interact face-to-face. Active participation is possible in such a communication, through two-way observation and discussion between the participants.

Fashion shows represent marketer-controlled fashion promotion.
(*WWD,* Faichild Publications)

THE ROLE OF IMPERSONAL COMMUNICATIONS

Impersonal communications of fashion information occur through national mass media (e.g., TV, national magazines), local media (e.g., local radio, newspapers), mailed promotions, catalogs, consumer education, and retailers' promotions at the point of sale, such as labels, tags on garments, displays, and fashion shows. Sponsors of these communications range from corporations marketing specific styles or brand names to consumer-interest groups, but marketer-dominated sources control most of these messages. Contents of messages can range from factual and educational presentations (objective presentations) to promotional and propagandistic appeals (subjective presentations). All these communications are formalized, impersonal, one-way transmissions of their chosen message from source (sponsors) to receivers (consumers).

Impersonal communications stimulate awareness of and interest in current fashions. The visual media of television, magazines, and newspapers have a particular ability to communicate new styles to the general public. They also educate consumers. Newspapers and magazines regularly carry features on fashions and fabrics, giving details on economic principles of choosing and wearing apparel. Since these are written by professional apparel specialists, the messages tend to be factual and authoritative. And finally, impersonal communications inform consumers of the specific styles and brand names available in the local market. This information can be useful to consumers as they form preferences for styles and select stores to shop.

Different sorts of impersonal communications may team up to present fashion information to the consuming public, as illustrated by the following example. Shortly after the seasonal showings of fashion designers, the most sensational new styles often receive media coverage through newspapers and perhaps television. Each month fashion magazines illustrate their editors' selections of leading designs. The emerging trends are also interpreted in local newspaper fashion pages, women's interest columns, men's fashion columns, general interest magazines—both men's and women's—and consumer educational media. These messages are further reinforced by newspaper fashion advertisements, ads that increase consumer awareness of local fashion trends, and currently available merchandise. Finally, retail store displays and information presented at the point of sale direct the consumer's attention to the promoted trends being offered. In this way, several kinds of impersonal communications act to complement each other in presenting and filtering information on styles currently available.

Retail shore displays inform consumers as to how new fashion can be worn.
(Enrico Coveri, Florence, Italy)

Other impersonal communications are of less promotional intent but still can be important. For instance, movies and television programs can indirectly communicate information, even though their purpose is neither promotional nor educational. Such programs communicate fashion information because they reflect the fashions of current life-styles. Indeed TV producers carefully monitor fashion trends and set their stages to reflect current ideals of appearance and occasional innovations. Further, the advertising of products other than clothing may incidentally employ actors wearing current fashions. A considerable amount of fashion information might be incidentally received and processed, even though these media are not directly attempting to convey fashion information.

In a different way, consumer education in clothing selection also stimulates interest in fashions. Although consumer education tries to encourage the development of skills related to economical consumption, a greater total involvement with current styles of dress can also result. Moreover, professional consumer educators frequently encourage consumers to appreciate the role of fashion in their clothing choices. These educational activities can reach a large part of the population, particularly through newspapers and consumer publications.

Selecting the messages to be communicated through impersonal communications is a crucial decision. There is an almost endless supply of specific styles, brand names, fashion trends, and product characteristics that might be emphasized. Of necessity, only a carefully selected amount of information can actually be communicated. For example, a fashion editor can promote only a few styles, those considered the most promising fashion trends for the coming season, together with some of the more risky innovations (not too many, for one cannot be wrong too often). Likewise, a retailer can promote only a few styles thought to be consistent with fashion trends in the local market. Or, the consumer educator must assess the informational needs of consumers and plot an educational strategy consistent with these needs. Therefore, such sources must judge the appropriate communications to transmit, and their judgments can have considerable impact on consumer decision making in the market.

How effectively can impersonal communications influence consumer decisions? Many people think the impersonal media are powerful. For instance, fashion editors stress the importance of their judgments in helping establish fashion trends. Television advertisers, a minority in the fashion field, emphasize the impact of their messages in maintaining brand awareness and brand loyalty. Retailers point to the successful effects of newspaper ads and store displays, the results of which can often be seen in increased sales. Consumer educators point to the increasingly knowledgeable

MTV has helped shape a new generation of fashion (Cindy Crawford, host of MTV's *House of Style*).
(MTV; Photographer, Jay Strauss)

and sophisticated consumer, the product of consumer education. Unquestionably, many messages are reaching their audiences, informing, persuading, and influencing consumers.

There are also reasons why impersonal communications do not always have a direct effect on their audiences. First, the media compete for the consumer's attention, and some messages are never received by their intended audiences. Second, promotional communications present one-sided arguments favoring their sponsors, and are susceptible to questions of credibility for that reason. Third, many mediating factors in the environment can intervene to reduce any direct causal effect of a communication. And finally, a communication may present inadequate factual information, thereby limiting its potential influence on receivers.

Research is needed to demonstrate the effects of impersonal communications on consumer behavior. Though much research on this topic has been conducted,[2] evidence that impersonal communications can be consistently effective in controlling consumers' choices of fashions is scarce. However, some basic research suggests that impersonal communications can be particularly effective in reaching *fashion change agents,* influencing these leaders to initiate the fashion process.

Several studies illustrate this idea. King's (1964, 1965) research on fashion communications suggests that early buyers of fashion during the fashion season are moderately higher in media exposure than the later buyers and nonbuyers. Exposure to general-interest magazines, fashion magazines, newspapers, and radio tended to be higher among early buyers. However, television exposure was actually lower among early buyers than among late buyers. Grindereng (1967) supports these findings in her research on early adopters, which also found early adopters of new styles more likely to use mass media than personal sources for fashion information.

Summers (1970, 1972) has focused on the media-exposure patterns of fashion innovators and opinion leaders and found the exposure patterns for these two market segments remarkably similar. Both innovators and opinion leaders read more general-interest magazines, news magazines, home magazines, women's magazines, and especially fashion magazines than other consumers. However, among both innovators and opinion leaders, exposure to television, radio, intellectual journals, and romance magazines was found to be no different from exposure to these media of other consumers.

Reynolds and Darden (1972) have also presented data on the roles of media in disseminating fashion information. In measuring sources of first awareness of a new style, they found opinion leaders to be more exposed to fashion magazines than nonleaders. However, nonleaders reported newspapers and television as first sources of awareness significantly more than did opinion leaders.

These investigations suggest that fashion leaders are more exposed to impersonal communications, predominantly printed media, than are other consumers. However, a large part of the population is not exposed to fashion-oriented media, regardless of their innovator or opinion-leader status. For instance, Summers (1972, 47) notes that although exposure to fashion magazines can be concentrated among innovators, over 65 percent of respondents reported they rarely or never read these magazines. Nevertheless, the content of such magazines, when they reach the highly fashion-oriented sector of the population, appears to be important in starting the fashion process.

Impersonal communications also provide messages that can be transmitted from one consumer to another in personal communications. This has become known as the "two-step flow" of communication (Katz and Lazarsfeld 1955). This hypothesis says that information is first communicated from mass media to opinion leaders, and then from opinion leaders to other segments of the population. In this manner, communication occurs in two steps, with opinion leaders first acting as receivers and then later acting as channels of communications when they discuss messages from media with others. The two-step situation means that channels of communication interact, and there are many other situations where other channel and receiver interactions might occur. The two-step hypothesis draws attention to a multitude of more complex flows of communication that can occur.[3]

Recent research by Chowdhary (1989) also indicates media use varies by age and sex. Media were broadly defined to include many differing marketer-dominated, consumer-dominated and neutral sources, most related to mass media communications. In a large-scale survey of 950 older adults and 750 younger adults, the younger consumers of both sexes made significantly greater use of a broad range of media than those who are older. However, older consumers did appear to make greater use of several selected media, including fashion columns and ads in newspapers. With regard to sex, females made significantly greater use of most forms of communications, including fashion media and other marketer-dominated sources. Perhaps most interesting is the consistent finding that all age and sex categories made greater use of consumer-dominated than marketer-dominated sources. Obviously such personally relevant sources have credibility, but since mass media sources were included in both categories, we can conclude that mass media have a strong effect extending well past the traditional marketer-dominated promotions of newspapers, magazines, and stores.

Research by Kaiser and Chandler (1985) offers another interesting perspective on media use and influences, specifically by older fashion consumers. Their study focused on a sample of 209 consumers above age 50. They found that television, magazines, and newspapers were likely to be used for ideas on normative (appropriate) styles of dress. Positive portrayals of media characters and older adults (e.g., George Burns, Johnny Carson, Miss Elli on *Dallas*) appeared to be influential for some subjects. Newspapers and magazines were also judged more influential than TV, yet they offer fewer senior role models. These subtle aspects of media use are not yet conclusive, but the one conclusion we may draw is that mass media may have a more pervasive impact on senior consumer behavior than is sometimes supposed, and on the maturing fashion-oriented consumer in general.

THE ROLE OF PERSONAL COMMUNICATIONS

The trends in fashions begun by impersonal communications can further diffuse through personal communications. Personal communications occur where people interact directly with each other. The most obvious case is

Television shopping channels, such as QVC, provide fashion information to consumers.

(*WWD*, Fairchild Publications)

two or more persons engaged in verbal discussion, either in each other's presence or by telephone. Another case is visual observation of other people. The observer can receive visual but unspoken cues or bits of information—symbolic communications—simply by watching other people. Personal appearance is a significant part of that communication.

Personal communication has several features that enhance its impact on consumer decisions. Informal and relaxed discussion of information is possible, and the participants can share their opinions, evaluations, and accumulated knowledge with each other. The consumer may ask for and receive information whenever desired, whereas information from impersonal communications is not always readily available when it is needed. Styles can be observed and discussed in the actual settings of their use; for instance, information on the appropriate styles for a social gathering might be obtained by noting and discussing actual behavior at a party, club meeting, and other social occasions. The consumer may seek personal information such as what accessories to wear with a style, how it would look on the wearer, where to buy it, and what others think of its fashionability. Furthermore, the credibility of each person communicating information can be immediately assessed. These communications can legitimize a style as a candidate for adoption. For this reason, personal communications can be an informative and persuasive kind of communication.

Verbal Discussion

Research shows that personal discussions can be one of the most active and influential of fashion communications. For example, Katz and Lazarsfeld (1955), in the first major investigation of personal communication in fashion, found that about two-thirds of the women in their study had made a recent fashion change, and personal influence had entered into most of these decisions. Their study also pointed to the importance of opinion leaders in verbally communicating with their friends about fashion and influencing their friends' choices. They found that fashion opinion leaders existed at all status levels of the consumer population, were concentrated in younger age groups, were high in fashion interest, and tended to be highly gregarious. It was also found that personal influence usually occurred between persons of equal social status and age—social peers. These findings established personal influence and opinion leadership as powerful and widespread influences on fashion diffusion.

King and Summers (1967) conducted similar research on the dynamics of personal communications in the diffusion of fashion information. The investigation focused on the identification of two-person dyads where an exchange of fashion information had occurred between a pair of friends or family members. The subjects in the investigation were 507 women in Boston. The researchers collected data on the sort of information people discussed, whether the interaction was between family or nonfamily members, and demographic characteristics of the participants. The total volume of communications was substantial, with 66 percent of the sample indicating they had engaged in a fashion discussion either as a source, a receiver, or both. Topics of discussion were in three areas. First, 32 percent of the women had talked about general fashion trends, such as popular styles, colors, and materials for the coming season. A total of 23 percent had discussed shopping information, such as availability and price of styles at local stores. Finally, 45 percent of the respondents discussed individual fashion information, such as what would look good on the person, what friends were wearing, and styles for particular occasions. The topics discussed were quite similar in interactions among family and nonfamily members (King and Summers 1967, 28, 33).

They also analyzed age and social-class characteristics of the people engaging in a personal discussion. In discussions among family members, 44 percent were between persons of approximately the same age (no more than eight years apart). In those between friends, 79 percent were between people of about the same age. When socioeconomic status was examined, 80 percent of the discussions occurred between individuals within one status category of each other (seven categories of status were used). Also, when the participants were not in the same category, there appeared to be an equal tendency for information to flow from higher to lower or lower to higher status (King and Summers 1967, 36, 38, 41).

The King and Summers study reinforces the findings of Katz and Lazarsfeld. It points out that personal communications on fashion are very active, and a variety of potentially influential subjects are discussed. It was also found that personal communications are active both among family members and among friends, and that discussion frequently occurs as a two-way exchange between individuals. Finally, discussions most frequently occur between individuals similar in age and socioeconomic status, and who therefore could be expected to have much of relevance to say to each other.

Research by Reynolds and Darden (1972) focused on personal communications in influencing the rejection of a particular new style, the midi-length dress, which was heavily promoted but eventually rejected in the late 1960s and early 1970s (but widely adopted in the late 1970s to 1980s). Among 81 subjects who engaged in personal communications on the midi, 233 negative comments on the style were identified. A total of 25 percent of the comments involved the general fashion trend, suggesting the midi was "old-fashioned," "faddish," and that other people might not adopt the style. Personalized information was discussed by 38 percent of the respondents, including comments that the style would not look good, was bulky and uncomfortable, and would be unsuitable for many occasions. On the economics of the style, 7 percent of the discussions were on the high cost of buying a new wardrobe with new accessories. Perhaps most significant, 93 percent of the respondents reported their discussions of the midi had been largely negative. This high level of negative personal communications undoubtedly contributed to the failure of the midi in the early 1970s (Reynolds and Darden 1972, 42-43).

Visual Observation

A lot of information on fashions is communicated when a person observes the dress of others. In fact, visual observation of dress can be the most important kind of fashion communication. The reason is that when people regularly engage in social interaction, or encounter strangers, conscious or unconscious observation of others becomes an active and ever-present channel of communication. As indicated in earlier chapters, visual observation in anonymous situations of massed collective behavior may be the most prevalent form of influence here.

Visual communication in fashion diffusion has received little research. However, some investigations in nonverbal communication suggest some hypotheses. In one important area (as discussed in chap. 9), investigators frequently note that dress is a nonverbal cue in the formation of first impressions of a person.[4] For example, a great deal of the identity of strangers, upon their meeting for the first time, will be established by nonverbal cues. The observer might identify the stranger's occupation, social status, social role and many other features based on nonverbal cues or symbols of dress. In the absence of other information on the stranger's identity, an observer tends to rely on such visual cues.

Research has also called attention to clothing as a nonverbal communicator of similarities in attitudes, values, and sociopolitical orientations among people (Thomas 1973; Buckley and Roach 1974; Lind and Roach-Higgins 1985). That is, similarities in dress among people tend to symbolize their similarities in social orientations and styles of life. This function of clothing may often be seen by individuals and be used to determine which people will be accepted into group membership and which will not.

Another study specifically suggests that individuals wearing currently fashionable dress may be perceived as more sociable than those who are out of fashion (Johnson, Nagasawa, and Peters 1977). This was found to be true for both male and female college students, who evaluated photographs of a female student model wearing fashionable and unfashionable outfits. The researchers noted that their findings contradict the supposition that the importance of fashionable dress is being de-emphasized in contemporary society.

Thus, clothing communicates information nonverbally in a number of ways. It may help form first impressions, serve as a visible social symbol of personal identity, and communicate sociability, attitudes, and values. But a visual communication does not always convey accurate information. The wearer can manipulate clothing cues to present fraudulent impressions, and the person making the interpretation may not know the cues or may make inaccurate judgments of their meanings. Also, in a society where status symbolism is ambiguous or perceived as less important, it can become increasingly difficult to interpret the nonverbal meaning of dress. Therefore, although dress can communicate some basic information about its wearer, the interpretation of nonverbal cues is subject to many biases and intervening variables which act to obscure the meaning of the communication.

How does nonverbal communication become a factor in the transmission of fashion information? From visual observation and symbolic interpretation, the consumer picks up many cues or bits of information that might influence later purchases. Whether or not the consumer accurately interprets the meanings of these cues is not as important as the mere fact that he or she receives some information. If the consumer simply, even innocently, sees that a symbolic cue conveys prestige or perhaps a shared pattern of attitudes and values relevant to his or her social situation, then this interpretation may encourage adoption of the style. These are situations where the subsidiary effect of nonverbal communications is to stimulate awareness and diffusion of fashions. However, we must also keep in mind the fact that many styles will diffuse merely because certain adopters visually display the style and others then copy it because of its attractiveness.

SUMMARY

This chapter has discussed a wide range of fashion communications that consumers receive and use in deciding to adopt or reject a fashion. Fashion communications that actively disseminate information are advertising and promotion in the mass media, nonpromotional content in the mass media, retailer promotions at the point of sale, consumer education, visual observation, and verbal discussions. These may be divided into the broad categories of impersonal and personal communications.

The different kinds of communications can perform different and complementary roles in the fashion process. In general, a variety of impersonal communications (e.g., mass media, retailer promotions) appear to team up in creating awareness and stimulating interest in current styles. These communications can then be important in initiating fashion diffusion. Personal communications through visual observation and verbal discussion appear to be effective in diffusing information on the actual styles accepted in the consumer's social world. These communications can legitimize the style as a candidate for adoption. Personal communications can reinforce the social appropriateness of the style and stimulate the style's diffusion to other consumers.

NOTES

1. For details on concepts in this chapter, there are many relevant readings. On the general processes of communications in the adoption and diffusion of innovations, see Rogers (1983) and Wilkie (1990). On interpersonal communications in the diffusion of fashion and other types of information, see the classic research of Katz and Lazarsfeld

(1955) and the summaries of many historical studies by Robertson (1971). A large body of theory and research on consumer information seeking, reception, processing, and use developed during the 1970s and 1980s. For various perspectives on these subjects, see Hughes and Ray (1974), Wilkie (1975), Sproles, Geistfeld, and Badenhop (1978a and b), Bettman (1979), and Wilkie (1990). Current research in this field is found in such publications as *Advances in Consumer Research, Journal of Consumer Research, Journal of Consumer Affairs,* and other scholarly periodicals.

2. See the *Journal of Advertising Research, Journal of Consumer Research,* and *Journal of Marketing Research,* each of which has regularly reported studies on varied responses to advertising stimuli.

3. See Katz and Lazarsfeld (1955) and Robertson (1971) for further discussion of the two-step hypothesis and other more complex hypotheses on the flows of communication.

4. For examples, see Douty (1963), Hamid (1968), Gibbins (1969), Knapp (1972), Lambert (1972), Rosencranz (1972), and Eicher and Kelley (1974). Also, see Kleinke (1975) and Kaiser (1990) for comprehensive surveys of literature on this general topic. Chapter 9 also introduces concepts relevant to symbolic communications by fashions.

DISCUSSION QUESTIONS

1. Describe the various sources that transmit information that may influence consumers' decisions. What types of information (e.g., factual, propaganda, types of contents) does each transmit? What types of consumers are likely to seek and receive each source? How effective is each in (a) transmitting information and (b) actually influencing decisions?

2. Discuss the specific roles of various impersonal sources in transmitting information.

3. Discuss the specific roles of personal sources in transmitting information. How do these differ in their potential influence on consumers as compared to impersonal sources?

4. What fashion communications are most likely to be received and used by (a) fashion innovators, (b) opinion leaders, (c) later adopters, (d) young adults, (e) senior citizens, and (f) socially active consumers?

5. Design a research project that will identify the *specific* sources of information used by specific groups or market segments of consumers

(e.g., do innovators read *Vogue, Gentlemen's Quarterly*, the local newspaper, other sources; do teenagers use friends, shopping the stores, or others as principal sources?).

6. This chapter shows there are numerous sources of fashion communications in the consumer's environment. To what extent does this lead to information overload, or too much information for consumers? What is your assessment of the overall quality or adequacy of this informational environment?

SUGGESTED READINGS

Bettman, James R. *An Information Processing Theory of Consumer Choice.* Reading, Mass: Addison-Wesley, 1979.

Chowdhary, Usha. "Fashion Information Seeking by Younger and Older Consumers." *Clothing and Textiles Research Journal* 8 (Fall 1989): 49-55.

D'Antoni, Joseph S., and Howard L. Shenson. "Impulse Buying Revisited: A Behavioral Typology." *Journal of Retailing* 49 (Spring 1973): 63-76.

Kaiser, Susan B. and Joan L. Chandler. "Older Consumers' Use of Media for Fashion Information." *Journal of Broadcasting and Electronic Media* 29 (1985): 201-7.

Katz, Elihu, and Paul F. Lazarsfeld. *Personal Influence.* Glencoe, IL: The Free Press, 1955.

King, Charles W. "The Innovator in the Fashion Adoption Process." In *Reflections on Progress in Marketing,* edited by L. George Smith. Chicago: American Marketing Association, 1964.

Robertson, Thomas S. *Innovative Behavior and Communication.* New York: Holt, Rinehart and Winston, 1971.

Summers, John O. "The Identity of Women's Clothing Fashion Opinion Leaders." *Journal of Marketing Research* 7 (1970): 178-85.

11

Consumer Decision-Making Processes

OBJECTIVES

◆ To show how various sources of information team up to inform consumers and assist them in their consumer decision-making processes.
◆ To show that consumers use and find helpful a wide range of differing information sources and contents as they make their decisions to adopt new fashions.

As we have indicated in preceeding chapters, the choice of a new fashion requires a decision-making process by the consumer. This chapter examines how consumers seek and use information on new fashions in the course of decision-making, and as such builds on the principles developed in the preceeding chapter. Our principal theme is that consumer decision-making can involve an active and purposeful seeking and use of information to help choose fashions.

We begin with an explicit look at how information is used during the actual decision-making process. The starting point is informational use during the individual consumer's adoption process. We also must pay special attention to behavior at the point of purchase, ususally the retail store, for this is an informationally rich environment and the potential for its use here is considered significant by retailers. Then we turn to the question of whether there may be typical patterns that some consumers use, such as focusing on one type of information (e.g., media or personal sources). Finally we ask the question of what information consumers perceive as helpful to their decisions, and summarize several large studies giving perspectives on this question focusing on particular sources and informational contents.

INFORMATIONAL USE DURING THE ADOPTION PROCESS

Several studies indicate that consumers use different sources of information at different stages of the adoption process. Recall that an individual's decision to adopt or reject an innovation can be viewed as a five-stage mental process involving awareness, interest, evaluation, trial, and adoption or rejection (see chap. 3). At each of these stages, different sorts of information sources and message contents are used by the consumer in coming to a decision.

This idea is illustrated in an exploratory investigation by Beal and Rogers (1957). Their research focused on identifying sources of information used by rural women in their decisions to adopt fabrics containing nylon, Orlon acrylic, and Dacron polyester (these were relatively new fibers to consumers in the 1950s, the time of this classic research). Sources of information used by consumers were divided into five categories: mass media, agencies (home economics classes and Extension Service), personal communications, commercial communications (e.g., retail stores, garment labels, store salespersons), and "self" (personal experience with the product). They found that each of these categories of sources had different levels of use at each stage of the adoption process:

1. **Awareness Stage** Mass media were by far the most important source creating awareness, with 59 percent of respondents mentioning this source. Among other categories, personal communications were mentioned by 16 percent of the people surveyed and commercial sources were mentioned by 15 percent.
2. **Interest Stage** (Information Stage) Both mass media and personal communications were equally used at this stage, with both mentioned by 34 percent of the people surveyed. Commercial sources were mentioned by 16 percent of the respondents.
3. **Evaluation Stage** At this stage, when the consumer is evaluating information in contemplation of a decision, personal communications were the major source of information, mentioned by 39 percent of the respondents. Commercial sources were second, with 31 percent of the respondents mentioning these sources. Mass media were mentioned by only 12 percent of the people.

Commercial sources of information are often used by consumers at the trial stage of fashion adoption.
(*WWD*, Fairchild Publications)

4. **Trial Stage** At this stage, the individual is about to make the purchase decision. Therefore, it should not be surprising that commercial sources were by the far the most frequently mentioned, with 40 percent of all mentions. Second in mentions were personal communications, with 18 percent of the respondents indicating this source.

5. **Adoption Stage** Personal satisfaction with a product is obviously important to the continued purchase and use of a product, and this source was mentioned by all the respondents. However, the investigators did not attempt to determine if further use of other sources occurred in a decision to continue adoption (Beal and Rogers 1957).

These findings are reinforced by research on fashion adoption by Reynolds and Darden (1972). They found that impersonal media sources, including fashion magazines, television, and newspapers, were most frequently mentioned as creating awareness of a new style. The media became progressively less significant at the informational and evaluative

Consumers seek and use information at the point of purchase in their decision-making.
(Fairchild Books & Visuals)

stages, and personal sources increased in importance. In general, these data support the role of media in creating awareness and informational interest. Other sources become increasingly important as the evaluative process continues.

Research by Polegato and Wall (1980) on information seeking by fashion opinion leaders and followers expands and reinforces these findings. Focusing on a sample of 187 women college students, they found considerable use of many marketer-dominated, consumer-dominated and neutral sources of information. Overall fashion leaders made significantly greater use of information than followers; clearly leaders read, see, and hear more. At the awareness stage, both leaders and followers make greater use of marketer-dominated sources, particularly advertising and store displays. Fashion magazines were cited much more frequently by leaders than followers as first sources of awareness, and leaders did not cite consumer-dominated sources of first awareness. At the comprehension stage (similar to the interest stage; see chap. 3), leaders more frequently used marketer sources, while followers frequently cited consumer sources, primarily female friends. In the legitimation stage (similar to the evaluation stage; see chap. 3), informational use declined, particularly among followers, but some leaders continued to consult a variety of sources. Marketer and consumer-dominated sources were consulted by leaders and followers, with store displays and magazines cited frequently. Visually monitoring and talking with friends were cited often, but considerably more by leaders,

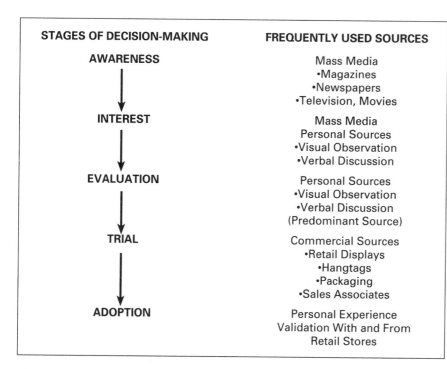

STAGES OF DECISION-MAKING

AWARENESS

INTEREST

EVALUATION

TRIAL

ADOPTION

FREQUENTLY USED SOURCES

Mass Media
•Magazines
•Newspapers
•Television, Movies

Mass Media
Personal Sources
•Visual Observation
•Verbal Discussion

Personal Sources
•Visual Observation
•Verbal Discussion
(Predominant Source)

Commercial Sources
•Retail Displays
•Hangtags
•Packaging
•Sales Associates

Personal Experience
Validation With and From
Retail Stores

FIGURE 11.1   Sources of Information Used During the Consumer's Decision-Making Process—A Model

showing the increased potential role of personal sources for them as decision-making progressed.

In addition to illustrating that consumers use many sources of information, these investigations point to the important principle that different sources of information may perform complementary functions in the consumer's decision process. Mass media seem to be effective in stimulating awareness and interest; personal sources add an evaluation of the product; and commercial sources provide specific information necessary to make the final decision to buy. Each source thus appears to perform a specialized role in transmitting kinds of information needed at each stage of the decision. Based on these conclusions, we may construct a basic model of which sources of information are likely to be used at each stage of decision-making (see fig. 11.1).

INFORMATION SEEKING AT THE POINT OF PURCHASE

Consumers seek information, compare alternative choices, and make decisions at the point of purchase—the retail store. Before shopping the consumer may define the broad outline of the decision, such as what stores to shop, style preferences, color preferences, price ranges, and level of quality. Some consumers may form a definite idea of what to purchase, but for many others the prospective choice will be vaguely defined. But no one can make the final choice until he or she sees the alternatives available. Then some of the most active information seeking can take place.

Consumers are exposed to potentially influential information at the point of purchase (Davis 1987; Eckman, Damhorst and Kadolph 1990; Jacobi and Walters 1958). For example, retailers are well aware of the persuasive power of window and in-store displays. These promotional techniques communicate information on the most current styles and accessories featured by the store, and displayed styles frequently sell quickly. Packages, tags, and labels on garments communicate specific details on characteristics of each alternative selection. Salespersons offer descriptions and promotional advice on specific choices. Consumers do their personal evaluations of alternative choices, and occasionally a shopping companion is consulted for his or her opinions. As the consumer gathers the desired information, the number of alternative styles considered is narrowed to a manageable number, and the final decision is made based on certain critical attributes (product characteristics such as style, styling details, color, brand name) of the alternatives. Theoretically, the fashion-oriented consumers make the choice based on critical attributes of style and fabric, while others emphasize brand, labels, price, or other non-fashion factors.

Some evidence indicates that consumers substantially narrow the number of stores to shop before making a shopping trip. In a study of 2,578 consumer decisions, most of which were fashion-related purchases, researchers found over half the purchases were made by shopping only one store (Dommermuth and Cundiff 1967). From 33 to 38 percent of the consumers had shopped two or more stores for such fashion-oriented purchases as women's and girls' dresses, coats, and jewelry. In less expensive categories such as men's shirts and women's blouses, only 20 percent had shopped two or more stores (Dommermuth and Cundiff 1967, 33). Well under one quarter of the purchases, on the average, were made by shopping three or more stores. Thus it appears that shopping one or two stores is an optimal number for many consumers, and substantial narrowing of store choices takes place in any particular consumer purchase. Proprietary studies by malls bear this out, and while some consumers shop three or four stores, many time-pressed or store-loyal consumers can shop only one or two carefully selected alternatives.

One reason for limited shopping may be that consumers see little benefit in extensive shopping compared to the costs in time and travel needed to shop many stores. Considerable narrowing of the choice of stores may also happen as consumers receive communications through advertising or

Consumers evaluate fashion in styling, workmanship, fit, and color/pattern prior to purchase behavior.
(Fairchild Book & Visuals)

personal discussions about stores carrying specific styles or brands. Finally, whatever information is available at the stores picked by the consumer could be particularly influential, since it is immediately available and is not competing with promotional or information messages of other stores.

What information does a consumer seek and use in decision-making at the point of purchase? Several investigations give us some answers. Research by Whitlock, Ayres, and Ryan (Ryan 1966, 170-73) illustrates the information-seeking process in women's shopping for blouses. A total of 380 shoppers were observed as they made purchases. Fit of the blouses was one of the most frequently sought pieces of information, but only 38 percent of the shoppers actually assessed the fit. A total of 14 percent asked their shopping companion's advice, and 15 percent requested information from a salesperson. Significantly, only 6 percent examined the product's construction, only 7 percent checked labels, and only 10 percent mentioned using advertisements or displays as informational sources. However, in a follow-up study, nearly 40 percent of the consumers reported they remembered removable tags, with two-thirds of these finding label information useful.

An investigation by Martin (1971) examined the specific types of information consumers seek in making a fashion purchase. In a controlled

The store-intensive searcher is most likely to look at how clothes are displayed in retail stores.

(Folic, Rio de Janeiro)

laboratory experiment, female subjects were shown line drawings of basic apparel styles and were asked to make "purchase decisions" based on this one bit of information; the subjects were told to assume the style would fit them correctly. Following this initial decision, respondents were then informed that they could gather other information on the style to help them decide whether or not they would buy the item. The subjects were given a list of nine informational factors from which they could choose a maximum of five factors.

Table 11.1 presents the nine informational factors and the percentage of subjects choosing each one. Price and physical characteristics of the garments were by far the most frequently sought information. In comparison, marketing-related information and salesperson's evaluation of the product received a modest number of choices. Another important finding was that subjects who decided to buy sought more information than those deciding not to buy. Finally, 25 percent indicated that style was the primary reason for making their decision, while 67 percent indicated that other information factors were primary influences. Price was mentioned as the prime factor in decision-making by 55 percent of the subjects, and was most frequently the first bit of information subjects requested (Martin 1971, 68).

TABLE 11.1 TYPES OF INFORMATION REQUESTED IN FASHION PURCHASE DECISIONS

Information Requested	% of Respondents Requesting Information
Price	86%
Garment Characteristics	
Color	74%
Material content	64%
Garment care	35%
Marketing Information	
Brand name	44%
Store identification	35%
Department where sold	16%
Impersonal Communications	
Salesperson's style evaluation	9%
Salesperson's quality evaluation	9%

SOURCE: Summary of data presented by Martin (1971, 69)

This discussion has described some overt factors in consumer information seeking and decision-making at the point of purchase. A different approach involves identifying the consumer's covert thought processes as a purchase is made, and constructing protocols or transcripts of the actual decision process (O'Shaughnessy 1987). Exploratory research on fashion decisions exemplifying this method was conducted by Alexis, Haines, and Simon (1968), using female college students who volunteered for the study. To do the study, students were given money to make three actual shopping trips and clothing-purchase decisions. On each shopping trip, a subject was accompanied by an interviewer trained to observe the shopper's behavior and to record each action or comment made by the shopper. Subjects were asked to speak their thoughts at each step of the decision. In this manner, the researchers were able to construct transcripts of each step in the information-seeking and decision-making processes of the subjects.

Based on their analysis of these protocols, the researchers suggest that there are several basic steps in the shopping and decision-making process: (1) recalling previously received information and deciding what item or rank ordering of items to purchase, (2) developing a "data base" of information in the individual's memory, to use during the shopping trip, (3) choosing a store to shop, and (4) going through the actual decision-making process in the store. The researchers also presented transcripts of the consumer's decision-making processes at the point of purchase, which suggest that consumers engage in different but systematic information gathering and thinking as they reach a decision. Some of the basic information-seeking behaviors are summarized in table 11.2.

A variation to the protocol method is the in-store intercept survey, recently recommended in research by Eckman, Damhorst and Kadolph (1990). Their study focused on open-ended questioning of 73 female subjects who were actually trying on garments in several retail specialty stores. They focused on identifying evaluative criteria for purchase, which suggests the informational search involved as well. When asked about their evaluative criteria, subjects offered a variety of criteria relating to aesthetics. In order of importance, styling, workmanship, appearance, fit, and color/pattern were mentioned. Infrequently mentioned were criteria related to usefulness (e.g., appropriateness, versatility), brand, price, or availability at competitive stores. This does not mean that information on these factors is unimportant; indeed, the feasible set of alternatives to try on is probably determined by information on such criteria as usefulness and price. But when the final purchase is about to be completed, the power of fashion and aesthetics asserts itself dominantly.

Based on these and related findings, Eckman, Damhorst and Kadolph suggest a model of information seeking and decision-making at the point of purchase including three stages (Eckman, Damhorst and Kadolph 1990):

◆ At the interest stage the individual selects alternatives to consider based on color (a key criterion), pattern, style, fiber, fabric, price, and care requirements.
◆ At the trial stage, fit, which must be minimally satisfactory, and aesthetics then become the principal criteria of decision-making.
◆ In the third stage, buy or reject, positives are weighted against negatives and a choice is made. A few negatives may not matter, but too many with respect to aesthetics causes rejection.

Other studies are indicative of subtle complexities and trade-offs that enter decision-making at the time of purchase. Information on other variables such as store prestige, fiber content, country of origin, and care requirements are sometimes proposed as influences on consumers' judgments. There are consistent findings that store image and fiber content particularly influence positive judgments of apparel (Heisey 1990). Other studies using simulated shopping experiences suggest information seeking may often be limited, skipping half or more of the available information (Davis 1987). The focus of such searches may be on major attributes like style and price (Davis 1987), but other characteristics like fabric, fit and store where purchased are sought and used by significant numbers of consumers.

TABLE 11.2 TYPES OF INFORMATION USED AT POINT OF PURCHASE

Product Characteristics
1. Is my size available?
2. What styles are available?
3. Do I like this style? Question major characteristics of:
    a) Silhouette—straight, round, "A," etc.
    b) Garment dimensions—sleeve and dress length, etc.
    c) Fabric weave and pattern
    d) Color and color combination—Is the dominant color favored?
    e) Details—Are details such as sleeves, collars, pockets, buttons, belts, etc. *liked?*
4. Does it fit me properly in necessary respects?
5. Is it comfortable?
6. Is it easy to care for?
7. What kind of material is it?
8. Is it well made?
9. Is this a good brand?
10. Is this item *different* from others?

Product Use
1. Is this item needed?
2. Do I have a similar item in my current wardrobe inventory?
3. How will I wear this style?
4. Is this style versatile?
5. Is it right for my age?

Price Evaluations
1. What is the price?
2. Is it a sale item?
3. Am I willing to pay this price?
4. Am I able to pay this price?
5. Does the item look cheap?
6. What are the prices of other choices?

Social Evaluations
1. What are my friends' experiences with similar styles?
2. How will my shopping companion evaluate this style?
3. What are other women or salespersons in this store wearing?
4. What kinds of impressions have my friends made with similar styles?
5. WIll this be a socially approved style?
6. Will this item flatter me?
7. Will this item make me feel good?

The Current Fashion Trend
1. What are other people wearing?
2. Have I seen this advertised in the newspapers?
3. What have I seen on this style in the current fashion news?
4. Is this too new or radical for me?
5. Is this going out of style?
6. Is this a fashionable choice?
7. Does this look good on me?
8. Do I like this style better than other available style choices?

SOURCE: Based on a reanalysis and summarization into basic categories of information-seeking behaviors from protocols developed by Alexis, Haines, and Simon (1968, 200–5)

One final study of present interest has suggested that some consumers are relatively receptive to receiving information in the store, while others are relatively insulated or negative to receiving information (Stone, Form, and Strahan 1954). In general, the study indicates that the consumer who receives information and influence at the point of purchase is a window shopper (one who attends to store front displays), enjoys shopping, is uncertain as to the preferred choice, and might discuss the proposed purchase with companions or salespersons. Insulated consumers are those who have well-defined purchasing plans when they shop and who assign little credibility to persuasive communications aimed at changing their preferences.

Thus information seeking is varied, sometimes dramatically, in depth as well as breadth of search, with all sources playing selective roles in one consumer or another's decision process. All information sources seem important to some type of consumer at some time or another, and these varied roles for each cannot be ignored.

PATTERNS OF INFORMATION SEEKING

Consumers may develop typical patterns of information seeking based on their life-style, psychological characteristics, and preferred or frequently consulted sources of information in particular. Research by Shim and Drake (1988, 1989) exemplifies this. Their study identified five different information search patterns among a sample of 1,034 employed women. Although focused on search for information in the special category of employment apparel, these search patterns likely have general applicability as well. The five searcher profiles were identified as:

1. The print-oriented searcher
2. The audio-visual oriented searcher
3. The store-intensive searcher
4. The professional-advice searcher
5. The pal-advice searcher.

The basic principle is that each type of searcher concentrates on a particular category of information, although a broader range of sources can be used as well (there is no evidence that any consumer type focuses exclusively on a single source, e.g. print media alone). A more complete profile of each searcher type, including relevant information sources and life-style characteristics, is summarized in table 11.3.

Some patterns of search may be demographically associated as well, although there is only limited evidence on this in the context of fashion.

TABLE 11.3 INFORMATION SEEKER PROFILES

The Print-Oriented Searcher
Most likely to read several kinds of magazines such as business, fashion and general-interest magazines, and newspapers for information on clothing.
Less likely to be confident on dress.
Tends to use socially directed criteria when selecting an outfit (i.e., prestige, sexy, brand and store name, and fashionability).
Has a fashion-conscious life-style.
More likely to have a self-confident life-style.
Considers herself an opinion leader.
Tends to plan before shopping.

The Audio-Visual–Oriented Searcher
Most likely to watch TV commercials and programs for information.
Most likely to listen to radio advertisements for information.
More likely to use socially directed criteria.
Less likely to consider appropriateness criteria when shopping for apparel.
Less likely to buy expensive outfits.

The Store-Intensive Searcher
Most likely to look at displays of clothing in retail stores.
Most likely to read retail store catalogs.
Less likely to have self-confidence in dress.
Less likely to use socially directed criteria when selecting apparel.
More likely to have fashionable life-style, and to look attractive.
Tends to think dressing well is an important part of her life.
More likely to have a contemporary life-style.

The Professional-Advice Seeker
Most likely to talk to personal shoppers or wardrobe consultants.
Tends to participate in seminars on "dress for success."
More likely to use socially directed criteria when selecting an outfit.
Most likely to buy expensive outfits.
Tends to have a self-confident life-style.
More likely to seek out the advice of her friends regarding brands or products.
More likely to plan before shopping.

The Pal-Advice Seeker
Most likely to talk to her friends, colleagues and family about clothes and stores.
Likely to lack self-confidence in dress.
Likely to lack a self-confident life-style.
More likely to seek out information from friends about brands or products.

SOURCE: Summary of data presented by Shim and Drake (1988).

The classic Thorelli studies on "the information seekers" suggest that consumers making extensive use of information are significantly among the better-educated, higher-income, and higher-occupational-status groups (Thorelli, Becker and Engledow 1975; Thorelli and Thorelli 1977). There may also be differences between the sexes in overall patterns of information seeking as well as use of specific sources, with women

TABLE 11.4   SOURCES CONSIDERED HELPFUL IN KEEPING INFORMED ON CURRENT FASHIONS

Sources of Information Concerning Women's Fashion[b]	New York[a] % of Total Mentions	Cleveland[a] % of Total Mentions	Boston	
			% of Total Mentions	% of Respondents Mentioning
Specialized Fashion Sources[c]	41	41	36	81
Going Shopping in Stores	18	18	25	57
General Mass Media	18	18	19.5	45
Personal Communication	22	23	19.5	45
Other	1	-	-	
	100	100	100	d
Base	(2,541)	(1,056)	(507)	

[a]Based on reanalysis of data presented by Rich (1963, 68)
[b]Identical measuring procedures were used by Rich, in New York and Cleveland, and King in Boston.
[c]Read: Of those sources mentioned as "helpful" by respondents interviewed in New York, 41 percent were specialized fashion sources.
[d]Exceeds 100 percent because of multiple mentions.

SOURCE: King and Summers (1967)

showing more overall involvement. For example, research by Bruner (1988) suggests women are more aware of clothing decisions, use more information, rate many key sources of information as more important, and get more involved in the shopping process than do men. Much of this difference in search pattern is likely encouraged by the larger market of apparel available to women, the extensive range of information sources dedicated to women's fashions, and acculturation.

WHAT INFORMATION IS HELPFUL?

The preceding discussion suggests that consumers use a variety of sources and messages during the course of decision-making. But what do they view as truly helpful to their choices? King and Summers (1967) reviewed findings of several studies in which adult women identified sources of information they saw as helpful in keeping informed on current fashions. Each of the studies used identical methods for identifying helpful sources. The studies were conducted in New York, Cleveland, and Boston, and findings are summarized in table 11.4. In each of the studies, specialized fashion sources like fashion magazines and fashion shows received the most mentions as helpful sources. Also receiving a substantial number of

TABLE 11.5 MOST HELPFUL SOURCES OF FASHION INFORMATION

TV commercials or programs	5.1%
Radio commercials or programs	0.1
Newspapers	23.3
Fashion magazines (e.g., *Vogue*)	21.4
Women's magazines (e.g., *McCalls*)	7.9
Home magazines (e.g., *Good Housekeeping*)	2.1
General interest magazines (e.g., *Life*)	0.7
Retail store displays	18.3
Retail store sales associates	1.8
Mail advertisement or coupons	0.0
Gifts or samples	0.0
Talking with friends or relatives	4.6
Store or manufacturer's catalogs	3.2
Information on package (including hangtags)	5.4
Fashion shows	6.1
	100.0

Base: 976 Respondents

SOURCE: New Product Adoption Research Program, Purdue University.
Coresearchers: Charles W. King, John O. Summers, and George B. Sproles

mentions was information seeking through personal communications, the more general rather than specialized fashion media, and shopping in retail stores. In a similar investigation by King, Summers, and Sproles, a sample of 976 adult women in Indianapolis was asked to identify a single "most helpful" source of fashion information (table 11.5). Again, a large number of differing information sources were identified, with newspapers, fashion magazines, and retail store displays receiving the largest number of mentions as "most helpful."

Gilkison (1973) examined teenagers' perceptions of the relative importance of different informational sources in influencing their clothing purchases. The study was first conducted in 1961, and then repeated in 1971, among samples of males and females from sixteen to nineteen. In each of those studies, teenagers were asked to rank the importance of five informational sources: parents, friends, salesclerks, magazines and newspapers, and television. The differences between the rankings for 1961 and 1971 are interesting. Among males, in 1961 parents were most frequently mentioned as the most important source, followed in order by friends,

TABLE 11.6 CONSUMERS' PERCEIVED USE OF FASHION COMMUNICATIONS

Categories of Communication	Seldom or Never Important	Sometimes Important	Often or Always Important
Mass Media			
Looking through women's magazines like *Good Housekeeping* or *Family Circle*	22.8%*	30.2%*	46.2%*
Reading newspaper ads on fashions	18.2	35.2	45.8
Reading magazine ads on fashions	21.2	37.8	40.3
Reading newspaper articles on fashions	25.6	33.8	39.8
Reading magazine articles on fashions	26.5	34.3	37.9
Watching clothing advertisements on TV	37.0	30.1	31.9
Reading sewing columns in newspapers	46.6	22.4	29.9
Looking through fashion magazines like *Vogue* or *Harper's Bazaar*	63.4	17.2	18.9
Looking through fashion magazines like *Glamour* or *Mademoiselle*	62.2	20.0	17.0
Personal Sources			
Watching what other women are wearing	14.5	30.9	53.6
Talking with family members	21.1	35.5	42.4
Talking with friends about current fashions	29.4	42.3	27.6
Seeing what movie and TV celebrities wear	48.0	24.9	26.4
Retailing			
Shopping the local stores	7.1	24.3	67.8
Observing clothing store displays	9.0	32.6	58.0
Looking through mail order catalogs	24.7	26.8	47.7
Talking with store salespersons	49.1	32.8	17.5
Going to fashion shows	73.9	18.5	6.9
Consumer Education			
Reading home economics publications	66.5	20.8	11.5
Attending clothing programs offered by fabric stores or companies like Singer	84.5	9.7	4.9
Attending home economics programs	85.8	8.6	4.8

*Interpretation: Of a random sample of 989 women throughout Indiana, 22.8% indicated they seldom or never looked for fashion information in women's magazines; 30.2% indicated they used women's magazines sometimes; and 46.2% indicated they used women's magazines often or always. Rows do not add to 100.0% because of missing answers by a small number of respondents.

SOURCE: Sproles (1977)

TABLE 11.7 IMPORTANCE OF DIFFERENT INFORMATIONAL CONTENTS

Type of Information	Seldom or Never Used	Sometimes Used	Often or Always Used
Styling			
Where to wear certain styles	13.5%*	25.6%*	60.0%*
Current fashion trends in my home town	32.3	32.4	34.5
Fashion trends in big cities like New York	70.6	17.6	11.2
The very newest styles or well-known fashion designers	65.6	23.0	10.1
Product Features			
How to care for my clothing (washing, dry cleaning, spot removal, etc.)	1.3	5.8	92.3
The price of specific items	2.3	16.7	80.5
Fiber content of the fabric	15.2	18.8	65.2
Comparing quality of different brand names	14.8	24.7	59.6
Planning and Selection			
Selecting a well-made "quality" fabric	2.1	10.5	86.6
How to plan and coordinate my wardrobe	9.1	19.6	70.6
How to budget my clothing purchases	12.8	20.9	66.0
Current sales in the stores	7.8	27.6	63.7
Selecting accessories (belts, scarves, etc.)	14.6	29.7	55.2
Selecting children's clothing	32.2	14.4	52.3
Selecting men's clothing	21.8	30.0	46.8
Where to buy specific fashion brand names	26.4	33.6	39.6
Selecting clothing for the elderly	65.2	16.5	17.7
Sewing at Home			
How to sew	31.5	12.1	55.6
Pattern preparation for home sewing	34.6	10.4	54.0
Remodeling or repairing clothing items	24.0	25.0	50.5
Quick sewing techniques	34.5	17.7	47.1
How to use advanced sewing techniques	41.9	17.3	39.8
How to make patterns	58.6	15.2	25.2

*Interpretation: Of a random sample of 989 women throughout Indiana, 13.5% indicated that information on "where to wear certain styles" was seldom or never important; 25.6% indicated this type of information to be sometimes important; and 60.0% indicated this information was often or always important. Rows do not add to 100.0% because of missing answers by a small number of respondents.

SOURCE: Sproles (1977)

magazines and newspapers, sales clerks, and television. In comparison, in 1971 the male subjects ranked friends as most important, followed by magazines and newspapers, salesclerks, parents, and television. Females showed a similar pattern. In 1961 females rated parents as the most important source, followed by friends, salesclerks, magazines, and television. In 1971 they ranked friends most important, followed by salesclerks, television, parents, and magazines. These findings underscore the importance of personal sources—parents, friends, and salesclerks—in influencing teenagers' clothing purchases. Also of interest is the decreasing importance of parents, and the increasing importance of friends, observed in the 1971 study. This finding supports the notion that friendships exercise an important socializing influence on the individual's decision-making.

Research by Sproles (1977) has further explored consumer perceptions of helpful sources. The research involved a survey of 989 randomly selected adult women in Indiana. Table 11.6 summarizes findings for major sources of fashion information. These data suggest that consumers realize that they use a wide range of informational sources on a regular basis. However, certain kinds of communications through mass media, personal contacts, and the retailing system clearly are seen as the most frequently used.

This study also investigated women's perceptions of the importance of different types of informational messages. Table 11.7 summarizes these findings for several categories of information. Information on product features, wardrobe planning, and product selection was viewed as most important. Information on the social appropriateness—where to wear certain styles—was also seen as important by a majority of women. Many other informational contents are valued by substantial percentages of consumer as these figures indicate. In total, these studies indicate consumers' desires for extensive information is high, and much of it is valued in making purchase decisions.

SUMMARY

This chapter emphasized the principle that consumer information seeking and decision-making are often relatively purposeful and systematic acts. Consumers see many sources and informational messages as helping their decisions, and research indicates that nearly all kinds of communications can be used as the decision is approached. For instance, mass media appear to be important in creating awareness and interest, verbal discussions with other people are used in evaluation, retailing sources appear to gain importance as the purchase decision approaches, and personal experience with the product influences the continued adoption or rejection of the product. Thus the different types appear to team up in communicating different sorts of information a consumer needs in making a final decision. Each type of communication appears to have a specialized function and effect on the consumer's decision process.

Some consumers may focus their attention on certain information sources, such as the print-oriented information seeker, the store-intensive searcher, and professional advice searcher. Research also suggests that consumers find a wide range of informational sources and contents to be helpful in their decision-making. Studies document the importance of the mass media, especially newspapers, fashion magazines, and women's magazines, but even more important may be retailing sources and personal sources such as watching what people are wearing. The informational contents that consumers find helpful to their decisions range from information on planning and selection of wardrobes, which appears very important to decisions, to information on where to wear styles and product features.

DISCUSSION QUESTIONS AND PROJECTS

1. Outline the steps in the consumer's decision-making process. What sources of information are most likely to be used and influence choices at each step? How does the types of informational contents sought change as the decision-making process progresses?
2. Choose any market segment or group of consumers having special needs (e.g., professional working people, teenagers, retired senior citizens, handicapped consumers). List the sources of information and types of informational contents most likely to be sought and received by this target market. Find and analyze the effectiveness of an advertisement or other communication toward this audience.
3. Collect five advertisements of current fashions from magazines and newspapers. Do a content analysis of each advertisement, assessing such things as design and layout of the communication, amount of content, type of message (factual, propaganda, extent of emotional appeal versus rational appeal, use of sexual appeals), and likelihood that the ad will be received and "processed" (read and understood) by consumers. Test the ads on several friends by showing each ad, observing their reactions, and asking their evaluations of each ad.
4. Go on a shopping trip and take a hand-held protable tape recorder. As you enter the store, verbalize and tape every thought that enters your mind as you proceed throught the shopping experience. (This verbal

transcript is sometimes called a shopping protocol.) Analyze your completed tape and compare it to table 10.2. What types of information did you use in arriving at your choices?

5. Research suggests that some consumers may specialize in a particular source of information when making decisions (e.g., the print-oriented searchers, the pal-advice searcher). Do you find evidence of this in your own behavior? Discuss this possibility with classmates as a classroom exercise, and tabulate the extent to which your classmates concentrate their information seeking in a single category of informational sources.

SUGGESTED READINGS

Beal, George M., and Everett M. Rogers. "Informational Sources in the Adoption Process of New Fabrics." *Journal of Home Economics* 49 (1957): 630-34.

Eckman, Molly, Mary Lynn Damhorst, and Sara J. Kadolph. "Toward a Model of the In-Store Purchase Decision Process: Consumer Use of Criteria of Evaluating Women's Apparel." *Clothing and Textiles Research Journal* 13 (Winter 1990): 13-22.

Martin, Claude R. Jr. "The Elderly Fashion Consumer: A Forgotten Market." *Working Paper No. 53,* University of Michigan, Bureau of Business Research, December 1971.

Polegato, Rosemary, and Marjorie Wall. "Information Seeking by Fashion Opinion Leaders and Followers." *Home Economics Research Journal* 8 (1980): 327-38.

Reynolds, Fred D., and William R. Darden. "Fashion Theory and Pragmatics: The Case of the Midi." *Journal of Retailing* 49 (Spring 1972): 51-62.

Shim, Soyeon, and Mary Frances Drake. "Apparel Selection by Employed Women: A Typology of Information Search Patterns." *Clothing and Textiles Research Journal* 6 (Winter 1988): 1-9.

12

Forecasting
Future Trends

OBJECTIVES

◆ To identify general and fashion-specific methods for predicting new trends in fashions.

◆ To suggest the future of the fashion phenomenon—what we may expect in years to come from this ever-changing phenomenon of human behavior.

Forecasting is like trying to drive a car blindfolded and following directions given by a person who is looking out of the back window.
Philip Kotler (1972, 192)

Forecasting the new trends in fashions is exceedingly difficult, and has more than just a touch of mystery to it. The obvious reason is that fashions are constantly subject to change, often at what seem to be the whims of consumers. Fashion has a notorious reputation for unpredictability, and the only safe prediction is that the fashion will ultimately change. To forecasters the challenge becomes one of anticipating *what* changes will take place, *when* they will happen, *who* will be the adopters (leaders, followers), and the *why* of this acceptance and diffusion. Because seeing the future is critical to our understanding of fashion-oriented behavior, we close this book with a synopsis of proven and evolving approaches to forecasting future fashions.

Making predictions of future fashions is both an art and a science. It is an art because forecasts are often made purely on good judgment, intuitions, and past experience. It is a science when forecasters use analytical concepts and models to analyze forthcoming trends on a systematic quantitative basis. This concluding chapter briefly introduces methods of forecasting employing both art and sophisticated scientific methods, identifying specific concepts and analytical approaches useful in forecasting fashion trends.

PRINCIPLES OF FORECASTING

Two sets of principles provide a basis for forecasting: (1) **general principles** of forecasting based on an analysis of the changing environment of consumers; and (2) **fashion-specific principles** that can be used in forecasting coming trends in consumers' acceptance of specific styles. A complete forecast of the future requires many of these principles, and successful forecasters use combinations of the following methods to make detailed and refined estimations of the most likely trends.

General Principles

Many forces from the consumer's environment can affect future patterns of consumer demand for fashions. Therefore, it is mandatory at the start to understand the broad trends in society from which fashions may spring. Some of the most significant are the changing state of the national economy, demographic trends, technological developments, and the changing sociocultural environment. Tracking these broad trends in society has become very popular and is now used to derive broad forecasts of all trends in consumption (Naisbitt 1982; Behling 1985-1986; Naisbitt and Aburdene 1990; Celente and Milton 1990).

The Economy   A changing economy has a fundamental influence on aggregate consumer demand. Factors such as the rate of inflation and changes in consumers' personal incomes determine the buying power of consumers. Factors of psychological economics, such as consumers' confidence in their financial future, also affect consumers' plans for future consumption. These economic factors combine to determine consumers' ability and willingness to engage in discretionary consumption of products like fashions.

During recessions or periods of high unemployment, affected consumers spend less on fashions. During these periods consumer demand can be expected to center on classics or other functional styles that are wearable for a long time. Conversely, when consumers' confidence and incomes rise, so do discretionary consumption and the demand for novel fashions.

Demographic Trends Changes in the population can affect future trends in fashion. For instance, some current demographic trends appear to be potential influences on the future of fashions. Of particular importance is the growing proportion of adults between thirty and fifty, a major market for fashions. The elderly population, also growing, is an increasingly important segment of the fashion market. In other trends, the United States will probably continue toward becoming a largely middle-class, middle-income, well-educated society. This trend can mean a lowered emphasis on status-symbolic consumption and greater similarities of dress among large numbers of people. Finally, there is a growing movement of the population away from central cities in favor of more rural areas, and to western and sunbelt states. In addition to creating new fashion markets, these mobile consumers have new life-styles that can shape orientations to fashions.

Technological Developments The development of new technology for the creation of products is a continuing goal of science and industry. Each invention of a "new" or "improved" product can make previous products obsolete and create demand for newer and superior products.

There are almost continuous innovations and technological developments in the production of textiles and clothing. Most have come from textile science, through physical modifications to fibers, new chemical finishes for fabrics, and new fabric-production techniques. Innovations in garment construction have evolved more slowly, but computerized techniques for apparel design and construction have been adopted by many apparel manufacturers. New developments stimulate consumer demand for products of higher quality and superior performance, with the concomitant result that there is an opportunity for new styles to be promoted.

The Socio-Cultural Environment Changes in the consumer's socio-cultural environment—in life-styles, standards of living, and social values—can be powerful influences on future fashions. Modern life-styles are constantly changing as a result of increased leisure time, new social opportunities, physical mobility, and changing roles of men and women. Standards of living are also subject to changes as we enter an age of declining natural resources, a societal demand for conservation, and a social climate of antimaterialism. The new morality of individualism and personal

ConsumerSpeaks

Edited by Peter Walsh

Teen Spending: It's a Lot to Digest

Teens are big spenders and food, surprisingly, is high on the menu

Last summer, a 1992 poll revealed that there were 20.5 million teens in the U.S. The poll, from the market research firm Teenage Research Unlimited, also found that those teens were spending $57 billion of their own money and $36 billion of their family's money.

But instead of spending the money on movies, CDs and concert tickets, surprisingly they spent most of that money on food and on health and beauty aids.

Another survey, this one from the International Council of Shopping Centers (ICSC)/Gallup Organization, found that teens are almost as value-conscious as adults, and by the age of 18 many are already brand loyal and they exercise those loyalties when they go to the grocery store, department store and drug store to shop.

Food shopping ranks high on the scale of purchases for several reasons, the ICSC survey said. First is that teens are at a stage when their bodies are growing fast, and therefore they require larger intakes of food. They need to replenish the calories they are burning up.

Next, the survey claimed that food stores and convenience stores are often located near schools and recreation areas because store planners know that teens tend to be heavy snack-food purchasers. Finally, food stores are usually one of the first store types that children visit with their parents.

The increase in single-parent households (requiring teens to take on additional responsibilities such as food shopping) is also important to note, the survey said.

While it is true that they prefer malls over any other type of shopping location and especially like shopping in small shops, today's teens are experimenting with off-price and manufacturers' outlet stores, it was found. The survey issued a warning to retailers based on the information pollsters uncovered: "... youths' store preferences today may in part determine the successful retailing outlets of tomorrow."

The ICSC survey of 200 teens found that when it comes to clothes, girls buy more than boys do and their preferences vary when it comes to the type of store they shop.

Men's apparel was purchased by 45 percent of all teenagers, with boys buying most of their own clothes, the survey said.

While both prefer shopping in malls, girls favor small specialty stores like The Limited or the Gap while boys like to shop in apparel-oriented sporting goods stores such as Herman's or Athlete's Foot.

Stores such as Chess King were the next choice for male teens, followed by the traditional department stores and warehouse clubs.

Teen boys also prefer small, mall-type stores when they buy electronics like stereos, Walkmans and video cams.

The least important products for teens were children's

Continued on Page 23

Products Purchased by Teens

Groceries 59%
Health and Beauty Aids 52%
Women's Clothing 48%
Men's Clothing 45%
Electronics 28%
Children's Clothing 19%
Home Furnishings 13%

Shopping Location Choices

Teens vs. Adults

■ Teens ■ Adults

	Teens	Adults
Malls	71%	64%
Strip Centers	40%	61%
Either Mall or Strip	76%	85%
Downtown	33%	20%
Stand-Alone Stores	68%	78%

Men's Apparel Purchases

By Teens, By Outlet

Outlet	%
Small Specialty Store	100%
Sears, Ward's or J.C. Penney	37%
Discount Department Store	29%
Traditional Department Store	26%
Manufacturer's Outlet	25%
Off-Price Store	22%
Warehouse Club	13%

Source: ICSC Research Bulletin

freedom could redefine and relax future norms of society. Cultural diversity is also a force favoring introduction and popularization of the new. Such sociocultural changes, when affecting large segments of the population, can modify consumers' future orientations toward changing fashions.

Some of these forces can counter one another. For instance, trends toward active life-styles and increased leisure appear to be open invitations to the consumption of casual and informal fashions. Similarly, trends toward increasing emphasis on self—the individualization of personal identity—self-expression, and hedonism would seem to favor an increasing variety and use of fashions. But the trends toward antimaterialism and less emphasis on status symbolism can result in a reduced interest in fashions. The forecaster is thus confronted with the challenge of identifying the most dominant trends and using these to forecast consumer demand.

Fashion-Specific Principles

The general principles of forecasting can be used to construct a broad picture of future consumer demand. There are numerous specific methods to forecast future fashions, and these are used particularly in the fashion business (Perna 1987). Now for a look at scientific, analytically-based principles that can be used in forecasting specific trends in fashion.

Historical Continuity of Fashion Change　New fashions evolve from previously existing fashions in a continuous manner. That is, each new fashion may be viewed as a modification or elaboration of previously existing styles. Therefore, if the forecaster has studied trends of the recent past, say the last five to ten years, estimates of future trends might be made from this baseline of information.

Research on historical patterns of fashion change has indicated that basic components of styling such as skirt lengths and widths follow a relatively continuous pattern of change. Long-run changes in these components have also appeared to cycle from one extreme to another in an evolutionary manner. Although the concept of historical continuity has not been systematically applied to analyzing short-run changes in design details and colors, it appears that this principle could be usefully applied to forecasting changes in these areas as well. Some analysts even suggest this is among the most important and reliable principles for forecasting fashions (Robinson 1975).

Measurement of Fashion Diffusion　One of the most useful approaches for forecasting specific trends involves the measurement of fashion diffusion, based on the concept of the fashion life cycle. Using this approach, the forecaster identifies a specific fashion trend and constructs a diffusion curve for the trend. A diffusion curve is constructed by counting the number of adopters (buyers and wearers) of a style during several consecutive points in time. A graphic representation of the object's diffusion (consumer acceptance) can then be constructed (see chap. 4).

A forecast of the coming trend can then be made from the diffusion curve. By analyzing the rate of acceptance and the current level of acceptance, the analyst can estimate how much further the trend may extend. For instance, the diffusion curve may indicate whether the style is growing, reaching market saturation, or beginning its decline. A forecast is then made, based on the current extent of diffusion indicated by the curve and the amount of consumer demand (number of potential adopters) remaining.

In making a forecast from the diffusion curve, the analyst must be particularly aware of the current strength of the trend at the time the forecast is made. Is the trend strong enough to go several more months, or to carry over to the next season? How many potential adopters have not yet adopted the style? Is the style faddish or does it reflect elements of a historically continuous trend? Will adopters make repeat purchases? The diffusion curve cannot answer these questions perfectly, and other information is needed to make the final forecast. But the diffusion curve is a basic reference for determining the future strength and duration of the trend.

Consumer Surveys Surveys can be used to measure a variety of behavioral dimensions relevant to fashion trends. Consumers' cognitive orientations toward new styles and their current levels of fashion consciousness (innovativeness, interest, and knowledge) are basic data that can be gathered through surveys. Current norms of dress can be measured to determine which fashions are strongly endorsed in the consumers's social environment. Consumers' psycho-social motivations toward individuality or conformity might also be measured and used to infer whether the current environment favors a continuation of existing trends (conformity) or emergence of new trends (individuality). These varied measures could then be used to make prediction of consumers' receptivity to new styles in the near future and the kinds of consumers most likely to accept these changes.

Consumer Panels Panels of consumers can be used to monitor changing patterns of consumer demand for fashions. A panel may include thousands of consumers who keep regular (typically monthly) records of their clothing acquisitions. The pattern of consumer acquisitions can be charted over a continuous period of time to identify trends in consumption. Another approach might be to focus strictly on panels composed of

Fashion-specific fore-casting: textile companies forecast consumer preferences for colors and fabrics based upon trends of the recent past.

Textile salespersons present their fabric lines to fashion designers and apparel manufacturers. Decisions as to which fabrics to purchase are based upon their short-range forecasting of consumer preferences.

fashion innovators. Such a specialized panel could be particularly valid in identifying and predicting new trends in fashions or temporary fads.

Test Marketing of New Styles   Each fashion season, manufacturers introduce some new and innovative designs. Some larger manufacturers also have a separate division specializing in producing only the most creative and avant-garde styles. One purpose of these activities is to test the market, to identify potential trends in fashion.

Based on the results of these limited tests, a manufacturer can plan to produce and promote the apparently successful styles on a larger scale during the next fashion season. Similarly, retail stores forecast consumer preferences based on limited test marketing of new styles, without taking the risk of committing a large amount of inventory to the new style when it is first available. However, test marketing has dangers, for a new design might sell very well to fashion innovators or faddists during a test but not appeal to the mass market. On the other hand, the overly conservative producer or retailer who avoids new styles may miss the whole trend of the market and lose an opportunity for profit.

Monitoring Major Centers of Fashion Creativity   One of the most frequent methods of forecasting involves monitoring major centers of fashion creativity. Executives at all levels of the fashion industry constantly watch the new designs of high-fashion designers, new styles offered by firms with a reputation for leading new trends, and new fashions in cities with a leading fashion reputation like London, Paris, New York, and Los Angeles. Sales trends in bellwether retail stores are also monitored and used as leading indicators of new trends in mass fashions. Many people in the fashion industry believe monitoring these sources of creativity is a valuable way to identify new trends.

A similar approach involves monitoring patterns of fashion acceptance in certain segments of the population that have a reputation for fashionability: African-Americans, young people, prestigious groups in local social environments, professional working women, and the clientele of fashionable restaurants and clubs. Monitoring consumer choices in these market segments provides predictions of new fashions for the mass market.

Trends in Consumer Expenditures   A general method for forecasting consumer demand involves compilation of historical data on aggregate consumer expenditures. These data may be broken down into expenditures by different categories of merchandise, levels of expenditures in different types of stores (department, specialty, chain, and discount), and proportion of total consumer expenditures on clothing. Trends in these data may then be used to project trends in fashion demand.

One potentially useful approach may center on analysis of purchases to replace worn-out clothing versus those that are additions resulting from changing fashions. In every fashion season some part of consumer expenditures will be replacements based on needs, and this may be a relatively stable portion of consumer demand from year to year. However, other purchases will be directly related to changing fashions and consumers' demand for newness, which may be based on discretionary choice rather than an objectively identified need. Analyzing these trends may provide an indication of the current strength of consumer demand for newness (fashion change), which may be projected for the near future.

Forecasts Using Quantitative Models Predicting consumer behavior is a complex problem involving the identification and use of many variables. To cope with this problem, some analysts are now developing precise mathematical and statistical models with an array of variables to predict consumer behavior. For example, Bhat (1985) proposes we can analyze and forecast fashion demand, the total sales for an item, using math models including the ratio of sales for a period (e.g., a week) to inventory for the period. The proposition is that sales are also a mathematical function of price, time in the season, depth of stock (colors, sizes), and special seasonal effects (e.g., Christmas). However, such models have not been used much for predicting fashion demand, primarily because most models have focused on predicting levels of consumer demand (number of units sold, say, or total dollar expenditures). This sort of forecasting is needed, but fashion forecasters also have a critical qualitative interest in forecasting style and design trends. No quantitative models for generating such forecasts currently exist, other than simple fashion counts of what people are actually wearing or what is selling (these only indicate current fashion, but may signal the future in a limited way). Nevertheless, experimentation with quantitative models has been active among economists and marketing researchers, and fashion forecasters can be expected to take greater interest in quantitative forecasting models in years to come.

Forecasts Using Qualitative Approaches Qualitative methods have accelerated in acceptance by fashion forecasters, particularly in the industry. While there are many such methods (Hirschman 1989), all center on studying people (consumers) in their natural settings and/or "in their own words." It does not involve complex math, but does involve the complex problems of watching what consumers are actually doing,

listening to what they say, and from this information interpreting and forecasting their behavior.

Most popular of the qualitative methods is the *focus group,* which brings a group of eight to twelve consumers together to have a synergistic conversation on some specific topic, such as new and popular fashions for the next six months. Another approach, widely used and advocated by forecasters and some executives we have interviewed, simply involves immersing oneself in the society around you, observing, taking notes, taking pictures, watching trendsetting TV programs and movies, traveling, making clipping files from newspapers and magazines, and synthesizing all this knowledge gained from experience. One executive told us that he gains the best perspective simply by observing fashions around Union Square in downtown San Francisco; others gain it by traveling to Paris to see the fashionable boutiques, clubs, and people in restaurants. Still others

find innovations in once unheard-of places: MTV videos, gay clubs, museums, ethnic festivals. So much of today's and tomorrow's fashions are tipped by these visible sources, if one will only immerse himself or herself in the culture with open eyes and mind.

Store-Specific Forecasts   Each store or fashion business will use a selection of these techniques that, based on their experiences, help forecast new trends. In addition, internal records and information of the store shape a more precise forecast. Certainly the store must begin with complete knowledge of its target market or market segment, the unique group of consumers to whom they appeal. We should expect to know, for example, their level of fashion involvement (very innovative to very conservative), benefits sought, needs, price sensitivity, and preferred brands or designers, all of which are indicators of what fashions may or may not be accepted. Forecasts are further sharpened by knowing the life-styles, attitudes, values, and demographics of the target market.

Promostyl's forecasting system for fashion trends includes predictions 12 to 18 months ahead of the fashion season.

(Promostyl/New York Inc.)

Most stores focus on immediate past sales of the store to plan their near-term forecasts. What styles sold fast, slow? How much did they sell? What styles did customers inquire about, and what did they return or complain about? Of course the store's fashion director, buying office, salespeople, and resources (suppliers) will offer potentially valid perspectives as well. The pace of a fashion season can be so hectic that these internal sources are overlooked, yet these are easily cultivated sources of information and data with the added advantage of being most relevant to the store. For the retail forecaster, these are ultimately the first sources to be used, and among the most effective in achieving a high probability of successful forecasting.

Concluding Comments   No method of forecasting fashions is fool-proof; however, with the combined general and fashion-specific principles for forecasting, the analyst can construct a broadly valid estimate of future consumer behavior.

TYPES OF FORECASTS

Differing types of forecasts may be developed depending on the objectives of the individual or organization requiring the forecast. Forecasts fall into two types, short-range and long-range, and differ not only in the period of time covered but also in degree of accuracy. As the period of time included in the forecast increases, it is less likely that the forecast will be perfectly accurate and more likely that unpredictable events will change the prospective pattern of consumer behavior.

Short-Range Forecasts

The field of fashion is most interested in the development of short-range forecasts. The period of time covered by these forecasts may range from several months to two years. These short-range forecasts seek to identify specific styles and levels of demand for these styles, and to pinpoint the times when consumer demand for the styles can be expected. Several types of short-range forecasts are used. The longest of these are made by fiber and fabric manufacturers. They must forecast consumer preferences for fabrics at least twelve months and often as much as two years into the future, since design and manufacturing of fabrics must be done well before apparel manufacturing is planned.

The apparel producer's forecasts are usually for six to twelve months into the future. Frequently, apparel producers work with fabric producers, who make longer forecasts of fashion trends. The apparel producer's forecast is critical; it is the basis for choosing the styles to produce and promote for the next fashion season.

Retail stores make forecasts for three to six months into the future, focusing on the coming fashion season. Buyers will use them to plan their purchases of merchandise. From these forecasts a store will choose specific price ranges to emphasize, styling and colors to offer, producers from which to purchase specific styles, and merchandising tactics for promoting styles during the fashion season.

Thus, a number of differing short-term forecasts are used by fabric producers, apparel manufacturers, and retailers. Each of these forecasts has to be precise in terms of quantity to produce or order, styling trends to emphasize, and the market segments of consumers who will, it is hoped, adopt the styles. Many fashion-specific principles of forecasting discussed earlier are used in making these predictions.

Long-Range Forecasts

Long-range forecasts require a view into the more distant future, perhaps three to five years, and often decades. These longer-term forecasts do not necessarily concentrate on precise prediction of styling trends, but typically focus on developing a broad managerial guide for the future. Forecasting may be used to establish long-range goals, such as styling, markets, and marketing strategy to emphasize, plan for future production, and develop a program for reaching the organization's goal in light of expected changes in the future.

A long-range forecast cannot draw an exact picture of the future. Some dimensions of the future, such as demographic trends, might be predicted with reasonable certainty, but most long-run social and economic trends can only be estimated. Therefore, the long-range forecast may often place attention on forecasting the alternative possibilities of change which might occur. Obviously there are many possibilities, such as the invention of new technology, changes in the sociocultural environment, changes in the competitive environment, and new trends in the economy. The forecast estimates the most probable changes in these factors, and uses these estimates in general planning for the future.

THE FUTURE OF FASHION

What is the future of fashion for the remainder of this century? Here are some general predictions of the factors that might influence the future of fashion. Of course, any forecast can become rapidly obsolete; therefore, the following should be viewed as suggestions of fashion's potential existence in the years to come.

Appearance performs a central role in affecting an individual's personal identity and social acceptance among other people. Clothing performs a role in this psycho-social phenomenon, and it is reasonable to forecast that dress and fashion will continue to be manipulated with these psychological and social goals as underlying motivations.

Future fashions will reflect the life-styles and related values of their wearers. Social norms regarding the social appropriateness of fashions for different activities and roles will continue to become more flexible, leading to the simultaneous existence of many fashion trends. Consumers will have great latitude in fashion adoption—it will be difficult to make an inappropriate choice, though a broadly defined norm for dress will underlie most aspects of future life.

The desire for novelty and personal stimulation appears to be a fundamental characteristic of human behavior. This underlying demand for change sets the stage for future innovations in fashion to evolve continuously into acceptance. It is unlikely that fashion change will cease to exist in a society that so values creativity and innovation. However, revolutionary or highly innovative styles will probably not be developed with frequency. Rather, a majority of future innovations in fashions may be expected to evolve from previously known and experienced objects.

Fashions will continue to respond to economic conditions in the environment. A compelling force favoring new fashions is the existence of a strong economy and a rising standard of living. Conversely, fashion consumption will decline in periods of reduced economic growth and more restricted standards of living.

Fashion is a business in which many small firms compete for consumer attention, and this may be expected to continue well into the future. The result of this competitive environment is that many differing styles and designs will continue to be made available for selection. However, there is also a trend in growth of some relatively large fashion producers controlling a big share of the market. These producers can have an important influence on future definitions of mass fashion.

There appears to be a continuing role of celebrities, elites, and fashion designers as influencers of taste. However, their roles as dictators and arbiters of fashion trends has declined. Social norms and personal preferences within the consumer's own social environment are taking the place of the elite or designer in determining fashion trends. However, designers are centers of fashion creativity, and an active community of fashion designers and designer brand names may be expected in the future. Also, designers and elite consumers might continue to have an indirect effect on mass fashions through the continued use of knockoff copying of successful designs.

Future fashion trends will be influenced by the behavior of change agents (fashion innovators and opinion leaders) operating within their own social environments. This is a fundamental principle of fashion theory, and the fashion analyst must look to the choices of these consumers as principal influences on new fashion trends. The regularities evident in the fashion process could conceivably cease without the powerful inspirations of these tastemakers.

Fashion theory centers on the proposition that styling and design, and particularly the styling currently receiving social acceptance, are fundamental in consumers' choice and use of dress. However, the consumer also keeps in mind many other important product characteristics, such as practicality of function, comfort, ease of maintenance, versatility, and value for the money. At any given time, some of these may be particularly important to consumer decision-making. For instance, in the 1970s it was fashionable for some consumers to say they purchased styles based on their "individuality, practicality, and comfort," with the implicit denial of a *fashion-oriented* or conformist influence on their choices. This temporary orientation to dress has had some long-range consequences for some consumer markets, but the 1980s saw a return in consumer orientation to fashionable behavior and dressing up. Thus, the fashion analyst must be aware of the particular product characteristics endorsed by consumers at any given time in developing a forecast of future consumer behavior.

At times, fashion has implied uniformity or even identicality in dress; for example, a conservatively tailored business suit (dress for success) for "everyone." However true this may have been in the past, it is unlikely to be so in the future. Rather, one can expect a diversity of designs to pervade any dominant fashion trend, and the analyst of the future must look for general fashion concepts or ideals in styling that can find expression in a variety of individualistic ways. For instance, such concepts as casual dress, pant suits for women, the mod look, and counterculture dress have included the acceptance of many individualistic variations within those essentially singular fashion trends. To identify fashion trends in the future the analyst must look for the commonality in general themes that will underlie each uniquely designed object of fashion.

Overall, these propositions do not suggest the emergence of a new world of fashion radically different from the present. However, any view of the future requires regular updating. Students of fashion should test the adequacy of these propositions and construct their own predictions of future trends in fashions.

DISCUSSION QUESTIONS

1. Identify a new fashion trend you believe is about to start. What type of consumers will be the innovators and opinion leaders in this trend? What stores will lead and follow the trend? Where will the trend be adopted first, and later? How long will the trend last and what will be its total level of acceptance at each time in this diffusion (draw your predicted diffusion curve).
2. What demographic changes do you see in society during the next ten years? What demographic groups will be especially dominant in this market? What implications do these demographic factors have for the design and marketing of changing fashions?
3. Social trends and changing life-styles are also major factors shaping the styles we wear. Form groups in class to discuss current life-styles and identify five major trends shaping tomorrow's fashions.
4. Discuss how the concept of historial continuity in fashion change can help forecasters predict new fashion trends. Give an analytical example from the past ten years, and use this to suggest the trend for the next year.
5. What are the strengths and limiations of using diffusion curves as predictive tools?
6. Considering the wide range of fashion-specific forecasting tools, which ones do you think are most appropriate for forecasting new trends in (a) women's dressy outerwear, (b) men's casual sportswear, (c) running shoes, (d) men's underwear, and (e) colors of dress shirts and blouses. Be prepared to defend your choices with explanations.
7. Study the literature of forecasting by visiting your library to seek out books, magazines and trade journals specializing in forecasts (see literature such as *American Demographics*, *Futures*, *Women's Wear Daily*, *DNR*, and many others). What types of forecasts do these make, and how would you use each to help predict changing trends?
8. Discuss the use of long-range versus short-range forecasts in different parts of the fashion business (e.g., large specialty retailers, mass retailers, mass manufacturers of apparel, high fashion designers, textile producers, dye manufacturers). What are the differing forecasting needs of each group?

SUGGESTED READINGS

Behling, Dorothy. "Fashion Change and Demographics: A Model." *Clothing and Textiles Research Journal* 4 (1985-86, No. 1): 18-24.

Bhat, Rajendra R. *Managing the Demand for Fashion Items.* Ann Arbor, MI: University of Michigan Research Press, 1985.

Celente, Gerald, and Tom Milton. *Trend Tracking.* New York: John Wiley, 1990.

Naisbitt, John, and Patricia Aburdene. *Megatrends 2000: Ten New Directions for the 1990s.* New York: William Morrow and Company, 1990.

Perna, Rita. *Fashion Forecasting.* New York: Fairchild Publications, 1987.

Robinson, Dwight E. "Style Changes: Cyclical, Inexorable, and Foreseeable." *Harvard Business Review* 53 (November-December 1975): 121-31.

Bibliography

Aaker, David A., and George S. Day, eds. *Consumerism.* New York: The Free Press, 1971.

Adler, France-Michele. *Sportsfashion.* New York: Avon Books/Hearst, 1980.

Aiken, Lewis R. "The Relationships of Dress to Selected Measures of Personality in Undergraduate Women." *Journal of Social Psychology* 59 (1963): 119-28.

Alexis, Marcus, George H. Haines, and Leonard Simon. "Consumer Information Processing: The Case of Women's Clothing." In *Marketing and the New Science of Planning,* edited by Robert L. King. Chicago: American Marketing Association, 1968.

Allen, Charlene Duch, and Joanne B. Eicher. "Adolescent Girls' Acceptance and Rejection Based on Appearance." *Adolescence 8* (1973): 125-38.

Allport, Gordon W. *Personality: A Psychological Interpretation.* New York: Holt, Rinehart and Winston, Inc., 1937.

Allport, Gordon W., Philip E. Vernon, and Gardner Lindzey. *Study of Values.* 3d edition. Boston: Houghton Mifflin Co., 1970.

Allport, George W. *Pattern and Growth in Personality.* New York: Holt, Rinehart, and Winston, 1961.

American Home Economics Association. "Aesthetics and Clothing, An Annotated Bibliography." Washington: American Home Economics Association, 1972.

Anderson, Barbara, and Cletus Anderson. *Costume Design.* New York: Holt, Rinehart, and Winston, 1984.

Angelino, Henry, Lenorah A. Barnes, and Charles L. Shedd. "Attitudes of Mothers and Adolescent Daughters Concerning Clothing and Grooming." *Journal of Home Economics* 48 (1956): 779-82.

Anspach, Karlyne. "Clothing Selection and the Mobility Concept." *Journal of Home Economics 53* (1961): 428-30.

Anspach, Karlyne. "The American in Casual Dress." *Journal of Home Economics 55* (1963):255-257.

Anspach, Karlyne. *The Why of Fashion.* Ames, Iowa: The Iowa State University Press, 1976.

Anthony, Pegaret, and Janet Arnold. *Costume, A General Bibliography.* London: The Costume Society, Victoria and Albert Museum, 1974.

Asch, Solomon E. "Effects of Group Pressure Upon the Modification and Distortion of Judgments." In *Groups, Leadership and Men,* edited by H. Guetzkow. Pittsburgh, Penn: Carnegie Press, 1951: 177–90

Atkin, C. K. "Observation of Parent-Child Interaction in Supermarket Decision-making." *Journal of Marketing 42* (1978): 41-5.

Banner, Lois. *American Beauty.* New York: Alfred A. Knopf, 1983.

Barber, Bernard. *Social Stratification.* New York: Harcourt, Brace and World, Inc., 1957.

Barber, Bernard, and Lyle S. Lobel. "'Fashion in Women's Clothes and the American Social System." *Social Forces 31* (December 1952): 124-31.

Barnett, H.G. *Innovation: The Basis of Cultural Change.* New York: McGraw-Hill Book Co., Inc., 1953.

Barr, Estelle De Young. "A Psychological Analysis of Fashion Motivation." *Archives of Psychology 26* (June 1934): 1-100.

Barthes, Roland. *The Fashion System.* New York: Hill and Wang/Farrar, Straus, and Giroux, 1983.

Baugh, Dawna F., and Leslie L. Davis. "The Effect of Store Image on Consumer Perceptions of Designer and Private Label Clothing." *Clothing and Textiles Research Journal 7* (Spring 1989): 15-21.

Baumgarten, Steven A. "The Innovative Communicator in the Diffusion Process." *Journal of Marketing Research 12* (February 1975): 12-18.

Baumgartner, Charlotte Wolff. "Factors Associated With Clothing Consumption Among College Freshmen." *Journal of Home Economics 55* (1963): 218.

Beal, George M. and Everett M. Rogers. "Informational Sources in the Adoption Process of New Fabrics." *Journal of Home Economics 49* (1957): 630-34.

Beaton, Cecil. *Fashion: An Anthology.* London: Victoria and Albert Museum, 1971.

Beaton, Cecil. *The Glass of Fashion.* Garden City, N.Y.: Doubleday and Company, Inc., 1954.

Beckett, Kathleen. "A New Groove." *Vogue,* September 1985, 474.

Behling, Dorothy. "Fashion Change and Demographics: A Model." *Clothing and Textiles Research Journal 4,* (Fall 1985): 18-24.

Bell, Quentin. *On Human Finery.* London: The Hogarth Press, 1947.

Benedict, Ruth. "Dress." *Encyclopedia of the Social Sciences.* New York: MacMillan, 1931.

Berg, Sanford V. "Independent Tastes and Fashion Behavior." *Quarterly Review of Economics and Business 13* (1973): 49-58.

Bergler, Edmund. *Fashion and the Unconscious.* New York: Robert Brunner, 1953.

Bergler, Edmund. "A Psychoanalyst Looks at Women's Clothes." *Cosmopolitan,* February 1960, 52-55.

Berk, Richard A. *Collective Behavior.* Dubuque, Iowa: Wm. C. Brown Company Publishers, 1974.

Berkman, Harold W., and Christopher Gilson. *Consumer Behavior: Concepts and Strategies* (3d Ed.). Boston: Kent Publishing, 1986.

Bettman, James R. *An Information Processing Theory of Consumer Choice.* Reading, Mass: Addison-Wesley, 1979.

Bhat, Rajendra R. *Managing the Demand for Fashion Items.* Ann Arbor, MI: UMI Research Press, 1985.

Bigelow, Marybelle S. *Fashion in History.* Minneapolis: Burgess Publishing Co., 1970.

Blumberg, Paul. "The Decline and Fall of the Status Symbol: Some Thoughts on Status in a Post-Industrial Society." *Social Problems 21* (1974): 480-98.

Blumer, Herbert. "Fashion." *International Encyclopedia of the Social Sciences.* New York: The MacMillan Company, 1968.

Blumer, Herbert. "Fashion: From Class Differentiation to Collective Selection." *Sociological Quarterly 10* (1969): 275-91.

Bogardus, Emory S. "Social Psychology of Fads." *Journal of Applied Sociology 8* (1924): 239-43.

Borror, Merna Jane, and Anna M. Creekmore. "Relation of Physical Coloring and Personality Characteristics to Color Preferences for Clothing." *Journal of Home Economics 57* (1965): 447-50.

Boucher, Francois. *20,000 Years of Fashion: The History of Costume and Personal Adornment.* New York: H.N. Abrams, 1967.

Branson, Donna H., and Maureen M. Sweeney. "Clothing Comfort Conceptualization and Measurement: Toward a Metatheory." In *Critical Linkages in Textiles and Clothing: Theory, Method, and Practice,* edited by S.B. Kaiser and M. L. Damhorst. ACPTC: Monument, CO, 1991, 94-105.

Brenninkmeyer, Ingrid. *The Sociology of Fashion.* Paris: Libr airie de Recueil Sirey, 1963.

Brett, Joyce, and Anne Kernaleguen. "Perceptual and Personality Variables Related to Opinion Leadership in Fashion." *Perceptual and Motors Skills 40* (1975): 775-79.

Brockman, Helen L. *The Theory of Fashion Design.* New York: John Wiley and Sons, Inc., 1965.

Brown, Lawrence A. *Innovation Diffusion.* New York: Methuen, 1981.

Bruner, Gordon C. II. "Singles and Sex Roles: Are There Differences in Clothing Prepurchase Process?" *Clothing and Textiles Research Journal 7* (Fall 1988): 3-9.

Bryant, Nigel J. "Petitioning: Dress Congruence Versus Belief Congruence." *Journal of Applied Social Psychology 5* (1975): 144-49.

Buckley, Hilda M. "Toward An Operational Definition of Dress." *Clothing and Textiles Research Journal 3* (Spring 1985): 1-10.

Buckley, Hilda Mayer, and Mary Ellen Roach. "Clothing as a Nonverbal Communicator of Social and Political Attitudes." *Home Economics Research Journal 3* (December 1974): 94-102.

Bush, George, and Perry London. "On the Disappearance of Knickers: Hypotheses for the Functional Analysis of the Psychology of Clothes." *Journal of Social Psychology 51* (1960): 359-66.

Byrne, D. *The Attraction Paradigm.* New York: Academic Press, 1971.

Calasibetta, Charlotte. *Fairchild's Dictionary of Fashion* (Second Edition). New York: Fairchild Publications, 1988.

Carman, James M. "The Fate of Fashion Cycles in Our Modern Society." *In Science, Technology and Marketing,* edited by Raymond M. Haas. Chicago: American Marketing Association, 1966.

Carson, Richard. *Fashions in Hair.* New York: Hastings House Publishers Inc., 1965.

Casselman, Marsha A., and Mary L. Damhorst. "Relationship of Sport Involvement and Role Knowledge to Female Bicyclists' Use of and Interests in Sport Apparel." Presentation at the Annual Meeting of the Association of College Professors of Textiles and Clothing, Denver, 1990.

Cattell, R. B. *Personality: A Systematic, Theoretical, and Factual Study.* New York: McGraw-Hill, 1950.

Celente, Gerald, and Tom Milton. *Trend Tracking.* New York: John Wiley, 1990.

Chaiken, Alan L., Valerian J. Derlega, John Yoder, and David Phillips. "The Effects of Appearance on Compliance." *Journal of Social Psychology 92* (1974): 199-200.

Chowdhary, Usha. "Fashion Information Seeking by Younger and Older Consumers." *Clothing and Textiles Research Journal 8* (Fall 1989): 49-55.

Christiansen, Karen, and Anne Kernaleguen. "Orthodoxy and Conservatism—Modesty in Clothing Selection." *Journal of Home Economics 63* (1971): 251-55.

Clum, Terry L., and Joanne B. Eicher. "Teenagers' Conformity in Dress and Peer Friendship Groups."

Michigan State University Agricultural Experiment Station, Research Report 156, March 1972.

Cobliner, W. Godfrey. "Feminine Fashion as an Aspect of Group Psychology: Analysis of Written Replies Received by Means of a Questionnaire." *Journal of Social Psychology 31* (1950): 283-89.

Cocks, Jay. "Scarves and Minds." *Time,* March 21, 1988, p72.

Coleman, James S., Elihu Katz, and Herbert Menzel. *Medical Innovation: A Diffusion Study.* Indianapolis: The Bobbs-Merrill Company, 1966.

"Comfort in Casuals." *Textile Horizons 5* (1985): 35-38.

Compton, Norma H. "Personal Attributes of Color and Design Preferences in Clothing Fabrics." *Journal of Psychology 54* (1962): 191-95.

Compton, Norma H. "Clothing Fabric Preferences in Relation to Selected Physical and Personality Characteristics." *Journal of Home Economics 55* (1963): 218-19.

Compton, Norma H. "Body Image Boundaries in Relation to Clothing Fabric and Design Preferences of a Group of Hospitalized Psychotic Women." *Journal of Home Economics 56* (1964): 40-45.

Compton, Norma H. "Body Build, Clothing and Delinquent Behavior." *Journal of Home Economics 59* (1967): 655-59.

Compton, Norma H., and Olive A. Hall. *Foundations of Home Economics Research: A Human Ecology Approach.* Minneapolis: Burgess Publishing Co., 1972.

Cooley, Charles H. *Human Nature and the Social Order.* New York: Charles Scribner's Sons, 1902.

Corliss, Richard. "Coming on Strong: The New Ideal of Beauty." *Time* August 30, 1982, p72-77.

Cox, Donald F., ed. *Risk Taking and Information Handling in Consumer Behavior.* Cambridge, Mass.: Harvard University Press, 1967.

Cox, D. F., and S. U. Rich. "Perceived Risk and Consumer Decision Making — The Case of Telephone Shopping." *Journal of Marketing Research 1* (1964): 32-39.

Crane, Diana. "Fashion in Science: Does It Exist?" *Social Problems 16* (1969): 433-41.

Crawford, M. D. C. *Philosophy in Clothing.* New York: Brooklyn Museum, 1940.

Crawford, M.D.C. *The Ways of Fashion.* New York: G.P. Putnam's Sons, 1941.

Crawford, M.D.C. "The Eyed Needle." In *Dress, Adornment, and the Social Order,* edited by Mary Ellen Roach and Joanne Bubolz. New York: John Wiley and Sons, Inc., 1965.

Creekmore, Anna M. "Clothing Related to Body Satisfaction and Perceived Peer Self." Michigan State University Agricultural Experiment Station, Research Report 239, March 1974.

Creekmore, Anna M. *Methods of Measuring Clothing Variables.* Michigan State University Agricultural Experiment Station, 1971.

Cremers van der Does, Eline C. *The Agony of Fashion.* Poole, Great Britain: Blanford Press, 1980.

Damhorst, Mary L. "Meanings of Clothing Cues in Social Context." *Clothing and Textiles Research Journal 3* (Spring 1985): 39-48.

Damhorst, Mary L. "In Search of a Common Thread: Classification of Information Communicated Through Dress." *Clothing and Textiles Research Journal 8* (Winter 1990): 1-12.

D'Antoni, Joseph S., and Howard L. Shenson. "Impulse Buying Revisited: A Behavioral Typology." *Journal of Retailing 49* (Spring 1973): 63-76.

Daniels, Alfred H. "Fashion Merchandising." *Harvard Business Review 29* (May 1951): 51-60.

Darden, William R., and Fred D. Reynolds. "Generalized Innovation Factors in Men's Apparel Fashions." *In Combined Proceedings, 1971 Spring and Fall Conferences of the American Marketing Association,* edited by Fred C. Allvine. Chicago: American Marketing Association, 1972, 434-38.

Darden, William R., and Fred D. Reynolds. "Predicting Opinion Leadership for Men's Apparel Fashions." *Journal of Marketing Research 9* (1972): 324-28.

Darden, William R., and Fred D. Reynolds. "Backward Profiling of Male Innovators." *Journal of Marketing Research 11* (1974): 79-85.

Darley, John, and Joel Cooper. "The 'Clean for Gene' Phenomenon: The Effects of Students' Appearance on Political Campaigning." *Journal of Applied Social Psychology 2* (1972): 24-33.

Daves, Jessica. *Ready-Made Miracle.* New York: G.P. Putnam's Sons, 1967.

Davis, Daphne. *Stars!* New York: Simon and Schuster. 1983.

Davis, Fred. "Clothing and Fashion as Communication." In *The Psychology of Fashion,* edited by M. R. Solomon. Lexington: Heath/Lexington Books, 1985, 15-27.

Davis, Leslie L. "Effects of Physical Quality and Brand Labeling on Perceptions of Clothing Quality." *Perceptual and Motor Skills 61* (1985): 671-77.

Davis, Leslie L. "Consumer Use of Label Information in Ratings of Clothing Quality and Clothing Fashionability." *Clothing and Textiles Research Journal 6* (Fall 1987): 8-14.

Davis, Leslie L. "Social Salience: What We Notice First About a Person." *Perceptual and Motor Skills 71* (1990): 334.

Davis, Leslie L., and Franklin G. Miller. "Conformity and Judgments of Fashionability." *Home Economics Research Journal 11* (1983): 337-42.

Dearborn, George V. *The Psychology of Clothes.* Princeton: Psychological Review Co., 1918.

Dearborn, George Van Ness. "The Psychology of Clothing." *Psychological Monographs 26* (1918-1919): 1-72.

DeCaro, Frank. "Untouchables to Put the Arm on Fashion-Conscious Males." *The Denver Post* Thursday, July 2, 1987, 2D.

DeLong, Marilyn. *The Way We Look.* Ames: Iowa State University Press, 1987.

Deutsch, Morton, and Harold Gerard. "A Study of Normative and Informational Social Influences Upon Individual Judgment." *Journal of Abnormal and Social Psychology 51* (1955): 629-36.

Dichter, Ernest. "Psychology of Textiles." *Journal of the Textile Institute 51* (1960): 486-598.

Dichter, Ernest. *Handbook of Consumer Motivations.* New York: McGraw-Hill Book Co., 1964.

Dichter, Ernest. "Fashion, Fabrics, and Erogenous Zones." *American Fabrics* Summer 1967, 87.

Dittes, James E., and Harold H. Kelley. "Effects of Different Conditions of Acceptance Upon Conformity." *Journal of Abnormal and Social Psychology 53* (1956): 100-107.

Dommermuth, William P., and Edward W. Cundiff, "Shopping Goods, Shopping Centers, and Selling Strategies." *Journal of Marketing 31* (1967): 32-36.

Donnelly, James H. Jr., and Michael J. Etzel. "Degrees of Product Newness and Early Trial." *Journal of Marketing Research 19* (1973): 295-300.

Dooley, William H. *Clothing and Style.* New York: D.C. Heath and Company, 1930.

Doughty, John Carr. "The Art of Fashion Colour Forecasting." *Textile Institute and Industry 6* (1968): 97-100.

Douty, Helen I. "Influence of Clothing on Perception of Persons." *Journal of Home Economics 55* (1963): 197-202.

Duka, John. "Detente Dressing." *Elle,* July 1986, 116-18.

Dunlap, Knight. "The Development and Function of Clothing." *Journal of General Psychology 1* (1928): 64-78.

Ebeling, Maloa and Mary Lou Rosencranz. "Social and Personal Aspects of Clothing for Older Women." *Journal of Home Economics 53* (1961): 464-65.

Ebin, Victoria. *The Body Decorated.* New York: Thames and Hudson, 1979.

Eckman, Molly, Mary Lynn Damhorst, and Sara J. Kadolph. "Toward a Model of the In-Store Purchase Decision Process: Consumer Use of Criteria for Evaluating Women's Apparel." *Clothing and Textiles Research Journal 8* (Winter 1990): 13-22.

Eco, Umberto. *A Theory of Semiotics.* Bloomington: Indiana University Press, 1979.

Edmonds, Ed M., and Delwin D. Cahoon. "Female Clothes Preference Related to Male Sexual Interest." *Bulletin of the Psychonomic Society 22* (1984): 171-73.

Eicher, Joanne B., and Eleanor A. Kelley. "A Longitudinal Study of High School Girls' Friendship Patterns, Social Class, and Clothing." Michigan State University Agricultural Experiment Station, Research Report 222, February, 1974.

Elliott, Huger. *Fashions in Art.* New York: Appleton-Century, 1937.

Emswiller, T., K. Deaux, and J. Willits. "Similarity, Sex and Requests for Small Favors." *Journal of Applied Social Psychology 1* (1971): 284-91.

Evans, S. Evelyn. "Motivations Underlying Clothing Selection and Wearing." *Journal of Home Economics 56* (1964): 739-43.

Fallers, Lloyd A. "A Note on the 'Trickle Effect.'" *Public Opinion Quarterly 19* (1954): 314-21.

Festinger, Leon. *A Theory of Cognitive Dissonance.* Evanston, Illinois: Row, Peterson and Co., 1957.

Festinger, Leon. "Informal Social Communication." Psychological Review 57 (1950): 271-282. In *Behavioral Science Foundations of Consumer Behavior,* edited by Joel B. Cohen. New York: The Free Press, 1972.

Festinger, Leon. "A Theory of Social Comparison Processes." *Human Relations 7* (1954): 117-40.

Field, George A. "The Status Float Phenomenon: The Upward Diffusion of Innovation." *Business Horizons 13* (August 1970): 45-52.

Fiske, Susan T., and Shirley E. Taylor. *Social Cognition.* Reading, MA: Addison-Wesley, 1984.

Flaccus, Louis W. "Remarks on the Psychology of Clothes." *Pedagogical Seminary 13* (1906): 61-83.

Flowers, William Henry. *Fashion in Deformity, As Illustrated in the Customs of Barbarians and Civilized Races.* London: MacMillan and Co., 1881.

Flugel, John Carl. *The Psychology of Clothes.* London: Hogarth Press, International Psychoanalytic Library, 1930.

Focht, Brenda M., and Geitel Winakor. "Collecting Clothing Consumption Data." *Journal of Home Economics 59* (1967): 788-93.

Foley, Caroline A. "Fashion." *Economic Journal 3* (1893): 458-74.

Ford, C. S., and F. A. Beach. *Patterns of Sexual Behavior.* New York: Harper and Row, 1951.

Form, William H., and Gregory P. Stone. "The Social Significance of Clothing in Occupational Life." *Technical Bulletin 247,* Michigan State College Agricultural Experiment Station, June, 1955.

Form, William H., and Gregory P. Stone. "Urbanism, Anonymity and Status Symbolism." *American Journal of Sociology 62* (1957): 504-14.

Forsythe, Sandra M., Mary F. Drake, and Charles Cox. "Dress as an Influence on the Perceptions of Management Characteristics in Women." *Home Economics Research Journal 13* (1984): 112-21.

Fowles, J. "Why We Wear Clothes." *ETC: A Review of General Semantics 31* (December, 1974): 343-52.

Francis, Sally, and Leslie Davis Burns. "Effect of Consumer Socialization on Clothing Shopping Attitudes, Clothing Aquisition, and Clothing Satisfaction." *Clothing and Textiles Research Journal 10* (Summer 1992): 35-39.

Franken, Richard B. "Advertising Appeals Selected by the Method of Direct Impression." *Journal of Applied Psychology 8* (1924): 232-44.

Freudenberger, Herman. "Fashion, Sumptuary Laws, and Business." *Business History Review 37* (Spring-Summer 1963): 37-48.

Fromkin, Howard L. "The Psychology of Uniqueness: Avoidance of Similarity and Seeking of Differentness." Institute for Research in the Behavioral, Economic, and Management Sciences, Purdue University, Paper No. 438, December, 1973.

Fromkin, H. L., and R. Lipshitz. "A Construct Validity Method of Scale Development: The Need for Uniqueness Scale." Institute for Research in the Behavioral, Economic, and Management Sciences (Paper No. 591). West Lafayette, Ind.: Purdue University, 1976.

Fromkin, H. L., J. C. Olson, R. L. Dipboye, and D. Barnaby. "A Commodity Theory Analysis of Consumer Preferences for Scarce Products." Paper presented at the American Psychological Association Convention, Washington, September 1971.

Fromkin, H. L., J. J. Williams, and R. L. Dipboye. "Birth Order, Responses to Need for Uniqueness Scale Items, and Valuation of Scarce Commodities." Unpublished Manuscript, Purdue University, 1974.

Garma, Angel. "The Origin of Clothes." *Psychoanalytic Quarterly 18* (1949): 173-90.

Gatignon, Hubert, and Thomas S. Robertson. "A Propositional Inventory for New Diffusion Research." *Journal of Consumer Research 11* (1985): 849-67.

Gibbins, Keith. "Communication Aspects of Women's Clothes and Their Relation to Fashionability." *British Journal of Social and Clinical Psychology 8* (1969): 301-12.

Gibbins, Keith. "Social Psychological Theories of Fashion." J*ournal of the Home Economics Association of Australia 3* (1971): 3-18.

Gibbins, Keith, and Jeffrey R. Coney. "Meaning of Physical Dimensions of Women's Clothes." *Perceptual and Motor Skills 53* (1981): 720-22.

Gibbins, Keith, and Tonya K. Gwynn. "A New Theory of Fashion Change: A Test of Some Predictions." *British Journal of Social and Clinical Psychology 14* (1975): 1-9.

Gilkison, Paul. "Teen-agers' Perceptions of Buying Frames of Reference: A Decade in Retrospect." *Journal of Retailing 49* (Summer 1973): 25-37.

Goethals, George R. "Social Comparison Theory: Psychology From the Lost and Found." *Personality and Social Psychology Bulletin 12* (1986): 261-78.

Goffman, Erving. *The Presentation of Self in Everyday Life.* Garden City, NY: Doubleday Anchor Books, 1959.

Gold, Annalee. *How to Sell Fashion.* New York: Fairchild Publications, Inc., 1968.

Greeno, Daniel W., Montrose S. Sommers, and Jerome B. Kernan. "Personality and Implicit Behavior Patterns." *Journal of Marketing Research 10* (1973): 63-69.

Gregory, Paul M. "Fashion and Monopolistic Competition." *Journal of Political Economy 56* (1948): 69-75.

Gress, Edward G. *Fashions in American Typography 1780-1930.* New York: Harper & Brothers, 1931.

Grindereng, Margaret P. "Fashion Diffusion." *Journal of Home Economics 59* (1967): 171-74.

Gurel, Lois M. "The Function of Dress." In *Dimensions of Dress and Adornment,* edited by Lois M. Gurel and Mariannne S. Beeson. Dubuque, Iowa: Kendall/Hunt Publishing Co., 1975, 3-6.

Gurel, Lois M., June C. Wilbur, and Lee Gurel. "Personality Correlates of Adolescent Clothing Styles." *Journal of Home Economics 64* (1972): 42-47.

Haley, Elizabeth G., and Norejane J. Hendrickson. "Children's Preferences for Clothing and Hair Styles." *Home Economics Research Journal 2* (1974): 176-93.

Hall, Edward T. *The Silent Language.* Garden City, NY: Doubleday and Co., Inc., 1959.

Hamid, Paul N. "Style of Dress as a Perceptual Aid in Impression Formation." *Perceptual and Motor Skills 26* (1968): 904-6.

Hamilton, Janice, and Jessie Warden. "The Student's Role in a High School Community and His Clothing Behavior." *Journal of Home Economics 58* (1966): 789-91.

Hanmer, Davina, and Tim Graham. *Diana: The Fashion Princess.* New York: Holt, Rinehart and Winston, 1984.

Harms, Ernest. "The Psychology of Clothes." *American Journal of Sociology 44* (1938): 239-60.

Harris, Christie, and Moira Johnson. *Figleafing Through History: The Dynamics of Dress.* New York: Atheneum, 1971.

Harris, Mary B., and Gail Bays. "Altruism and Sex Roles." *Psychological Reports 32* (1973): 1002.

Hart, Edward W., and Jacob Jacoby. "Novelty, Recency, and Scarcity as Predictors of Perceived Newness." In *Proceedings, 81st Annual Convention,* American Psychological Association, 1973.

Hartmann, George W. "Clothing: Personal Problem and Social Issue." *Journal of Home Economics 41* (1949): 295-98.

Hatfield, Elaine, and Susan Sprecher. *Mirror, Mirror: The Importance of Looks in Everyday Life.* Albany, NY: State University of New York Press, 1986.

Hawes, Donice A., and D. Lois Gilmore. "Clothing Utilization." *Journal of Home Economics 59* (1967): 112-15.

Hazlitt, William. "On Fashion." In *The Collected Works of William Hazlitt,* 11, edited by A.R. Waller. London: J.M. Dent and Co., 1904, 437-42.

Heisey, Francesann L. "Perceived Quality and Predicted Price: Use of the Minimum Information Environment in Evaluating Apparel." *Clothing and Textiles Research Journal 8* (Summer 1990): 22-28.

Hendricks, Suzanne H., Eleanor A. Kelley, and JoAnne B. Eicher. "Senior Girls' Appearance and Social Participation." *Journal of Home Economics 60* (1968): 167-72.

Hensley, Wayne E. "The Effects of Attire, Location, and Sex on Aiding Behavior: A Similarity Explanation." *Journal of Nonverbal Behavior 6* (1981): 3-11.

Hertz, D.B., and K.H. Schaffir. "A Forecasting Method for Management of Seasonal Style-Goods Inventories." *Operations Research 8* (1960): 45-52.

Hill, Margot Hamilton, and Peter A. Buckness. *The Evolution of Fashion.* London: B.T. Batsford Ltd., 1967.

Hirsch, Paul M. "Processing Fads and Fashions: An Organization-Set Analysis of Cultural Industry Systems." *American Journal of Sociology 77* (1972): 639-59.

Hirschman, Elizabeth C. "Comprehending Symbolic Consumption." In *Symbolic Consumer Behavior,* edited by Elizabeth C. Hirschman and Morris B. Holbrook. Ann Arbor, MI: Association for Consumer Research, 1980, 4-6.

Hirschman, Elizabeth C., Ed. *Interpretive Consumer Research.* Provo, UT: Association for Consumer Research, 1989.

Hoffman, R.M. "Measuring the Aesthetic Appeal of Textiles." *Textile Research Journal 35* (1965): 428-34.

Hoffman, Hans-Joachim. "How Clothes Communicate." *Media Development 4* (1984): 7-11.

Hollander, Anne. "Movie Clothes." The *New York Times Magazine*, December 1, 1974, p68, 70-71.

Hollander, Stanley C. "A Note on Fashion Leadership." *Business History Review 37* (1963): 448-51.

Horn, Marilyn J. *The Second Skin.* (2d ed.) Boston: Houghton Mifflin Co., 1975.

Horn, Marilyn J. and Lois M. Gurel. *The Second Skin.* (3d ed.) Boston: Houghton Mifflin, 1981.

Horridge, Patricia, and Mary Lynne Richards. "Relationship of Fashion Awareness and Clothing Economic Practices." *Home Economics Research Journal 13* (1984): 138-52.

Horridge, Patricia, and Mary Lynne Richards. "Awareness of the Social Implications of Clothing in Relation to Fashion Awareness and Clothing Economic Practices," *Psychology, A Quarterly Journal of Human Behavior 23*, no. 2 (1986): 5-15.

Houck, Catherine. *The Fashion Encyclopedia.* New York: St. Martin's Press, 1982.

Howell, Georgina. *In Vogue.* New York: Schoken Books, 1975.

Hughes, G. David, and Michael L. Ray, eds. *Buyer/Consumer Information Processing.* Chapel Hill, N.C.: The University of North Carolina Press, 1974.

Humphrey, Carolyn, M. Klassen, and A.M. Creekmore. "Clothing and Self-Concept of Adolescents." *Journal of Home Economics 63* (1971): 246-50.

Hurlock, Elizabeth. "Motivation in Fashion." *Archives of Psychology 17*, no. 111 (1929).

Hurlock, Elizabeth B. *The Psychology of Dress.* New York: The Ronald Press, 1929.

Jacobi, John E. and S. George Walters. "Social Status and Consumer Choice." *Social Forces 36* (1958): 209-14.

Jacobi, John E., and S. George Walters. "Dress Buying Behavior of Consumers." *Journal of Marketing 23* (1958): 168-72.

Jacobson, Wilhelmina E. "Human Motives Underlying Fashion Changes." *Practical Home Economics 14* (1936): 230-31.

Jacoby, Jacob. "Multiple-Indicant Approach for Studying New Product Adopters." *Journal of Applied Psychology 55* (1971): 384-88.

Jacoby, Jacob, George J. Szybillo and Carol Kohn Berning. "Time and Consumer Behavior: An Interdisciplinary Overview." *Journal of Consumer Research 2* (1976): 320-39.

Jacoby, Jacob, and L. B. Kaplan. "The Components of Perceived Risk." In *Proceedings of the 3rd Annual Conference of the Association for Consumer Research 3*, edited by M. Venkatesan. (1972): 382-93.

James, William. *The Principles of Psychology.* New York: Holt, Rinehart and Winston, 1980.

Janney, J.E., "Fad and Fashion Leadership Among Undergraduate Women," *Journal of Abnormal and Social Psychology, 36* (1941): 275-78.

Jarnow, Jeannette A., and Beatrice Judelle. *Inside the Fashion Business.* (2d ed.) New York: John Wiley and Sons, 1974.

Jarnow, Jeannette A., Beatrice Judelle, and Miriam Guerreiro. *Inside the Fashion Business.* (3d ed.) New York: John Wiley, 1981.

Jarnow, Jeanette, and Miriam Guerreiro. *Inside the Fashion Business.* (5th ed.) New York: John Wiley, 1991.

Jasinski, Frank J. "How They Dress on the Job: Clues to Informal Organization." *Personnel 34* (November-December 1957): 35-41.

Jenkins, Martha C., and Lois M. Dickey. "Consumer Types Based on Evaluative Criteria Underlying Clothing Decisions." *Home Economics Research Journal 4* (March 1976): 150-62.

Johnson, Barbara Hunt, Richard N. Nagasawa, and Kathleen Peters. "Clothing Style Differences: Their Effect on the impression of Sociability." *Home Economics Research Journal 6* (September 1977): 58-63.

Johnston, Moira. "What Will Happen to the Gray Flannel Suit?" *Journal of Home Economics 64* (1972): 5-12.

Joseph, Nathan. *Uniforms and Nonuniforms: Communication Through Clothing.* New York: Greenwood Press, 1986.

Joseph, Nathan, and Nicholas Alex. "The Uniform: A Sociological Perspective." *American Journal of Sociology 77* (1972): 719-30.

Kaiser, Susan B. "Toward a Contextual Social Psychology of Clothing: A Synthesis of Symbolic Interactionist and Cognitive Theoretical Perspectives." *Clothing and Textiles Research Journal 2* (Fall/Winter 1983-84): 1-9.

Kaiser, Susan B. *The Social Psychology of Clothing.* New York: Macmillan, 1985.

Kaiser, Susan B. *The Social Psychology of Clothing.* (2d ed.) New York: Macmillan, 1990.

Kaiser, Susan B., and Joan L. Chandler. "Older Consumers' Use of Media for Fashion Information." *Journal of Broadcasting and Electronic Media 29* (1985): 201-7.

Kann, Eric. "Manmade Fibers and the Consumer." *Textile Institute and Industry 1* (1963): 16.

Kassarjian, Harold H. "Personality and Consumer Behavior: A Review." *Journal of Marketing Research 8* (1971): 409-18.

Katona, George. *The Mass Consumption Society.* New York: McGraw-Hill Book Co., 1964.

Katz, Elihu. "The Two Step Flow of Communication: An Up-to-Date Report on an Hypothesis." *Public Opinion Quarterly 21* (1957): 61-78.

Katz, Elihu, and Paul F. Lazarsfeld. *Personal Influence.* Glencoe, Illinois: The Free Press, 1955.

Keane, Helen Faith. "Why We Dress as We Do: The Story of Fashion." *Forecast for Home Economics 77* (1961): 33-39.

Kefgen, Mary, and Phyllis Touchie-Specht. *Individuality in Clothing Selection and Personal Appearance.* New York: The MacMillan Company, 1971.

Kelley, Eleanor A., Caroline W. Daigle, Rosetta S. LaFleur, and Linda Jo Wilson. "Adolescent Dress and Social Participation." *Home Economics Research Journal 2* (1974): 167-75.

Kelley, Eleanor A., et al. "Clothing Acquisition and Use Practices of Early Adolescents." Louisiana State University Agricultural Experiment Station, Research Report No. 2, June 1973.

Kelley, Eleanor A., and Joanne B. Eicher. "Popularity, Group Membership, and Dress." *Journal of Home Economics 62* (1970): 246-50.

Kelley, Eleanor A., and Deanna N. Turner. "Clothing Awareness and Feelings of Deprivation and Satisfaction Among Lower Social Class First Grade Children." *Journal of Home Economics 63* (1970): 396-400.

Kelley, Harold H. "Two Functions of Reference Groups." In *Readings in Social Psychology,* edited by G.E. Swanson, T. M. Newcomb, and E. Hartley. New York: Henry Holt and Co., 1952, 410-14.

Kidwell, Claudia and Margaret C. Christman. *Suiting Everyone: The Democratization of Clothing in America.* Washington, D.C.: Smithsonian Institution Press, 1974.

Kiesler, C. A., and S. B. Kiesler. *Conformity.* Reading, Mass.: Addison-Wesley, 1970.

Kilborn, Susan King. "Perception and Creativity in Clothing." *Perceptual and Motor Skills 32* (1971): 24-26.

King Charles W. "Fashion Adoption: A Rebuttal to the Trickle Down' Theory." In *Toward Scientific Marketing,* edited by Stephen A. Greyser. Chicago: American Marketing Association, 1963.

King, Charles W. "The Innovator in the Fashion Adoption Process." In *Reflections on Progress in Marketing*, edited by L. George Smith. Chicago: American Marketing Association, 1964.

King, Charles W. *Communicating With the Innovator in the Fashion Adoption Process.* Institute for Research in the Behavioral, Economic, and Management Sciences, Herman C. Krannert Graduate School of Industrial Administration, Purdue University, Paper No. 121, September, 1965.

King, Charles W. "Adoption and Diffusion Research in Marketing: An Overview." In *Science, Technology, and Marketing,* edited by R. J. Haas. Chicago: American Marketing Association, 1966.

King, Charles W., and George B. Sproles. "Predictive Efficacy of Psychopersonality Characteristics in Fashion Change Agent Identification." *Proceedings,* 81st Annual Convention of the American Psychological Association, 1973, 845-46.

King, Charles W., and George B. Sproles. *The Explanatory Efficacy of Selected Types of Consumer Profile Variables in Fashion Change Agent Identification.* Institute for Research in the Behavioral, Economic, and Management Sciences, Purdue University, Paper No. 425, October, 1973.

King, Charles W., and John O. Summers. *Interaction Patterns in Interpersonal Communication.* Institute for Research in the Behavioral, Economic, and Management Sciences, Herman C. Krannert Graduate School of Industrial Administration, Purdue University, Paper No. 168, March, 1967.

King, Charles W., and John O. Summers. *The New Product Adoption Research Project.* Institute for Research in the Behavioral, Economic, and Management Sciences, Purdue University, Paper No. 196, 1967.

Kirkpatrick, Curry. "Wow!" *Sports Illustrated,* July 8, 1985, 22-23.

Klapp, Orin. *Collective Search for Identity.* New York: Holt, Rinehart and Winston, Inc., 1969.

Klein, Adolph I. "Fashion: Its Sense of History—Its Selling Power." *Business History Review 37* (Spring-Summer 1963): 1-2.

Kleinke, Chris L. *First Impressions: The Psychology of Encountering Others.* Englewood Cliffs, N.J.: Prentice-Hall, Inc., 1975.

Kleinke, Chris L. "Effects of Dress on Compliance to Requests in a Field Setting." *Journal of Social Psychology 101* (1977): 223-24.

Klietsch, Ronald G., "Clothesline Patterns and Covert Behavior." *Journal of Marriage and the Family 27* (1965): 78-80.

Knapp, Mark L. *Nonverbal Communication in Human Interaction.* New York: Holt, Rinehart and Winston, Inc., 1972.

Knapp, Mark L. *Nonverbal Communication in Human Interaction.* (2d ed.) New York: Holt, Rinehart and Winston, 1978.

Kness, Darlene, and Barbara Densmore. "Dress and Social-Political Beliefs of Young Male Students." *Adolescence 11* (1976): 431-42.

Koffka, K. *Principles of Gestalt Psychology.* New York: Harcourt Brace, 1935.

Kohler, W. *Gestalt Psychology.* New York: Liveright, 1929.

Konig, Rene. *A La Mode: On the Social Psychology of Fashion.* New York: The Seabury Press, 1973.

Kotler, Philip. *Marketing Management: Analysis, Planning, and Control.* Englewood Cliffs, N.J.: Prentice-Hall, Inc., 1972.

Kroeber, A.L. "On the Principle of Order in Civilization as Exemplified by Changes of Fashion." *American Anthropologist 21* (1919): 235-63.

Lambert, S. "Reactions to a Stranger as a Function of Style of Dress." *Perceptual and Motor Skills 35* (1972): 711-12.

Lambert, William W., and Wallace E. Lambert. *Social Psychology.* Englewood Cliffs, N.J.: Prentice-Hall, Inc., 1964.

Landon, E. Laird, Jr. "Self Concept, Ideal Self Concept, and Consumer Purchase Intentions." *Journal of Consumer Research 1* (1974): 44-51.

Lang, Kurt, and Gladys Lang. "Fashion: Identification and Differentiation in the Mass Society." In *Dress, Adornment, and the Social Order,* edited by Mary Ellen Roach and Joanne Bubolz. New York: John Wiley and Sons, Inc., 1965, 322-46. Reprinted from *Collective Dynamics.* New York: Thomas Y. Crowell Co., 1961, 465-87.

Langner, Lawrence. *The Importance of Wearing Clothes.* New York: Hastings House, 1959.

Lauer, Jeanette C., and Robert H. Lauer. "The Battle of the Sexes: Fashion in 19th Century America." *Journal of Popular Culture 13* (1980): 581-89.

Lauer, Robert, and Jeanette Lauer. *Fashion Power: The Meaning of Fashion in American Society.* Englewood Cliffs, NJ: Prentice-Hall, 1981.

Laver, James. *Modesty in Dress.* Boston: Houghton Mifflin Co., 1969.

Laver, James. *The Concise History of Costume and Fashion.* New York: Harry N. Abrams, Inc., 1969.

Lawler, Monica. "Cultural Influences on Preference for Designs." *Journal of Abnormal and Social Psychology 51* (1955): 690-92.

Leavitt, Clark, and Karen Kaigler-Evans. "Mere Similarity Versus Information Processing: An Exploration of Source and Message Interaction." *Communication Research 2* (1975): 300-306.

Lee-Potter, Charlie. *Sportswear in Vogue Since 1910.* New York: Abbeville Press, 1984.

Lennon, Sharron J. "Physical Attractiveness, Age, and Body Type." *Home Economics Research Journal 16* (1988): 195-203.

Lennon, Sharron J., and Leslie L. Davis. "Individual Differences in Fashion Orientation and Cognitive Complexity." *Perceptual and Motor Skills 64* (1987): 327-30.

Lennon, Sharron J., and Leslie L. Davis. "Clothing and Human Behavior from a Social Cognitive Framework. Part 1: Theoretical Perspectives." *Clothing and Textiles Research Journal 7* (Summer1989a): 41-48.

Lennon, Sharron J., and Leslie L. Davis. "Clothing and Human Behavior From a Social Cognitive Framework. Part 2: The Stages of Social Cognition." *Clothing and Textiles Research Journal 8* (Fall 1989b): 1-9.

Lennon, Sharron J., and Franklin G. Miller. "Attire, Physical Appearance, and First Impressions: More is Less." *Clothing and Textiles Research Journal 3* (Fall/Winter 1984-85): 1-8.

Lester, Katherine Morris, and Rose Netzorg Kerr. *Historic Costume.* 6th ed. Peoria, Ill.: Chas. A. Bennett Co., Inc., 1967.

Levin, Phyllis Lee. *The Wheels of Fashion.* Garden City, N.Y.: Doubleday and Co., 1965.

Levin, Jack, and Harvey Black. "Personal Appearance as a Reflection of Social Attitudes: Stereotype or Reality?" *Psychological Reports 27* (1970): 338.

Lind, Charlene, and Mary E. Roach-Higgins. "Fashion, Collective Adoption, and the Social-Political Symbolism of Dress." In *The Psychology of Fashion,* edited by Michael R. Solomon. Lexington, Mass: Lexington Books, 1985, 183-192.

Littrell, Mary A., and Elizabeth A. Berger. "Perceiver's Occupation and Client's Grooming: Influences on Person Perception." *Clothing and Textiles Research Journal 4* (Spring 1986): 48-55.

Littrell, Mary Bishop, and Joanne B. Eicher. "Clothing Opinions and the Social Acceptance Process Among Adolescents." *Adolescence 8* (1973): 197-212.

Livesly, W. J., and D. B. Bromley. *Person Perception in Childhood and Adolescence.* New York: Wiley, 1973.

Lowe, Elizabeth D., and Karlyne A. Anspach. "Toward a Definition of Freedom of Dress." *Home Economics Research Journal 1* (1973): 246-50.

Lowe, Elizabeth D., and Karlyne A. Anspach. "Freedom in Dress: A Search for Related Factors." *Home Economics Research Journal 7* (1978): 121-27.

Lowe, Elizabeth D., and Hilda M. Buckley. "Freedom and Conformity in Dress: A Two Dimensional Approach." *Home Economics Research Journal 11* (1982): 197-204.

Lowe, Elizabeth D., John W. G. Lowe. "Quantitative Analysis of Women's Dress." In *The Psychology of*

Fashion, edited by Michael R. Solomon. Lexington, Mass: Lexington Books, 1985, 193-206.

Lowe, John W. G., and Elizabeth D. Lowe. "Cultural Pattern and Process: A Study of Stylistic Change in Women's Dress." *American Anthropologist 84* (1982): 521-44.

Lowe, John W. G., and Elizabeth D. Lowe. "Stylistic Change in Women's Dress: Regularity or Randomness?" *Advances in Consumer Research 11* (1984): 731-34.

Lurie, Alison. *The Language of Clothes.* New York: Random House, 1981.

Mack, Raymond W., and Kimball Young. *Sociology and Social Life.* 5th ed. New York: Van Nostrand Reinhold Company, 1968.

Mack, Raymond W., and John Pease. *Sociology and Social Life.* 5th ed. New York: D. Van Nostrand Company, 1973.

Martin, Richard. *All-American: A Sportswear Tradition.* New York: Fashion Institute of Technology, 1985.

Martin, Richard. *Fashion and Surrealism.* New York: Rizzoli, 1987.

Martin, Claude R. Jr. "The Elderly Fashion Consumer: A Forgotten Market." Working Paper No. 53, University of Michigan, Bureau of Business Research, December 1971.

Martin, Claude R., Jr. "A Comparison of Fashion-Buying Behavior Between Teenage Girls and Middle-Aged Women." Working Paper No. 56, University of Michigan, Bureau of Business Research, February, 1972.

Martin, Claude R., Jr. "What Consumers of Fashion Want to Know." *Journal of Retailing 47* (1971-72): 65-71, 94.

Maslach, Christina, Joy Stapp, and Richard T. Santee. "Individuation: Conceptual Analysis and Assessment." *Journal of Personality and Social Psychology 49* (1985): 729-38.

Maslow, Abraham H. *Motivation and Personality.* New York: Harper & Row, 1954.

Maslow, Abraham H. *Toward A Psychology of Being.* Princeton, N.J.: Van Nostrand Company, Inc. 1962.

Mason, Joseph Barry, and Danny Bellenger. "Analyzing High Fashion Acceptance." *Journal of Retailing 49* (1973-74): 79-88.

Mathes, Eugene W. and Sherry B. Kempher. "Clothing as a Nonverbal Communicator of Sexual Attitudes and Behavior." *Perceptual and Motor Skills 43* (1976): 495-98.

Matthews, Lillian B. "Fabric Preferences, Perceptual-Personality Characteristics, and Obesity." *Journal of Home Economics 61* (1969): 177-82.

May, J. K., and Ardis W. Koester. "Clothing Purchase Practices of Adolescents." *Home Economics Research Journal 13* (1985): 226-36.

McCracken, Grant D. "The Trickle-Down Theory Rehabilitated." In *The Psychology of Fashion,* edited by Michael R. Solomon. Lexington, Mass: Lexington Books, 1985, 39-54.

McCracken, Grant. *Culture and Consumption: New Approaches to the Symbolic Character of Consumer Goods and Activities.* Bloomington, IN: Indiana University Press, 1988.

McCullough, Elizabeth, Mary Fran Miller, and Imogene M. Ford. "Sexually Attractive Clothing: Attitudes and Usage." *Home Economics Research Journal 6* (1977): 164-70.

McDowell, Colin. *McDowell's Directory of Twentieth Century Fashion.* Englewood Cliffs, NJ: Prentice-Hall, 1985.

McInnis, Jacquelyn Hobbs, and Jane Kelly Shearer. "Relationship Between Color Choice and Selected Preferences of the Individual." *Journal of Home Economics 56* (1964): 181-87.

Mead, George H. *Mind, Self, and Society.* Chicago: The University of Chicago Press, 1934.

Menge, John A. "Style Change Costs as a Market Weapon." *Quarterly Journal of Economics 76* (1962): 632-47.

Meyersohn, Rolf and Elihu Katz. "Notes on a Natural History of Fads." *American Journal of Sociology 62* (1957): 594-601.

Miller, Norman, and Donald C. Butler. "Social Power and Communication in Small Groups." *Behavioral Science 14* (1969): 11-18.

Miller, Franklin G., Richard A. Feinberg, Leslie L. Davis and Kathleen L. Rowold. "Measurement of Individual Differences in Sensitivity to Appearance." *Home Economics Research Journal 10* (1982): 381-90.

Miller, Franklin G., and Kathleen L. Rowold. "Attire, Sex Roles, and Responses to Requests for Directions." *Psychological Reports 47* (1980): 661-62.

Milsap, Roger E. "Issues in the Measurement of Values." In *Proceedings of the Division of Consumer Psychology Annual Convention*, edited by Joel E. Saegert. Washington, D.C. 1986, 118-22.

Moore, Wilbert E. *Social Change.* 2d ed. Englewood Cliffs, N.J.: Prentice-Hall, Inc., 1974.

Morton, Grace Margaret. "Psychology of Dress." *Journal of Home Economics 18* (1926): 584-86.

Moschis, George. *Consumer Socialization: A Life-Cycle Perspective.* Lexington, Mass: Lexington Books, 1987.

Moschis, G. P., R. L. Moore, and L. F. Stephens. "Purchasing Patterns of Adolescent Consumers." *Journal of Retailing 53* (1977): 17-26.

Murphy, P. "The Attitude of Buyers and Consumers to the Newer Fabrics." *Textile Institute and Industry 3* (June 1965): 152.

Naisbitt, John. *Megatrends: Ten New Directions Transforming Our Lives.* New York. Warner Books, 1982.

Naisbitt, John, and Patricia Aburdene. *Megatrends 2000: Ten New Directions for the 1990s.* New York: William Morrow and Company, Inc., 1990.

Neuhauser, Elyce. "Designs from the Big Screen Go Mainstream." *California Apparel News* April 22-28, 1988, 8.

"New Snap for Garters." *Time,* August 15, 1988, 33.

Newman, Joseph W., and Bradley D. Lockeman. *Consumers' Information-Seeking Processes for Fashion Goods: A Literature Review.* Ann Arbor, MI: University of Michigan, Bureau of Business Research, 1972.

Nicosia, Francisco M., and Robert N. Mayer. "Toward a Sociology of Consumption." *Journal of Consumer Research 2* (1976): 65-75.

Noesjirwan, J. A., and J. M. Crawford. "Variations in Perceptions of Clothing as a Function of Dress Form and Viewer's Social Community." *Perceptual and Motor Skills 54* (1982): 155-63.

Nystrom, Paul H. *Economics of Fashion.* New York: Ronald Press, 1928.

Nystrom, Paul H. *Fashion Merchandising.* New York: Ronald Press, 1932.

O'Shaughnessy, John. *Why People Buy.* New York: Oxford University Press, 1987.

Ostlund, Lyman E. "Role Theory and Group Dynamics." In *Consumer Behavior: Theoretical Sources*, edited by Scott Ward and Thomas S. Robertson. Englewood Cliffs, N.J.: Prentice-Hall, Inc., 1973, 230-75.

Painter, John Jay, and Kent L. Granzin. "Profiling the Male Fashion Innovator—Another Step." Paper presented at the Annual Conference of the Association for Consumer Research, November 1, 1975.

Painter, John Jay, and Max L. Pinegar. "Post-High Teens and Fashion Innovation." *Journal of Marketing Research 8* (1971): 368-69.

Pasnak, Mary Frances Drake, and Ruth W. Ayres. "Clothing Attitudes and Personality Characteristics of Fashion Innovators." *Journal of Home Economics 61* (1969): 698-702.

Patel, Ambalah S., and Jesse E. Gordon. "Some Personal and Situational Determinants of Yielding to Influence." *Journal of Abnormal and Social Psychology 61* (1960): 411-18.

Pegaret, Anthony, and Janet Arnold. *Costume: A General Bibliography.* London: The Costume Society, Victoria and Albert Museum, 1974.

Perna, Rita. *Fashion Forecasting.* New York: Fairchild Publications, 1987.

Pettigrew, Thomas F. "Social evaluation theory: Convergences and Applications." In *Nebraska Symposium on Motivation,* edited by D. Levine. Lincoln: University of Nebraska Press, 1967.

Petzel, Florence E. "Fifty Years of Research in Textiles." *Journal of Home Economics 51* (1959): 701-4.

Phillips, Gerald M., and Eugene C. Erickson. *Interpersonal Dynamics in the Small Group.* New York: Random House, 1970.

Picken, Mary Brooks. *The Fashion Dictionary.* Revised edition. New York: Funk and Wagnalls, Co., 1973.

Pistolese, Rosana, and Ruth Horsting. *History of Fashion.* New York: John Wiley and Sons, Inc., 1970.

Polegato, Rosemary, and Margorie Wall. "Information Seeking by Fashion Opinion Leaders and Followers." *Home Economics Research Journal 8* (1980): 327-38.

Polhemus, Ted. "Fashion, Anti-fashion and Body Image." *New Society 11* (1973, October): 73-76.

Polhemus, Ted, and Lynn Proctor. *Fashion and Anti-Fashion: An Anthropology of Clothing and Adornment.* London: Thames and Hudson, 1978.

Rahr, Frederic H. "Is the Fashion Approach to Color Old-Fashioned?" *Journal of Retailing 29* (Fall 1953): 109-14.

Read, Katherine H. "Clothes Help Build Personality." *Journal of Home Economics 42* (1950): 348-50.

Redlich, Fritz. "A Needed Distinction in Fashion Study." *Business History Review 37* (Spring-Summer 1963): 3-4.

Rees, D. W., L. Williams, and H. Giles. "Dress Style and Symbolic Meaning." *International Journal of Symbology 5* (1974): 1-7.

Reingen, Peter H. "Comment on Woodside." *Journal of Marketing Research 11* (1974): 223-24.

Reiss, Albert J., and A. Lewis Rhodes. "Status Deprivation and Delinquent Behavior." *Sociological Quarterly 4* (1963): 135-49.

Reynolds, Fred D. and William R. Darden. "Why the Midi Failed." *Journal of Advertising Research 12* (1972): 39-44.

Reynolds, Fred D. and William R. Darden. "Fashion Theory and Pragmatics: The Case of the Midi." *Journal of Retailing 49* (Spring, 1973): 51-62.

Reynolds, William H. "Cars and Clothing: Understanding Fashion Trends." *Journal of Marketing 32* (1968): 44-49.

Rhodes, Zandra, and Anne Knight. *The Art of Zandra Rhodes.* Boston: Houghton Mifflin Co. 1984.

Richards, Elizabeth A., and Ruth E. Hawthorne. "Values, Body Cathexis, and Clothing of Male University Students." *Journal of Home Economics 63* (1971): 190-94.

Richardson, Jane, and A.L. Kroeber. "Three Centuries of Women's Dress Fashions, A Quantitative Analysis." *Anthropological Records 5* (1940): 111-53.

Roach, Mary Ellen. "Adolescent Dress." *Journal of Home Economics 61* (1969): 690-97.

Roach, Mary Ellen. "Dress, Society, and Change." Address to the National Meeting of the Association of College Professors of Textiles and Clothing, Portland, Oregon, June, 1974.

Roach, Mary Ellen, and Joanne Bubolz Eicher, eds. *Dress, Adornment, and The Social Order.* New York: John Wiley and Sons, Inc., 1965.

Roach, Mary Ellen, and Joanne B. Eicher. *The Visible Self: Perspectives on Dress.* Englewood Cliffs, N.J.: Prentice-Hall, Inc., 1973.

Roach, Mary Ellen, and Kathleen Ehle Musa. *New Perspectives on the History of Western Dress.* New York: Nutri Guides, Inc., 1979.

Robenstine, Carol, and Eleanor Kelley. "Relating Fashion Change to Social Change: A Methodological Approach." *Home Economics Research Journal 10* (1981): 78-87.

Roberts, Helene E. "The Exquisite Slave: The Role of Clothes in Making of the Victorian Woman." *Signs: Journal of Women in Culture and Society 2* (1977): 554-69.

Robertson, Thomas S. *Innovative Behavior and Communication.* New York: Holt, Rinehart and Winston, 1971.

Robertson, Thomas S., and James H. Myers. "Personality Correlates of Opinion Leadership and Innovative Buying Behavior." *Journal of Marketing Research 6* (1969): 164-68.

Robertson, Thomas S., Joan Zielinski, and Scott Ward. *Consumer Behavior.* Glenview, Illinois: Scott, Foresman and Company, 1984.

Robinson, Dwight E. "Fashion Theory and Product Design." *Harvard Business Review 36* (November-December 1958): 126-38.

Robinson, Dwight E. "The Rules of Fashion Cycles." *Horizon*, March 1959, 113-17. Reprinted from *Harvard Business Review,* November-December, 1958.

Robinson, Dwight E. "The Styling and Transmission of Fashions Historically Considered. *Journal of Economic History 20* (1960): 576-87.

Robinson, Dwight E. "The Economics of Fashion Demand." *The Quarterly Journal of Economics 75* (1961): 376-98.

Robinson, Dwight E. "The Importance of Fashions in Taste to Business History: An Introductory Essay." *Business History Review 37* (1963): 5-36.

Robinson, Dwight E. "A Note on Fashion Leadership: Reply." *Business History Review 37* (1963): 451-55.

Robinson, Dwight E. "Style Changes: Cyclical, Inexorable, and Foreseeable." *Harvard Business Review 53* (November-December 1975): 121-31.

Robinson, Dwight E. "Fashions in Shaving and Trimming of the Beard: The Men of the Illustrated London News, 1842-1972." *American Journal of Sociology 81* (1976): 1133-41.

Rogers, Everett M. *Diffusion of Innovations.* Glencoe, Illinois: The Free Press, 1962.

Rogers, Everett M. *Diffusion of Innovations.* 3d ed. New York: The Free Press, 1983.

Rogers, Everett M. and F. Floyd Shoemaker. *Communication of Innovations.* New York: The Free Press, 1971.

Rogers, Everett M., and J. David Stanfield. "Adoption and Diffusion of New Products: Emerging Generalizations and Hypotheses." In *Application of the Sciences in Marketing Management,* edited by F.M. Bass, C. W. King, and E. A. Pessemier. New York: John Wiley, 1968.

Rokeach, Milton. *Beliefs, Attitudes, and Values.* San Francisco: Jossey-Bass, Inc., 1968.

Rokeach, Milton. *The Nature of Human Values.* New York: The Free Press, 1973.

Rosenbloom, Richard S. "A Conjecture about Fashion and Vertical Process Integration." *Business History Review 37* (1963): 94-97.

Rosencranz, Mary Lou Lerch. "A Study of Women's Interest in Clothing." *Journal of Home Economics 41* (1949): 460-62.

Rosencranz, Mary Lou Lerch. "Sociological Aspects of Clothing Studied." *Journal of Home Economics 42* (1950): 206-7.

Rosencranz, Mary Lou. "Clothing Symbolism." *Journal of Home Economics 54* (1962): 18-22.

Rosencranz, Mary Lou. "Social and Psychological Approaches to Clothing Research." *Journal of Home Economics 57* (1965): 26-29.

Rosencranz, Mary Lou. *Clothing Concepts.* New York: The MacMillan Co., 1972.

Rowold, Kathleen. "Sensitivity to the Appearance of Others and Projection as Factors in Impression Formation." *Home Economics Research Journal 13* (1984): 105-11.

Ruesch, J., and W. Kees. *Nonverbal Communication: Notes on the Visual Perception of Human Relations.* Berkeley: University of California Press, 1956.

Ryan, Mary Shaw. *Clothing: A Study in Human Behavior.* New York: Holt, Rinehart and Winston, 1966.

Samuel, W. "Response to Bill of Rights Paraphrases as Influenced by the Hip or Straight Attire of the

Opinion Solicitor." *Journal of Applied Social Psychology 2* (1972): 47-62.

Sapir, Edward. "Custom." *Encyclopedia of the Social Sciences,* 1931.

Sapir, Edward. "Fashion." *Encyclopedia of the Social Sciences*, 1931.

Schiavo, R. Steven, Barbara Sherlock, and Gail Wickland. "Effect of Attire on Obtaining Directions." *Psychological Reports 34* (1974): 245-46.

Schlenker, Berry R. *Impression Management: The Self-Concept, Social Identity, and Interpersonal Relations.* Monterey, CA: Brooks/Cole Publishing Co., 1980.

Schrank, Holly L., and D. Lois Gilmore. "Correlates of Fashion Leadership: Implications for Fashion Process Theory." *Sociological Quarterly 14* (1973): 534-43.

Seidel, Leon E. *Applied Textile Marketing.* Atlanta: W.R.C. Smith Publishing Co., 1971.

Sherbaum, C. J., and D. H. Shepherd. "Dressing for Success: Effects of Color and Layering on Perceptions of Women." *Sex Roles 16* (1987): 391-99.

Sherif, Muzafir. "A Study of Some Social Factors in Perception." *Archives of Psychology 27* (1935, no. 187): 1-60.

Sherif, Muzafer. *The Psychology of Social Norms.* New York: Harper, 1936.

Sherif, Muzafer, and Carolyn W. Sherif. *Reference Groups.* New York: Harper and Row, 1964.

Shim, Soyeon, and Mary Frances Drake. "Apparel Selection by Employed Women: A Typology of Information Search Patterns." *Clothing and Textiles Research Journal 6* (Winter 1988): 1-9.

Shim, Soyeon, and Mary Frances Drake. "Information Search Patterns in the Purchase of Apparel: A Synthesis of Two Theories." *Clothing and Textiles Research Journal 7* (Spring 1989): 40-46.

Shipley, Suzanne, and Mary Lou Rosencranz. "Older Women's Clothing Preferences." *Journal of Home Economics 54* (1962): 854.

Simmel, Georg. "Fashion." American Journal of *Sociology 62* (1957): 541-58. Reprinted from

International Quarterly 10 (1904): 130-55.

Simon-Miller, Francoise. "Commentary: Signs and Cycles in the Fashion System." In *The Psychology of Fashion*, edited by Michael R. Solomon. Lexington, MA: Lexington Books/D.C. Heath, 1985, 71-81.

Sistrunk, Frank. "Two Processes of Conformity Demonstrated by Interactions of Commitment, Set and Personality." *Journal of Social Psychology 89* (1973): 63-72.

Skinner, B.F. *About Behaviorism.* New York: Alfred A. Knopf, 1974.

Smith, A. D. *Social Change: Social Theory and Historical Processes.* London: Longman, 1976.

Smith, Thomas Spence. "Aestheticism and Social Structure: Style and Social Network in the Dandy Life." *American Sociological Review 39* (1974): 725-43.

Smucker, Betty, and Anna M. Creekmore. "Adolescents' Clothing Conformity, Awareness, and Peer Acceptance." *Home Economics Research Journal 1* (1972): 92-97.

Snyder, C. R., and Howard L. Fromkin. "Abnormality as a Positive Characteristic: The Development and Validation of a Scale Measuring Need for Uniqueness." *Journal of Abnormal Psychology 86* (1977): 518-27.

Snyder, C. R., and Howard L. Fromkin. *Uniqueness: The Human Pursuit of Difference.* New York: Plenum Press, 1980.

Solomon, Michael R. (ed.). *The Psychology of Fashion.* Lexington, Mass: Lexington Books, 1985.

Solomon, Michael. "Standard Issue." *Psychology Today,* December, 1987: 30-31.

Solomon, Michael R., and Susan P. Douglas. "Diversity in Product Symbolism: The Case of Female Executive Clothing." *Psychology and Marketing 4* (1987): 189-212.

Sproles, George B. "Fashion Theory: A Conceptual Framework." In *Advances in Consumer Research,* Vol. 1, edited by Scott Ward and Peter Wright. Urbana, Ill.: Association for Consumer Research, 1974, 463-72.

Sproles, George B. *Clothing Orientations of Adult Women in Indiana.* Research Bulletin #944, Agricultural Experiment Station, Purdue University, 1977.

Sproles, G.B. "Fashion Preferences and Store Patronage: A Longitudinal Study." *Advances in Consumer Research.* Volume 5. Association for Consumer Research 1978, 675-81.

Sproles, George B. *Fashion: Consumer Behavior Toward Dress.* Minneapolis: Burgess Publishing Company, 1979.

Sproles, George B. (ed.). *Perspectives of Fashion.* Minneapolis: Burgess Publishing Company, 1981.

Sproles, George B. "Analyzing Fashion Life Cycles— Principles and Perspectives." *Journal of Marketing 45* (1981): 116-24.

Sproles, George B. "Behavioral Science Theories of Fashion." In *The Psychology of Fashion,* edited by Michael R. Solomon. Lexington, Mass: Lexington Books, 1985, 55-70.

Sproles, George B., and Loren V. Geistfeld. "Issues in Analyzing Consumer Satisfaction/Dissatisfaction with Clothing and Textiles." *Advances in Consumer Research.* Volume 5. Association for Consumer Research, 1978, 383-91.

Sproles, George B., Loren V. Geistfeld, and Suzanne B. Badenhop. "Informational Inputs as Influences on Efficient Consumer Decision Making." *The Journal of Consumer Affairs 12* (Summer 1978a): 88-103.

Sproles, George B., Loren V. Geistfeld, and Suzanne B. Badenhop. "Types, Amounts and Sequences of Information Used by Efficient Consumers." *Proceedings*, American Council on Consumer Interests, 1978b, 28-37.

Sproles, George B., and Charles W. King. *The Consumer Fashion Change Agent: A Theoretical Conceptualization and Empirical Identification.* Institute for Research in the Behavioral, Economic, and Management Sciences, Purdue University, Paper No. 433, December, 1973.

Squire, Geoffrey. *Dress and Society.* New York: The Viking Press, 1974.

Stait, N.H. "Long Range Planning in a Fast Changing Fashion Market." *Long Range Planning 3* (1970): 55-60.

Steele, Valerie. *Fashion and Eroticism.* New York: Oxford University Press, 1985.

Steiner, Robert L., and Joseph Weiss. "Veblen Revisited in the Light of Counter-Snobbery." *Journal of Aesthetics and Art Criticism 9* (1951): 263-68.

Stone, Gregory P. "Appearance and the Self." In *Human Behavior and Social Processes,* edited by Arnold M. Rose. Boston: Houghton Mifflin Co., 1962.

Stone, Gregory P., William H. Form, and Hazel B. Strahan. "The Social Climate of Decision in Shopping for Clothes." *Journal of Home Economics 46* (1954): 86-88.

Storm, Penny. *Functions of Dress: Tool of Culture and the Individual.* Englewood Cliffs, N.J.: Prentice-Hall, 1987.

Sturdivant, Frederick D. "Subculture Theory: Poverty, Minorities, and Marketing." In *Consumer Behavior: Theoretical Sources,* edited by Scott Ward and Thomas S. Robertson. Englewood Cliffs, N.J.: Prentice-Hall, Inc., 1973.

Summers, John O. "The Identity of Women's Clothing Fashion Opinion Leaders." *Journal of Marketing Research 7* (1970): 178-85.

Summers, John O. "Generalized Change Agents and Innovativeness." *Journal of Marketing Research 8* (1971): 313-16.

Summers, John O. "Media Exposure Patterns of Consumer Innovators." *Journal of Marketing 36* (1972): 43-49.

Sybers, Ruth, and Mary Ellen Roach. "Clothing and Human Behavior." *Journal of Home Economics 54* (1962): 184-87.

Takahashi, Charlene L. and Audrey Newton. "Perceptions of Clothing Conformity." *Journal of Home Economics 59* (1962): 720-23.

Taylor, James W. "The Role of Risk in Consumer Behavior." *Journal of Marketing 38* (1974): 54-60.

Taylor, Lucy C., and Norma H. Compton. "Personality Correlates of Dress Conformity." *Journal of Home Economics 60* (1968): 653-56.

Tedeschi, J. T. *Impression Management Theory and Social Psychological Research.* New York: Academic Press, 1981.

Thomas, L.E. "Clothing and Counterculture: An Empirical Study." *Adolescence 8* (Spring 1973): 93-112.

Thompson, Thelma. "Fashion Therapy." *Journal of Home Economics 54* (1962): 835-36.

Thorelli, Hans B., Helmut Becker, and Jack Engledow. *The Information Seekers.* Cambridge, Mass: Ballinger, 1975.

Thorelli, Hans B., and Sarah V. Thorelli. *Consumer Information Systems and Consumer Policy.* Cambridge, Mass: Ballinger, 1977.

Tigert, Douglas J., Lawrence J. Ring, and Charles W. King. "Fashion Involvement and Buying Behavior: A Methodological Study." Paper presented at the Annual Conference of the Association for Consumer Research, November 1, 1975.

Tigert, Douglas J., Lawrence J. Ring, and Charles W. King. "Fashion Involvement and Buying Behavior." *Advances in Consumer Research 3* (1976): 46-52.

Tortora, Phyllis. "Fashion Magazines Mirror Changing Role of Women." *Journal of Home Economics 65* (1973): 19-23.

Troelstrup, Arch W. *The Consumer in American Society.* New York: McGraw-Hill Book Co., 1974.

Troxell, Mary D., and Beatrice Judelle. *Fashion Merchandising.* New York: McGraw-Hill Inc., 1971.

Tucker, Willi:am T. *Foundations for a Theory of Consumer Behavior.* New York: Holt, Rinehart, and Winston, 1957.

Turner, Ralph H. "Some Contributions of Muzafer Sherif to Sociology." *Social Psychology Quarterly 53* (1990): 283-91.

Turner, Ralph H., and Lewis M. Killian. *Collective Behavior.* 3d ed. Englewood Cliffs, N.J.: Prentice-Hall, 1987.

Unger, Rhoda, and Beth Raymond. "External Criteria as Predictors of Values: The Importance of Race and Attire." *Journal of Social Psychology 93* (1974): 295-96.

Veblen, Thorstien. *The Theory of the Leisure Class.* New York: MacMillan Co., 1912.

Vener, Arthur M., and Audray Weese. "The Preschool Child's Perceptions of Adult Sex-Linked Cultural Objects." *Journal of Home Economics 57* (1965): 49-54.

Venkatesan, M. "Experimental Study of Consumer Behavior Conformity and Independence." *Journal of Marketing Research 3* (1966): 384-87.

Venkatesan, M. "Cognitive Consistency and Novelty Seeking." In *Consumer Behavior: Theoretical Sources,* edited by Scott Ward and Thomas S. Robertson. Englewood Cliffs, N.J.: Prentice-Hall Inc., 1973.

Vreeland, Carl. "The Jantzen Method of Short-Range Forecasting." *Journal of Marketing 27* (1963): 66-70.

Walters, C. Glen. *Consumer Behavior: Theory and Practice.* Revised edition. Homewood, Ill.: Richard D. Irwin, 1974.

Ward, Scott. "Consumer Socialization." *Journal of Consumer Research 1* (1974): 1-14.

Ward, S., and D. Wackman. "Family and Media Influences on Adolescent Consumer Learning." *American Behavioral Scientist 14* (1971): 415-27.

Warner, Charles Dudley. *Fashions in Literature.* New York: Dodd, Mead and Co., 1902.

Wasson, Chester R. "How Predictable are Fashion and Other Product Life Cycles?" *Journal of Marketing 32* (1968): 36-43.

Wax, Murray. "Themes in Cosmetics and Grooming." *American Journal of Sociology 62* (1957): 588-93.

Weeden, Patricia. "Study Patterned on Kroeber's Investigation of Style." Dress-Journal of the *Costume Society of America 3* (1977): 9-19.

Wells, William D., ed. *Life Style and Psychographics.* Chicago: American Marketing Association, 1974.

Wells, William D., and Arthur D. Beard. "Personality and Consumer Behavior." In *Consumer Behavior: Theoretical Sources,* edited by Scott Ward and Thomas S. Robertson. Englewood Cliffs, N.J.: Prentice-Hall, Inc., 1973.

Wells, William D., and Douglas J. Tigert. "Activities, Interests and Opinions." *Journal of Advertising Research 11* (1971): 27-35.

Western Regional Research Cooperative Project W-98. "Relationship of Clothing to the Personal and Social Acceptability of Adolescents." Washington Agricultural Experiment Station, Washington State University, Bulletin 750, February, 1972.

Wilcox, R. Turner. *The Mode in Costume.* New York: Charles Scribner's Sons, 1958.

Wilkie, William L. *How Consumers Use Product Information.* Report Prepared for the National Science Foundation. Washington: U.S. Government Printing Office, 1975.

Wilkie, William L. *Consumer Behavior.* 2d ed. New York. John Wiley, 1990.

Wilkie, William L., and Edgar A. Pessemier. "Issues In Marketing's Use of Multi-Attribute Attitude Models." *Journal of Marketing Research 10* (1973): 428-41.

Williams, Madelyn C., and Joanne B. Eicher. "Teenagers' Appearance and Social Acceptance." *Journal of Home Economics 58* (1966): 457-61.

Wilson, Carrie. *Fashions Since Their Debut.* Scranton, Pa.: International Textbook Company, 1939.

Wilson, Elizabeth. *Adorned in Dreams: Fashion and Modernity.* London: Virago Press, 1985.

Winakor, Geitel. "Time Lag Between High Fashion and Accepted Fashion." *Journal of Home Economics 47* (1955): 343-44.

Winakor, Geitel. "Consumer Expenditures for Clothing in the United States, 1929-1958." *Journal of Home Economics 54* (1962): 115-18.

Winakor, Geitel. "The Process of Clothing Consumption." *Journal of Home Economics 61* (1969): 629-34.

Winakor, Geitel. "Economics of Textiles and Clothing, A Bibliography." Iowa State University, Textiles and Clothing Department, 1970.

Winakor, Geitel, and Barbara D. Goings. "Fashion Preference: Measurement of Change." *Home Economics Research Journal 1* (1973): 195-209.

Winakor, Geitel, Bernetta Canton, and Leroy Wolins. "Perceived Fashion Risk and Self-Esteem of Males and Females." *Home Economics Research Journal 9* (1980): 45-56.

Wise, Debra. "The Gekko." *GQ,* September 1988, 55.

Woods, Walter A., and Thomas C. Padgett. "Aesthetics Applied to Fashion Apparel." *Empirical Studies of the Arts 5* (1987): 15-30.

Woodside, Arch G. "Is There a Generalized Risky Shift Phenomenon in Consumer Behavior?" *Journal of Marketing Research 11* (1974): 225-26.

Workman, Jane E. "Fashionable Versus Out-of-Date Clothing and Interpersonal Distance." *Clothing and Textiles Research Journal 5* (Spring 1987): 31-35.

Young, Agnes Brooks. *Recurring Cycles of Fashion, 1760-1937.* New York: Harper and Brothers, 1937.

Zaltman, Gerald, Philip Kotler, and Ira Kaufman, eds. *Creating Social Change.* New York: Holt, Rinehart and Winston, Inc., 1972.

Subject Index

geographic aspects of, 82-4
high, defined, 13
historical continuity of, 19, 32-6, 128
and history, 19, 32
importance of, 22-4
innovation in, 70
interest in, 204
knowledge of, 204
life cycles, 95-104. *See also* Fashion diffusion curves
marketing of, 47-54, 98-100, 114-5, 125, 130
mass, defined, 13
motives for adoption of, 17-18, 179-80
principles, 18-20
sources of new, 44-7, 54-65
spread of. *See* Diffusion
symbolism of, 18, 20, 221-4. *See also* Fashion symbols
Fashion adoption
and collective behavior, 162-4
process of, 17-18, 75-8
satisfaction-of-needs approach to, 183-5
social psychology of, 180-2
Fashion change agents, 15-16, 85-9, 109-27, 253
Fashion cycle, 34-5
Fashion diffusion. *See* Diffusion
Fashion diffusion curves, 93-7, 99, 101, 104
acquisition and use curves, 95
detailed analysis, 97-104
principles of, 93-4
Fashion followers, 97, 99
Fashion forecasts, 283-5
Fashion industry, 24
competition in, 48-53
description of, 47-54
Fashion involvement, 203
Fashion isolates, 97
Fashion laggards, 97
Fashion leaders, 85-9, 97-8, 109-28, 154-6
Fashion leadership theories, 109-10
comparison of, 128-33
Fashion life cycle curves, 93-104

Fashion principles, 18-20
Fashion process, 69
defined, 13
social context of, 138-9
stages of, 15-17
Fashion seasons, 100-01, 119, 122
Fashion symbols, 217-20, 221-4
interpreting, 227-32
meaning of, 230-1
perceiving, 224-7
Fashion trends
defined, 12
diffusion of, 102-4
forecasting of, 185-95
termination of, 20, 169-76
Forecasting, 293-5
long range, 295
short range, 294-5
Functions of dress, 185-94

Gapbridgers, 124-5
Group identification, 152-4
Groups, 2, 4, 5, 80-1
social influence of, 142-4, 148-52
types of, 141-2

Hierarchy of needs, 183
High fashion, defined, 13
Historical continuity, 19, 32-6, 128
Horizontal flow theory, 116-7

Identity kits, 22
Immodesty, as a function of dress, 186-8
Impression management, 22, 237-9
Individuality, in dress, 19, 181
Information sources
impersonal, 245, 250-5
perceived as helpful, 276-80
personal, 245, 255-60
point-of-purchase, 267-74
prior to purchase, 264-7
searcher profiles, 274-6
Innovation-collective selection theory, 127-8
Innovations
adoption of, 17, 75-8
characteristics of, 71-5
defined, 70

diffusion of, 78-85
sources of, 45-8, 54-65
Innovative communicators, 87
Innovators, 63, 87, 109, 125, 126, 127, 131, 254-5
Intrinsic functions of dress, 185-91

Knock-off copying, 50, 166

Law of association, 228-9
Leadership. *See* Fashion leaders; Fashion leadership theories
Level of acceptance, 15, 93-4, 96
Lower classes
as fashion followers, 110-11
as fashion leaders, 126-7

Marketing channel, 47
Marketing of fashions, 98-100, 114, 119-23, 130, 246
Marketing research, 288-94
Market segment, 48, 293
Mass fashion, defined, 13
Mass-market consumers, 97, 99
Mass-market theory of fashion, 117-23, 130
Mass media, 119, 246, 250-5, 264, 277-8
Mass merchandisers, 53
Material, 10. *See also* Fabric
Membership group, 141
Merchandising. *See* Fashion diffusion curves; Fashion industry; Market segmentation; Marketing of fashions; Mass-market theory of fashion; Retail stores
Mobility, social, 82, 115-6
Modernism, 191
Modesty, as a function of dress, 176, 186-8
Movies, effect on fashion, 59-61
MTV, 62, 68, 253, 293
Musicians, as fashion leaders, 61-2

Newness, 70-1
Nonadopters, 98
Nonverbal communication, 221-4, 259
Norms, social, 133-41, 153, 162, 176

Nouveau riche, as fashion leaders, 115-6
Nudity, 72

Obsolescence, 17, 20, 99-100, 189-90
Occupational dress, 157-8
Off-price stores, 53
Opinion leaders, 87, 119-21, 128, 254-5, 266

Peer group, 141-2
Perceived risk, 74-5, 202-03
Personality, 180, 199-205
  and clothing interest, 204-05
  defined, 199
  of fashion leaders, 200-05
Physical attractiveness, 42
Prediction of fashions, 283-95
Prestige, 128, 130
Private label apparel, 50
Protection, as a function of dress, 183, 185-6
Psychoanalytic approach to fashion adoption, 195-8
Purchasing. *See* Adoption of fashions; Communications; Decision-making; Information sources

Quasi-uniforms, 157

Reference group, 141, 148-52
Retail stores, 50-3
Risk-taking, by consumers, 74-5, 88
Risky shift phenomenon, 144
Rule of excess, in fashion termination, 165, 169-70

Satisfaction-of-needs approach to fashion adoption, 183-5
Seasons, fashion, 100-01, 295
Seduction principle, 198
Self-concept
  defined, 208
  influence on dress, 181, 208-10
Self-expression, as a function of fashion, 181
Semiotics, 218-9
Sexual attraction, as a function of

dress, 188, 196-8
Shifting erogenous zones, theory of, 197-8
Silhouette
  as basic component of fashion, 6, 7
  defined, 7
  as related to mass-market theory of fashion, 122
Social affiliation, as a function of fashion, 194
Social change
  characteristics of, 36
  defined, 36
  related to fashions, 36-9, 44, 172-6, 192
Social class, 110-17, 129
Social cognition, 223-4
Social comparison, theory of, 207-8
Social differentiation, 172
Social events, effect on fashion, 54-6
Social groups, 4
  influence on dress, 142-4, 148-52
Social influence
  informational, 149-50
  normative, 150
Social mobility, and fashion diffusion, 81-2, 114-5
Social norms, 137-41, 162, 176
Social power, 144
Social-psychological function of fashion, 191-4
Social saturation, 16, 170-2
Socialization, 144
Sociograms, 80, 83
Socio-political events, effect on fashion, 56-7
Specialty stores, 51
Status symbols, 111, 232
Standardized dress, 157
Stereotype, 229, 234
Stores. *See* Retail stores
Style
  defined, 7
  social saturation of, 170-2
  variety of, 5, 7
Subcultural leadership, 123-7, 130-1
Subculture, 85, 123-4
Symbols. *See also* Fashion symbols

defined, 217
interpretation of, 227-32
sexual, as related to fashion, 196-7
social salience of, 220, 229
Symbolic consumption, 237
Symbolic differentiation, as a function of fashion, 193
Symbolic interaction, 223
Symbolic life cycle, 234

Target market, 48. *See also* Market segmentation
Technology, effect on fashion, 42, 44, 47, 285
Television, effect on fashion, 62-3
Termination of fashions, 3, 17, 20, 169-77
Textile industry, 48, 49
Trade associations, 53
Trade publications, 53-4
Traditions
  formal, 40
  informal, 41-2
Travel, effect on fashion, 82
Trickle-across theory, 110, 117-23, 128
Trickle-down theory, 109, 110-12, 129, 172
Trickle-up theory, 110

Uniforms, 156-8, 232
Uniqueness, theory of, 210, 213
Unisex dress, 37
Upper-class fashion leadership, 110-12

Values, 205, 232

Wealth, influence of on fashion, 88, 110-11
Women's clothing, sexual symbolism of, 196-8

Youth
  influence on fashion, 123-4, 125-6
  and socialization in dress, 145-8

Zeitgeist, 19, 22